T0278387

Gay Aliens and Queer Folk

GAY ALIENS AND QUEER FOLK

How Russell T Davies Changed TV

Emily Garside

2023

www.uwp.co.uk

British Library Cataloguing-in-Publication Data
A catalogue record for this book is available from the British Library.

ISBN: 978-1-915279-22-4

Cover artwork by Andy Ward
Typeset by Agnes Graves
Printed and bound by CPI (UK) Ltd, Croydon CR0 4YY

The publisher acknowledges the financial support of the Books Council of Wales.

For every teen who hid Queer as Folk VHS tapes,
and then found the Doctor to travel in time and space with.

Contents

Acknowledgements

Thank you to all my Whovian nerds over the years, from the uni crowd I'd gather every week to watch the new episodes with, to every stranger on the internet I've ever argued with over *Who*. Thank you to the information gatherers from '*Doctor Who* Set Reports' and those behind TardisWiki. Thanks also to everyone who ever wrote a *Torchwood* fanfic, you did great work.

Thanks to Lowenna Turner, my first-hand *Who* encyclopedia. Thank you, Rebecca Humphreys-Langford, for such insightful discussions on the Doctor and asexuality – I can't wait to read your work on the same. Thanks to Dai Hill, always there to analyse a combination of *Who* plotlines and Cardiff locations. Also, to Mads Misasi, my go-to nerd buddy who is always there when I doubt my nerd or writing ability.

Thank you to Jon Rainford for being a source of *Queer as Folk* quotes so obscure even Russell wouldn't remember them, and my go-to for 2000s queer culture, gay sense-checking, and all-around keeper of sanity.

Thank you, Beverley Slee, aka 'Mother Garside', for every *Doctor Who*-themed Cardiff pilgrimage, endless *Who* and *Queer as Folk* rewatches and as my sounding board and proofreader for this book.

And, of course, to Russell T Davies for the stories that made this book.

Introduction

Who is Russell T Davies to you? He is probably either the *Queer as Folk* one or the *Doctor Who* one, depending on your age. Alternatively, perhaps he is 'the Welsh one', which would, of course, be accurate for the man from Swansea, who started a career at Cardiff's Sherman Theatre and then brought the Doctor and his TARDIS back to Cardiff, helping to revitalise the film industry there (as well as some very particular TV tourism). Maybe he is the 'AIDS' one, having in 2021 brought the British side of the AIDS pandemic to our TV screens with *It's a Sin*. This story of one pandemic, from inside a pandemic, opened many people's eyes for the first time to that tragic chapter in queer history.

Or perhaps you know him for one or more of his many other contributions to British TV over the last two decades: *Casanova, Bob & Rose, The Grand, Mine All Mine, The Second Coming.* His contribution to the face of British TV is impactful. More crucially, his contribution to queer stories and queer TV is integral. On top of this, he is a Welsh voice at the heart of British TV.

At the time of writing, Davies is probably one of the most influential people in British TV. Not only is he now back at the helm of *Doctor Who* after a twelve-year break, steering the franchise into its sixtieth-anniversary celebrations and beyond, he is now also executive producing for other people alongside his writing work. In 2022 he started work as executive producer on *Three Little Birds* by Lenny Henry, perhaps a sign of more such work.

Davies has curated both a niche for himself and work that defies categorising, from overtly 'queer' dramas to kids' TV, ranging across

Shakespeare, historical drama and Welsh comedy. Following Davies's career from *Queer as Folk* through to *It's a Sin*, this book explores the vast cultural impact of his writing in representing queer lives on TV, from the breakthrough that was *Queer as Folk* – for many, the first time they had seen unapologetically gay characters on TV – through to his 'incidental' inclusion of queer characters in *Doctor Who* and the documenting of vital queer history in *It's a Sin*.

Structured around different TV shows, from the well-known to the more obscure, this book reflects on the contribution Davies's writing makes to the queer and British TV canons. After all, Davies changed how we see LGBTQ+ characters on TV and brought back an iconic TV franchise in *Doctor Who*, making it slightly queer, and slightly Welsh, too.

I start my journey with a look at Davies's early work and his path into writing for TV, and the elements of his style that can be traced back to this point. Following this, is the first of several 'coda' chapters, which delve into a specific aspect or essential character in Davies's work. These look at critical threads in his style that will continue across the book.

The first section of the book dives into the first of his iconic and queer works, *Queer as Folk*, the series that broke down barriers and opened doors to conversations about the long-ranging impact of the show. This section looks at where the rest of the world was at that time in terms of LGBTQ+ rights and where representation was in other TV shows, alongside examples from Davies's work, to illustrate how his writing paved the way for other shows with LGBTQ+ themes to be made.

Next, I move forward onto Davies's tenure with *Who* and his impact in revitalising both the franchise on Welsh TV, and queer and female representation in the show, taking an in-depth look into the Doctor and their representation of genderless identity and an asexual character. I follow on to the 'Whoniverse', as fans styled it, to *Torchwood* and the queer-aliens-for-grown-ups that invaded Cardiff. Along the way, I look at how all-encompassing the Whoniverse was for Cardiff then and the long-ranging impact these shows had.

The *Who* section ends with a coda focusing on women and how

Davies writes them, includes their stories, and respects them, in contrast to many other writers for TV. Then I look at the interlude in post-*Who* writing for Davies. I explore how Davies puts nerds, like women, at the centre of stories without mocking, but rather celebrating who they are.

Queer as Folk might be known as the queer story that broke the mould, but Davies has carried the queer mantra across all his work. While I look at queer characters separately, another chapter examines his other critical queer dramas, *Bob & Rose*, *Cucumber*, *Banana* and *Tofu*. It considers the power, similarities and differences in approaching queer narratives decades apart.

Welshness is referenced across Davies's stories and is considered, along with the impact his work has had on the Cardiff film economy, in a coda chapter, as is his take on politics and sex. While sex and queerness are not the same, they are inextricably linked in Davies's work, and a discussion of that, too, has its own chapter. That chapter looks at how he has created a variety of queer characters and how we cannot expect one writer to fix all our queer TV problems. However, that has not stopped Davies from trying.

In examining his recent works, *Years and Years, A Very English Scandal* and *It's a Sin*, I look at Davies's take on various queer issues and characters, and how he challenges audiences straight and queer through his writing. In *Years and Years*, he goes further, looking at a terrifying version of the future that is perhaps the darker side of *Who* that he never got to explore by asking 'what if' of humanity. However, in putting a queer storyline as a central element, Davies also reminds us that the fight is not won for equality and that the future might look increasingly dark for queer folks. Looking alongside this at his two historic queer dramas, *Scandal* and *Sin*, the drive to both 'know your history' for queer stories/audiences and 'learn from history' is apparent. That Davies loops around from telling the contemporary queer story of the moment in *Queer as Folk* to educating people on their history in *Sin* is an important through-line also. In this part of the book I ask, as a queer writer, did Davies have to earn the right to tell the story of AIDS on screen? Moreover, was it his kicking down the door with *Queer as Folk* that eventually enabled him to tell that story?

After all that, after getting to tell that story, and returning to the TARDIS…what next?

Chapter One

Canal Street to the TARDIS: Career overview

Davies's early career spent in children's TV would develop his creativity and also mark out some of the innovative and queer stories he'd later tell. From the stylistic elements, to working on his first queer characters, many of what we think of as 'Russell T Davies style' works, came from this early period. Like any writer does, he took a few missteps – with some works being written under another name because he didn't want to be associated with them. Essentially, in these early years we see the groundwork being laid during this time for the rest of his career.

Stephen Russell Davies was born in Swansea in 1963. He was always called by his middle name rather than his first. Later, he added the T to differentiate himself from another Russell Davies. In various interviews, he has talked of never being great at school (despite his parents being teachers). However, he did have a passion for drama, joining the West Glamorgan Youth Theatre as a teenager.

Davies studied English Literature at Worcester College, Oxford. This was followed by Theatre Studies at Cardiff University. In the early 1980s, he started his career, as many creatives in Cardiff do, as a volunteer at the Sherman Theatre. In 1985 he started working for BBC Wales on a series of short-form contracts, which included work as an illustrator for the show *Why Don't You?* It was for CBBC, too, that he had his one and only stint as a TV presenter, on 1 June 1987, in an episode of long-running children's show *Play School*. Over a period of around six months, he made several appearances. One ended in him walking off, declaring he was 'not doing that again'.[1] However, during his time at *Why Don't You?* Davies held several roles that would ultimately serve him well in the future – particularly the *Doctor Who* showrunner role. His roles (official and unofficial) included researcher, director, illustrator, assistant floor manager and publicist for fan mail.

During this time, too, Davies continued to write. He submitted a script to the soap *Crossroads* after hearing about a call for new writers. However, the show was cancelled in 1988 before the fruits of that could be determined. Davies's first professional scriptwriting job came in 1986 when producer Dave Evans offered him £100 to provide a replacement script for *Why Don't You.*[2] Off the back of that, he was offered various other CBBC jobs, culminating in 1988 in a six-month contract. At that point, Davies relocated to Manchester to work on the show.[3] One presciently 'Davies' script with a hint to the future *Who* years was where the presenter (Ben Slade) was trapped in a cafe by a supercomputer who tried to kill him.

Davies expanded his writing while at CBBC by working for shows including *DEF II*, *On the Waterfront*, and a documentary with kids TV icon Keith Chegwin about politics. This documentary is typical of Davies's work going forward – filmed in Norway, it took on politics and attitudes to politics, something Davies wouldn't shy away from in the 'family' show *Doctor Who* or, indeed, in his broader work. The crux of his approach is perhaps ingrained from the years he spent working in kids' TV, and that approach is to harness the power of TV to convey a message, and perhaps even change minds. CBBC was at this time – and indeed continues to be – a vehicle for education and information as much as entertainment (as the BBC's public broadcaster remit). But there was something, too, of a 'golden age' across the 1980s and 1990s, of which Davies was a part, where the BBC programming for kids pushed boundaries and didn't shy away from complex issues.

This type of writing shows up in Davies's work on BBC children's dramas *Dark Season* (1991) and *Century Falls* (1993), and his last stint on kids' TV with *Children's Ward* (1989–2000, Granada).

Dark Season can be seen as a *Doctor Who* precursor, partly as it contained a few similar storylines. However, what writer doesn't (rightly) steal from their own material? Also, Davies, as a lifelong Whovian, possibly saw it as a chance to write *Doctor Who*-style stories. These included episodes where teenagers were trapped by school computers (including a young Kate Winslet as 'Reet') and an episode where, crossing over with another supercomputer plot, the villain, Mrs Pendragon, crashes through the school stage. From elements such as the characters forming a group much like the Doctor and his companions to *Who*-like plot points, this period in his career feels a little like a bridge between the childhood *Doctor Who* fan and the future showrunner.

Davies followed *Dark Season* with *Century Falls* in 1993. It was set in an isolated village in the Yorkshire Dales/North York Moors and centred on a pair of psychic twins. *Century Falls* was a much darker work than its predecessor *Dark Season* and was created by the same director, Colin Cant.

While writing *Dark Season* and *Century Falls*, Davies sought freelance projects elsewhere; these included three scripts for the iconic BBC children's comedy *ChuckleVision* (1987–2009). However, he is probably better known to viewers from that generation through his work on Granada's *Children's Ward* (1989–2000), which would provide a springboard to his adult drama career. The children's medical drama was run by Tony Wood, who would later be best known for his work on *Coronation Street*. Similar to the BBC's adult medical drama *Casualty*, each episode of *Children's Ward* dealt with a 'disease of the week' alongside being an ongoing soap-like drama. By the mid-1990s, there was a push in the storylines to include issues that affected young people.

Davies won his first BAFTA in 1996 for his work on the one hundredth episode of *Children's Ward* (renamed *The Ward* in later series). Once again engaging with social issues, for this episode Davies wrote about grooming in online chatrooms – at this point, an emerging threat. In typically Davies fashion, the episode hinged on sci-fi fandom, with the character being groomed in an *X-Files* chatroom.

From this success, Davies would end up leaving the show for adult drama. He'd previously set his ambitions around soap opera writing, which he'd eventually realise by writing a straight-to-VHS *Coronation*

Street feature called *Viva Las Vegas!* (1997), in which long-standing couple from the show, Vera and Jack Duckworth, go on a trip to Vegas. In the interim in the mid-1990s, Davies would write for various programmes, including *Cluedo*, *Do the Right Thing* and *The House of Windsor*. The latter did poorly in reviews, and it seems Davies himself was unsure of their quality at the time, as for these shows he submitted scripts under a pseudonym. At the same time, Davies felt he had more freedom to write gay characters. In *Revelations* (a late-night soap opera), he wrote about a lesbian vicar with a coming-out storyline.

The Grand

Davies's next major project and first significant adult drama was *The Grand* (1997–8, Granada), a period soap drama set in a Manchester hotel during the interwar years. When another writer dropped out, the entire series fell to Davies to write. It's a reasonably dark piece despite being a seemingly generic period drama. The storylines reflect the unease and emotional trauma of the period. It aimed to show the real impact of those years: a soldier's execution for desertion, a destitute maid who threatens to abort her unborn child illegally, and also features a chambermaid called Monica Jones, played by Jane Danson, who is arrested and hanged for the murder of her rapist, who she killed in self-defence. The show was renewed for a second series despite the first season's dark tone. Considering the serious issues it addressed, the second series is slightly lighter in tone. *The Grand* was the first TV show where Davies included queer characters in his scripts. Long before *Downton Abbey*, in a similar era, gave us the 'gay butler', Davies gave us the gay barman. In the second series, there are a sequence of flashbacks of barman Clive Evans's life in the 1920s.

Davies himself has described this as a turning point in his writing of gay characters and his writing in general, as he says in an interview with the *Guardian* in 2003:

> I invented the story of Clive, the barman. Clive was a working-class lad struggling to express his sexuality in a time when the proper adjectives and nouns barely even existed. And

by focusing on Clive's sexuality instead of sub-plotting it, I wrote better.[4]

This was a shifting point for Davies, realising that he could write better, write perhaps more authentically if he 'wrote gay', as he continues to reflect:

> The Granada executives, Gub Neal and Catriona MacKenzie, were then appointed as heads of drama at Channel 4. Catriona pointed out that the Clive script was better than anything else I'd written. In essence, she was saying, 'Go gay!', but a lot more elegantly than that.[5]

'Go gay!' It is a brilliant imperative for any queer writer, and Davies's decision to 'Go gay!' would ultimately break down the doors for others to follow. But as a writer, it's an incredibly freeing notion: go gay. Or, more accurately, be who you are. Writers are told to write what you know and put yourself into the story, but that can be hard as a queer writer. This was true, particularly in the 1990s. How do you put yourself into the story or write what you know when what you know and who you are isn't accepted? Or, as Davies stated in the same interview with the *Guardian* cited above, 'Accept it or not, I'm going to write it.'[6]

Viewed from the perspective of the 2020s, that's fine. If you're Russell T Davies with many bankable projects behind you, many BAFTAs, and a production company that supports and trusts you, great. But as a young, relatively unproven writer in the early 1990s? It was a giant leap; nobody else was really 'going gay'.

Davies's early career showed elements of the style he'd develop over coming shows – from wry, dark humour, to a penchant for nerds and their stories, and even further, to his incorporation of queer stories. Nobody is entirely 'themselves' as a writer early in their career, particularly when trying to cobble together whatever work they can. But also, it takes time for a writer to grow into their voice, and Davies was curating this across these early projects.

Queer as Folk

This is the point at which Davies had his break-out hit *Queer as Folk* on Channel 4. On a personal level, this gave him the chance to recover from an accidental drug overdose (an event which made it into the series) and the opportunity to experience his first full-fledged celebration of his queer identity on screen. The first series was broadcast in 1999 and the second, shorter series, subtitled *Queer as Folk 2*, aired in 2000. Chapter Two: 'Can you show that on TV?' explores this queer drama in detail.

Bob & Rose

Following on from *Queer as Folk* was *Bob & Rose*, a very different style of queer drama, and one explored in Chapter Five: 'Other queer stories' as another approach to telling queer stories. It was overshadowed by world events, as it aired in September 2001, when the events of 9/11 dominated the TV schedules for weeks. The show was one of Davies's mum's favourites, with her describing it as 'possibly the best thing [he has] ever written'.[7] It was also the last thing she saw of his, as she died shortly after the fourth episode aired.

The Second Coming

For atheist Davies, writing about the second coming of Christ was perhaps not a logical step, but as with much of his work, here he was seeking to provoke debate. The series starred future Doctor Christopher Eccleston as a video store employee, who discovers he is the son of God with a few days to save the human race. *The Second Coming* had been several years in the making, enduring many rewrites since the first draft, and was presented to Channel 4 in 2000. At its core was the idea of a second coming of Christ in a human form. Screened over two successive evenings during TV prime time on Sunday, 9 February and Monday, 10 February 2003, *The Second Coming* had viewing figures of over six million.

After accepting the role, Eccleston observed that 'Baxter was getting lost amid his loftier pronouncements' and was keen to make him more sympathetic, and possibly more 'human' with it. Joining him was Lesley

Sharpe – off the back of her role in *Bob & Rose* – as the woman who was his downfall (Judith) and Mark Benton as the Devil. Its subject matter made it controversial from the start. It was the subject of a *Sunday Express* article a year before its original projected transmission date of late 2001.

Davies reportedly received death threats for the show's represent-ation of anti-religious messaging within the story, and criticism of the story itself. However, he also received multiple award nominations, for a National Television Award and a Royal Television Society Award.

Mine All Mine

Before his mother died, Davies returned home to Swansea frequently, and this provided inspiration for his next work, *Mine All Mine*. Essentially it is a show about family, and about Wales – the latter being a subject Davies hadn't really visited at this point. The show then is about a family in Wales, who in fact discover they own the entire city of Swansea. Airing in 2004, it was based on a folktale about the Welsh pirate Robert Edwards, who was famous for staking a claim to seventy-seven acres of Lower Manhattan. This series was a different direction to much of Davies's work up to this point and is still some-thing of an outlier in his work – more a mainstream comedy than a drama or science fiction. He also for the first time used a lot of Welsh actors, including a cameo from Swansea native Catherine Zeta-Jones.

Filmed in, and showing off, many areas of Swansea – which Davies was familiar with from his early life – it also mirrored his personal life in that the central family had two daughters and a gay son... just like Davies's family. Ultimately, it would be his least successful series commercially and not one that is often remembered even by fans of Davies – though some Swansea locals do remember it fondly. It aired in the four weeks running up to Christmas in 2003, ending with a 90-minute finale.

Casanova

Another often overlooked drama, but a fan favourite due to the inclusion of future Doctor David Tennant, was *Casanova*, which aired on BBC3 in 2005. Producers Julie Gardner, Michele Buck and Damien Timmer approached Davies to write *Casanova* (which was produced by London Weekend Television). It was to be a twenty-first-century adaptation of Casanova's memoirs. He agreed to script the series because it was 'the best subject in the world'. After reading the memoirs, instead of further perpetuating the stereotype of a hyper-sexual lover, he wanted to create a realistic depiction of Casanova. The series was initially written for ITV but after he could not agree on the serial length was turned down. Gardner took up a position as Head of Drama at BBC Wales and took the concept of *Casanova* with her to the new appointment. The BBC agreed to this arrangement only if the funding came from a regionally based independent production company. Davies turned to Nicola Shindler, who agreed to become the serial's fifth executive producer.

In Davies's script, two actors shared the title role: Peter O'Toole as the older Casanova and David Tennant as the younger version. In a departure from earlier adaptations like Dennis Potter's famous 1971 version, this series focused less on sex and misogyny and more on Casanova's respect for women. The series focused on three women for this: his mother (Dervla Kirwan), his lover Henriette (Laura Fraser) and his consort Bellino (Nina Sosanya). It followed Casanova through his early adulthood and the shaping of the man behind the legend.

When it premiered on BBC3 in March 2005, the first episode attract-ed 940,000 viewers, a record for a first-run drama on that channel. Of course, shortly after this, Casanova himself would take up the controls of the TARDIS when Tennant stepped into the role of the Doctor.

Doctor Who and *Torchwood*

We now enter the latter half of the 2000s, for Davies's *Who* and *Torch-wood* years. As I will show in Chapter Three: 'Gay aliens?' and Chapter Four: '*Doctor Who* for grown-ups', working on these programmes represented a childhood dream of Davies's. He embraced *Doctor Who*'s existing queer aesthetics and mixed it with twenty-first-century representation and a lot of Welshness. This, along with *Queer as Folk*, probably embodies what Davies was known for. During that time, the Welshness, the revival and the focus of the world's eye on Cardiff cannot be understated. It was a strange, yet brilliant (to borrow a phrase from the Tenth Doctor) time to be a lover of British sci-fi, Cardiff or Russell T Davies. That period tangentially shaped TV going forward, too, with the actors it supported in their careers, the writers and directors, and other people it nurtured. But also, the new generation of children it inspired through its storylines.

Torchwood and *The Sarah Jane Adventures*, the latter of which aired a year after the former, represent spin-offs from *Doctor Who* at both ends of the spectrum; one very much for adults and the other for kids. Both illustrate Davies's ability to spin many plates and adapt to multiple audiences. As mentioned above, it was an exciting time for TV and represented a high point in Davies's career. It enabled him to move forward with a pick of projects to work on in the next phase of his career.

Post-*Who*

In the post-*Who* landscape, there were many options for Davies.

His first project after *Who* was a book about his time on the show. In what would become a pattern throughout his career over the next few years, Davies never quite left *Who*, returning for audio dramas, short stories and social media takeovers. Then he simply took back the show in 2022. But as a punctuation to the series, he worked with journalist Benjamin Cook on an unusual and brilliant project.

The Writer's Tale

In September 2008, BBC Books published *The Writer's Tale*, a collection of emails between Davies and Cook, who worked on the *Radio Times* and *Doctor Who Magazine*. *The Writer's Tale* covers emails between February 2007 and March 2008. Cook and Davies referred to it as the 'Great Correspondence'. It mostly covers a mix of *Doctor Who* production and Davies's writing process across the fourth season of *Who*, including 'Voyage of the Dammed', 'Partners in Crime', 'Midnight', 'Turn Left', 'The Stolen Earth' and 'Journey's End' as focal points in the discussion. In the book's first chapter Cook also asks what he calls 'big questions' about Davies's writing and character development. In this, Cook discusses

Davies's character Donna Noble alongside *Skins* character Tony Stonem (who Davies did not write/create) as a contrasting character discussion. It becomes as much a writing-reflective-work/advice collection as it is a behind-the-scenes look at *Who*. Other 'big questions' include how he formulated ideas for stories, and the question, 'Why do you write?' After a few weeks, Cook assumed an unofficial advisory role in talking about the scripts and development of ideas with Davies. In the epilogue, there's another short exchange between them. Here, Cook changes from his role as 'Invisible Ben' to 'Visible Ben'. Following on from other successful series finales, 'The Parting of the Ways', 'Doomsday' and 'The Last of the Time Lords', which see the Doctor alone in the TARDIS, Cook advises mirroring this in 'Journey's End'. So instead of a cliff-hanger leading into 'The Next Doctor', we again see the Doctor alone. In the emails, after some days of deliberation, we see Davies accept that suggestion and thank Cook for his notes which improved the episodes.

Although initially planned as an insight into *Doctor Who*, the book is so much more; it is an exploration of every aspect of the writing process from the inside. It wasn't intended as a manual, but a writer could do a lot worse than reading this book and learning from Davies's techniques (and mistakes). It's peppered with gems of advice and ways of thinking about writing that make the process more transparent. (At the risk of breaking the fourth wall, this writer has, ever since reading that book, had a name for the weird intangible 'there but not' moments of writing that Davies calls 'the maybe' where, of course, a lot of this book existed for many months.)

There's also, naturally, a lot of *Who* content and many behind-the-scenes moments in the book that, despite the all-encompassing BBC coverage of *Who*, would never have seen the light of day if the book hadn't been published. In addition, it comes from the keyboards of Davies and Cook, both utter nerds for the Doctor and others, which brings it to life. Even the most cynical of fans would struggle not to find joy in their trading of tales from the TARDIS, and it feels like an apt way to end that period in Davies's writing life; by writing about it.

Post-*Who* writing

Davies stepped down from *Who* in 2009 and finished his tenure with four feature-length episodes. His departure from the show was announced, alongside a press release naming Steven Moffat as his successor, in May 2008. Davies's time in late 2008 was concentrated on writing the 2009 specials and preparing for the handover of leadership to Steven Moffat. He discusses this in 'The Final Chapter' of *The Writer's Tale* where he talks about departure plans for him, Gardner and Tennant. David Tennant's departure would be announced live during ITV's National Television Awards in 2008. Davies's last full script for *Who* was completed on 4 March 2009 and the filming of that episode was completed on 20 May, ending Davies's tenure (for now).

In June 2009, Davies moved with Gardner and Jane Tranter to the US and settled in Los Angeles, California. From there, he continued to oversee the production of *Torchwood* and *The Sarah Jane Adventures*. For *Sarah Jane* Davies also wrote the 2010 story 'Death of the Doctor' (season 4, episode 5). Davies also wrote the series opener and closer – 'The New World' and 'The Blood Line' – for *Torchwood: Miracle Day*. Across both series he was still giving informal assistance and story guidance. At this time too he was collaborating as script consultant on *Baker Boys*, a drama by former *Who* writer Helen Raynor and Welsh playwright Gary Owen. He was also approached by Lucasfilm to write for the proposed *Star Wars* live-action TV series, but he refused the commission.

Davies returned to the UK in 2011 after his partner, Andrew Smith, developed cancer, and this allowed him to work on a 'replacement' CBBC drama for *The Sarah Jane Adventures* (after Elisabeth Sladen's tragic and untimely death halted the series). Davies worked on this with *Who* and *Sarah Jane* writer Phil Ford. *Wizards vs Aliens* (2012–14), a CBBC drama about a teenage wizard and his scientist friend, was created by Davies and Ford as a 'genre clash' between sci-fi and supernatural fantasy. Davies also wrote for CBeebies on two other scripts for *Old Jack's Boat*, which starred *Doctor Who* alumni Bernard Cribbins and Freema Agyeman as a retired fisherman called Jack and his neighbour Shelley.

New queer dramas and old stories

From 2015 and beyond, we see Davies move back to queer drama in *Cucumber, Banana, Tofu, A Very English Scandal* and *It's a Sin* (explored in detail in Chapter Six: 'Queering history at the BBC', Chapter Seven: 'The future is a scary place' and Chapter Eight: 'Know your history'). All offer very different approaches to telling queer stories on TV, from an examination of true historical events in *Scandal* to an exploration of inter-generational identity in *Cucumber* and a fictionalisation of history in *Sin*. All are hugely important chapters in the development of queer TV and illustrate different approaches. To a degree, *Scandal* has somewhat been overlooked. It was perhaps not scandalous enough compared to other dramas, by this point, to grab attention. Or perhaps its more reserved historic approach made it less attention-grabbing than *Queer as Folk*. It was no less important. It presents a neat parallel in changes in politics to *Years and Years*, past and future, side by side in the timeline of Davies's work.

His other overlooked drama, *Cucumber* (2015), suffered with being compared to *Queer as Folk*, which it both was and wasn't destined to be by Davies. *Cucumber* is the natural successor in that it picks up the same generation decades on. But equally, the themes, the stories and the purpose of it sit elsewhere in the TV landscape. In Chapter Five: 'Other queer stories', I look at *Cucumber* alongside *Bob & Rose* to consider the different ways of telling queer stories that Davies embraced.

Finally, *It's a Sin* (2021), which was a decade or more in the making, both practically and, even more so, spiritually. Here Davies takes on the AIDS pandemic, something that feels very much like a rite of passage for him and his writing. It feels right that it took him so long to get to fulfil this rite of passage. Davies matured into writing here, what was a difficult piece of queer TV in every sense of the word, as explored in Chapter Eight: 'Know your history'.

A Midsummer Night's Dream

In 2016 Davies returned to the BBC with *A Midsummer Night's Dream*, an adaptation of the Shakespeare play for the channel. He had previously starred as Bottom in a school production of the play. *Dream* is the ultimate in a 'queering' take on the classic Shakespeare (with all its queer over- and undertones). *Dream* was a very 'Russell T Davies' reimagining of the play.

Post-*Sin*

What next, after completing the decade-long fight to get *It's a Sin* made, ticking off a bookend to his breakthrough hit of *Queer as Folk*? Davies's next project was *Nolly*, a biopic of iconic British soap opera star Noele Gordon, of *Crossroads* fame, with Helena Bonham Carter in the starring role. It aired on ITVX (ITV's streaming service) in February 2023. And as of 2023, Davies shows no sign of slowing down. He has announced a plan to write about sextortion, based on real-life incidents of blackmail. Davies has expressed interest in adapting for TV Charles Dickens's *The Old Curiosity Shop*. He is also attached to an ITV project, as mentioned above, as a script consultant and executive producer, titled *Three Little Birds*. This is a fictionalisation of Lenny Henry's mother's experiences arriving in the UK as part of the Windrush generation. As for the rest, in the uncertain world of TV, who knows...

Return to the TARDIS

Of course, that should be *Who* knows. It was announced in 2021 that Davies was returning to the helm of the TARDIS in 2022 for the sixtieth anniversary episode. See the Epilogue for reflections on that move and what it means for Davies's writing.

Coda

Style

The 'style' of Russell T Davies is a thread that runs through this book and, as with any writer, is integral to his work and somewhat impossible to quantify. In some ways, in the eye of the beholder too, what one person loves about Davies's style will be eyeroll inducing in another; what one person sees as his unique approach is a cliché trope to another. But we can agree that certain elements crop up repeatedly, forming a particular 'style' that, across his work, feels familiar and builds a picture of the storyteller he is.

Of course, Davies's real-life bleeds into his work – whether it's the tales from his past built on in *Queer as Folk* or that his partner's death is mirrored in the way Colin dies in *It's a Sin*. Or in writing Henry in *Cucumber*, we see a reflection on life as a middle-aged gay man. Davies's work is, of course, peppered by personal experience. That's a given for any writer. However, it's a dangerous line to tread, particularly with queer writers, to assume they are only writing from their experience. But in Davies's writing, we can perhaps see a streak of idealism. The Doctor always sees the world as redeemable; the human race as 'brilliant'. Perhaps there's something of that in Davies, too: an incurable streak of optimism through his work.

Humour
Humour is a hallmark of Davies's work. He can write the bleakest scenes and follow them with a belly laugh. The funeral in *Queer as Folk* is an excellent example of that. The reveal of Phil's death is devastating, as is his mother's response. The funeral opens sombrely, and then Vince has

14

to read 'D.I.S.C.O.' aloud. In some ways, this is a cliché of human life. As Davies says himself:

> You go to a funeral. Someone cracks a joke. I mean in the end we all die and it's a howling pit, but there's no point in writing that because in creating fiction you're actually creating something different, otherwise you'd be a documentary maker.[8]

But it's his deft handling of light and shade that makes Davies's work so very human. Just as with *Queer as Folk*, in *It's a Sin*, there are very, very funny moments at times before the tone shifts into seriousness. The fact that the series ends with a laugh is the best use of Davies's humour. In this case, we've just wept at the devastation of Ritchie's death. Still, in the final scene – a flashback to when he and all his friends were alive – we laugh because that's what life is, it's light and shade, and even if Ritchie is dead, especially then, it's still funny that a seagull stole his ice-cream.

Because, of course, the seagull stealing an ice-cream is funny, and the ridiculous sex scenes in *Queer as Folk* are funny, but so are the one-liners and the wit. There's something utterly unforgettable about Catherine Tate's delivery of 'A GIANT wasp' in *Doctor Who* that renders talking about a large stripy insect without doing a Donna Noble impression as near impossible. There's something hilarious and unforgettable about the dry wit of the quote, 'Paul McGann doesn't count.' For the following twenty years, this makes the poor Eighth Doctor the subject of a joke thanks to this line appearing in *Queer as Folk,* after Stuart is challenged to recite all the Doctors but leaves out McGann of the infamous movie version.

Humour is a great leveller and humaniser, and it is threaded throughout Davies's work. He has the skill in *Who* to make a children's show, one that appeals in both drama and humour to the whole family. There's a mix of child humour, farting Slitheen, and adult humour, such as a wink-wink about Shakespeare's queerness, and political humour. Elsewhere, when it's not humour in dark times, Davies has a knack for seeing the absurdity in humans in their behaviours and the way they speak. It could be the dry delivery of Julie Hesmondhalgh in *Cucumber*. Her comments on a variety of questions on sexual positions are dead-pan and that makes them hilarious. Or it might be that David Tennant can humorously interpret the subtle physical comedy written into the Doctor's approach to life and the universe. Sex can be inherently funny; writing in a variety of increasingly outlandish encounters for Stuart in *Queer as Folk* gives us a laugh. Davies has, in this respect, a rare, rounded view of comedy. Some writers specialise in dialogue, others in physical or set pieces; Davies manages to deliver all of these across his work.

Domesticity and the everyday

What Davies's humour manages is an all-encompassing look at human nature in all its quirks. There is another facet of Davies's work – domesticity. Davies's work for the most part is what could be termed 'kitchen sink drama', a term which describes a wave of 1950s and 1960s British theatre drama. Originally situated around the 'angry young men' plays of John Osborne (*Look Back in Anger*), it expands to encompass broader social realism plays. The inspiration for this style of play has continued. The line of such plays is often traced to British soaps like *Coronation Street*, where a realistic look at working-class everyday life is at the heart of the story.

Given Davies's love of *Corrie*, it's perhaps no surprise that the influence of this style of writing seeps into his work. Whenever or wherever his work is set, it's the human element that he focuses on. We see this in *Who*, where in contrast to the previous incarnation, the Doctor and their relationship to both the companions (in a platonic way) and their connection and fascination with the everyday lives of humans, takes centre stage. It's through the eyes of the Doctor, as an alien observing humans, that Davies can marvel at the human race, and celebrate and commiserate this on a bigger scale than perhaps would be 'acceptable' in other dramas. The Doctor can give voice to the fascination and wonder with humans and their everyday, and that comes through in Davies's other work.

In his other writing, Davies's specialty is everyday people. This is never more apparent than in *Years and Years*, in which we see a series of catastrophic world events through the domestic lens of one family's experience. As they say at the end, 'we just lived through it,' and in living through it, the everyday doesn't stop – from family dramas and affairs to simple dinners and cups of tea. The power of this lies in witnessing the small drama alongside the large, which is a factor that filters down through all of Davies's work. It's how homophobia and exclusion are talked about in *Queer as Folk* without being directly referenced. It's how *Cucumber* is entirely domestic in its concerns – the breakdown of a relationship, a man's mental health, the dynamics of a friendship group – but it is suitably gripping and dramatic, and also opens a host of broader thoughts and conversations. *Cucumber* is, in fact, arguably one of Davies's most compelling dramas, precisely for its domesticity. Whether or not we have experienced what Henry goes through, we can feel empathy and are drawn in. Davies centres on that across all his works.

What's critical here, as one of the most successful, and now arguably, influential writers in TV, Davies doesn't apologise for this. Somewhere along the line in the arts, 'kitchen sink' and 'domestic' became dirty words. Particularly today, in the era of high-concept work, with big-budget streaming dramas being the leaders again in TV, the work Davies does is perhaps not fashionable. That said, a writer who chose to reboot the much-maligned campy sci-fi that is *Doctor Who* probably cares very little about being 'fashionable'. The unapologetic domesticity and the drama of the everyday human condition have long defined his work. They are areas that should be celebrated.

Someone dies

In the domesticity of Davies's work, there is also the darker side; someone always dies. It happens right when you least expect it. In *Who*, it's an essential lesson: the Doctor cannot always save everyone. Indeed, we get how haunted they are by the deaths they've seen before. We get the celebratory 'everyone lives just this once' from the Ninth Doctor or River Song's voiceover reminding the Doctor that some days 'everyone lives' (and the Doctor revels at that moment). But we also see very real death in *Who*, not just on the Doctor's adventures but also in 'real life'. The episode 'Father's Day' best illustrates this when we see Rose come to terms with her father's death with the Doctor's help. In a twist supplied by the Doctor, we find that Rose was the mystery woman who sat with her dad until he died. We see her genuine grief, carried across the years to that point, and their real domestic impact, which mirrors Davies's skill.

Most of the deaths in *Who* are suddenly fleetingly seen as the result of Dalek attacks or similar. In classic sci-fi mode, we often see many beings or people die at once, in the disasters that the Doctor must avert. However, to emphasise this, Davies continually carries the tone back to the quiet domestic deaths, like in the case of Rose's dad, to bring home the real feelings of loss and remind us that the Doctor can't fix everything.

Elsewhere we get a surprise death, or a shocking one, as standard in most of Davies's work. We can question, how is it still a shock despite knowing how he operates? Skilful writing, for the most part, is the answer. The only death that perhaps falls a little flat is the death of Suzie in *Torchwood*, which, through no fault of Davies's, fell into a pattern of 'character is put in the promo and is killed off in the first episode'. This had been done in a lot of American TV at the time and most recently on another BBC flagship show, *Spooks* (who, in their defence, killed characters somewhat indiscriminately and regularly). Suzie's death didn't feel earned and was a plot point to get Gwen into the show. So perhaps like Davies's own joke about Paul McGann…Suzie's death doesn't count. *Torchwood* fills the 'killing off characters you care about' brief, with not one but three of the central team members killed off across three series. Those deaths felt earned and shocking (Ianto's death is explored in more detail in Chapter Four: '*Doctor Who* for grown-ups' for its broader implications). Owen and Toshiko's deaths certainly fulfil the 'didn't see it coming' and tragedy quota. While *Who* doesn't quite go in for the shock-death tactics in the same way (Davies manages some moderation for children), it doesn't shy away from death or if not death, at least loss. In *Who*, we lose River Song, Rose and Donna in tragic ways. They mostly find ways to come back, this being *Who*, but the tragedy is still there, tying into the domestic, love and loss themes that Davies uses so well.

Elsewhere, the 'didn't see it coming' death is there, ever-present, and ever a worry until it happens. We see it with Phil in *Queer as Folk*, we see it again in *Cucumber*, and we see it with Daniel in *Years and Years*. Even in *It's a Sin*, where we expect deaths, they take us by surprise. We don't expect sweet innocent Colin to be among the first to go; that's why it shocks us and is so tragic. In Davies's world, it's best not to get too attached to a character, just in case.

Pop culture/news culture

Elsewhere, Davies is also known for his pop culture references, cemented by his use of music, as explored below. Still, his worlds are firmly cemented in our reality. Whether it's Vince quoting *Doctor Who* or the Doctor quoting *The Lion King*, the characters are of our world. It never feels forced, and it's weaved together because nerds tend to rule Davies's world, too (as we'll see later). An array of fun pop culture references peppers his work.

We also see that Davies engages us with the media, using a meta technique, across his work. Explored in more depth in the section on politics, we see that Davies uses news broadcasts (usually fictionalised) to tell the bigger story, to the point in *Who* that regular newsreader Trinity Wells (played by Lachele Carl), became both a series regular, a fan favourite and a bit of a running joke. She witnesses every end of the world and mysterious save and yet never becomes suspicious of the alien with a blue box. Again, Davies is playing somewhat into how the media is controlled and controls us (a subject of the Ninth Doctor adventure 'The Long Game'). Elsewhere Davies incorporates news and media as a backdrop. We see snippets in *It's a Sin* where news and media add to the period feel of the piece. In *Queer as Folk*, a mix of *Doctor Who* and porn on TV provides the particular aesthetic of that show. Despite that humorous juxtaposition, the mix of the pornographic and sexual elements of the show, and the characterisation of Vince as a nerd, contributes to the creation of the world the characters inhabit. These examples show, too, the eye and ear Davies has for how media makes up our world and identities, which he uses to tell those stories.

Music

While it's not Davies's invention, he uses music, specifically a mix of pop music and original composition, within his stories as a driver of the narrative. Some writers leave the music to directors and post-production, but Davies doesn't do this, as for Davies, the music is integral. For some stories/series, an original composition is more appropriate – *Who* and *Torchwood*, particularly, for example, need the otherworldly music that original compositions provide. For these, and across most other series, Davies collaborates with Murray Gold. The latter's music ended up being the soundtrack to many people's *Who* experience, including the new theme tune, which he composed with the caveat that the new theme would divide fans, old and new, at regular intervals. But what would *Doctor Who* fandom be without a healthy dose of disagreement?

Davies is not above incorporating an original or pop song into the Whoniverse. A couple of original songs feature in episodes he wrote. For example, in 'The Runaway Bride', the song 'Love Don't Roam' (performed by Neil Hannon) is played at Donna's wedding. Hannon also performs vocals on other tracks, such as 'Song for Ten'.

Songs from the 'real' world have a different effect in *Who*. They remind viewers of the link the fictional world has to their world. Here they have a different effect from the use of pop songs in other series by Davies. However, he still effectively incorporates pop music, and the resultant pop culture links. He does this, firstly, to ground *Who* in reality, much like the companions ground the Doctor in the real world. The music reminds viewers that the world the stories are set in is 'our' world too. Secondly, pieces of music can be effective mood setters and storytelling moments. They can offer powerful backdrops, such as 'Abide with Me' playing in 'Gridlock' as a link to an almost long-lost humanity. Or 'He Who Would Valiant Be' sung by the Choir of Christ College in 'Human Nature', which gives a period piece moment and evokes an emotional response. Added to this are the various Christmas specials that include pop songs or hymns to invoke the season.

But possibly one of the greatest uses of pop music in *Who* was with the Master (John Simm's incarnation). Davies/the Master uses 'Voodoo Child' by Rogue Traders when the Master speaks the line from the song to announce the Toclafane's entrance. First, we hear the sound of drums building up in the Master's head, and then he shouts out the line, 'Here come the drums,' as the music begins, revealing the end of the world that he hopes for. The contrast with the invasion, the fear, and the sight of the TARDIS turning red and presumably dying, against the backdrop of a thumping drum and bass dance number, works as a disorienting but brilliant bit of TV storytelling. Later, the Master uses The Scissor Sisters 'I Can't Decide' as a satiric backdrop to murder. This is the tone of tongue-in-cheek camp drama that *Doctor Who* is the perfect vehicle for. Would a combination of The Scissor Sisters and a megalomaniac villain work in every show? No. But at least Davies's *Who* fits perfectly in *Who*.

Davies's use of music works best when he can fuse storytelling with pop song backdrops and a camp sensibility. In *Who* or *Queer as Folk* or *Cucumber*, we see a perfect storm of musical storytelling. This trope also works well in his darker works. Again, the dramatic use of a perfectly timed piece of familiar music in *Years and Years* works to evoke the mood. Also, in an almost 180-degree flip of *Who*, familiar music in dark post-apocalyptic drama has a chilling impact. The use of contemporary music moments in *Years and Years*, such as when Chumbawumba's 'Tubthumping' plays, is a throwback for viewers and a discordant moment of past meets future. 'Past meets future' features also in that the title track of *Years and Years* came from the band fronted by Olly Alexander, who would star in *It's a Sin*, and naturally sing in it.

It's a Sin offers the classic TV trope of using period music to help tell a story, something Davies hadn't been able to indulge in up to that point. This is an approach used to a degree in *A Very English Scandal*, which contained snippets of period pop songs along with the TV score by Murray Gold. However, *It's a Sin* doesn't only lean into the use of music to denote the period, but it features the kind of music that would have soundtracked the lives of the young characters. Much like *Queer as Folk* did with the music in the clubs of Canal Street, *It's a Sin* gives the audience, this time retrospectively, the music that the characters would listen to, and uses it to tell their story.

If anything, the 'traditional' use of music in Davies's dramas is the most effective. The title, *It's a Sin*, was a happy accident, given that the show was initially titled *Boys*. It was renamed as at that time, there was another similarly named drama. Calling it *It's a Sin* aligned with the camp queerness of the Pet Shop Boys' song 'It's a Sin' and allowed for the cross-promotion of Olly Alexander singing the title song. But beyond that, the show dives into music from the era, which also tells a story. *It's a Sin* is not only a musical time capsule steering us through the decade we spend with the characters, it also evokes emotions as we go. The series moves from 'Tainted Love' to 'Call Me' by way of 'Love Will Tear Us Apart', ending with 'Everybody Hurts'. It's a ride of classic pop tracks from the era. It's also a mix of camp queer classics, from Barry Manilow to Bronski Beat, and for anyone who was there, no doubt evoking memories of the time while also indicating clearly through the music just how queer a show and story this is at its roots.

Because queerness and music are important and interwoven in Davies's work, there's a strong tradition of queer people using music to express themselves, tell stories and even tell coded messages about themselves. In a world where, for example, queer TV wasn't as visible, music culture was a space where queer people could express themselves more freely. Pop stars, like Boy George or the Pet Shop Boys, were cultural icons leading the way in this. Particularly in terms of gender-non-conforming identities and expressing coded meanings in music, queer musicians embraced the space music gave them. Music and club scenes, from the 1920s and 1930s underground to the Canal Street of *Queer as Folk*, also clearly form an invaluable part of queer history. By bringing these two worlds together, using queer soundtracks pulled from the world they were set in to tell the stories of that world, Davies makes a powerful statement with his music.

Music, then, is a driving force in Davies's shows. *Queer as Folk* is an obvious example. The club scenes intersperse with hits associated with the period and feed the overall picture of a captured moment in queer history. But as a backdrop to the story, too, Davies carefully infuses the 'right' piece of pop music at the right time. The whole effect is much more calculated than simply a backdrop of pop hits; after all, each music moment costs money in royalties and time in administration and procuring the rights. This means that it's all carefully orchestrated.

We see a similar approach in *Cucumber*, where the music sometimes forms an antithetical backdrop. With us being mostly in Henry's head, the soundtrack is the music he likes, which is somewhat out of step with the popular music of the time. *Cucumber* also provides one of the finest examples of Davies using music to story-tell. In the opening episode, Henry gets ready for a date to a thumping pop soundtrack. For an entire five-minute scene, we all hear the pumping pop beats while he gets ready, showering, dressing, to the backdrop of his life about to fall apart. The events that unfold during that time are dark and impact the trajectory of his story. We watch it unfold to a Kylie soundtrack. It's a brilliant antithesis, but the disco soundtrack, overlaid by the story's visuals, is a great shorthand and compelling storytelling.

Cliff-hangers

Davies is a strong advocate for the continued use of the cliff-hanger ending and opposes advertising them, as letting people know about them dilutes the impact of the story, to the point where he also instructs editors to remove them from press copies of his episodes in case the impact is ruined. Cliff-hangers were removed from the review copies of the *Doctor Who* episodes 'Army of Ghosts', 'The Stolen Earth', and the first part of 'The End of Time', and Rose Tyler's unadvertised appearance in 'Partners in Crime' was excised. In an interview with BBC News shortly after the episode 'The Stolen Earth', Davies argued that the success of a popular TV series is linked to how well producers can keep secrets and create a 'live experience'.

> It's exciting when you get kids in the playground talking about your story, about who's going to live or die, then I consider that a job well done because that's interactive television, that's

what it's all about: it's debate and fun and chats. It's playing a game with the country, which is wonderful.[9]

This illustrates another interesting aspect about Davies, too; his messages or emotions are always hidden in plain sight and everyday moments, even in terms of his strategy. As *The Sunday Times* wrote about him in 2014:

> He wants to create something that will have people coming up to the channel's controller at a drinks party, wanting to talk about it. He's typically British in that he plays down his achievements. When you talk to him it's, 'Oh, I'm just a gay man. I don't really know what I'm doing – I'm just bumbling along', but the decisions he makes are not just artistic but strategic. He thinks big.[10]

The lists of top influencers repeatedly cement his legacy and indicate to whom we put his name against next. As he continued in *The Sunday Times*:

> On Saturday I met Martin Sherman – the seminal gay writer who wrote Bent. It was such an honour to meet him, and I thought, 'God, if I'm on some kind of list that includes people like that, which I think I might be, then that's really lovely.' If you can list me next to Martin Sherman, I'm a very happy man, and I'd be churlish to complain about any problems that come with that.[11]

In 2022, he was featured on a list of the most influential British artists of the last fifty years. He was number three, after David Bowie and Steve McQueen. If that's not style, what is?

Chapter Two

Can you show that on TV?
Queer as Folk

Queer as Folk was a breakout for Russell T Davies, Channel 4 and queer stories on TV. It offered a farewell to the hedonistic 1990s and a glimpse of what could be in the future. Following the (mis)adventures of Stuart and Vince provided a significant formative experience for many young queer people, both at the time of broadcast and later. Ask a queer millennial about what they watched in secret at home, and it is likely that they watched *Queer as Folk*, late at night on a bedroom TV, or alone on VHS at university or in their early twenties. Discussing the show became a quick way to tell if someone was 'your kind of person' (i.e. queer, or not a homophobe). *Queer as Folk* was initially one of those rebellious Channel 4 shows that wasn't for parents but gave a glimpse into queer life for those not yet living it: it was *Sex and the City* with gay guys who seemed like the ones you met (for better or worse) on a Friday night.

For all the fun and frivolity, too, Davies packed characteristic heart and seriousness into his landmark show. The audience ends up caring deeply for Vince and Stuart, and they lifted the lid on important conversations about queer life. The themes of the show include dangerous sexual encounters, early deaths, the shadow of AIDS, drug use and bad relationships. It also featured unconventional families, chosen families, friendship, sex and love. In short, it had the makings of great drama packed into ten short episodes. It's a show of its time, and also a show that defined a time in TV.

Channel 4

The show was massively sexual, fitting in well with Channel 4's 'racy' image at the time, and frankly, since. Set up in 1982, the channel was a teenager when *Queer as Folk* aired. The history of Channel 4 and where it sits today is integral to the history of queer TV and, indeed, Russell T Davies's history in broadcasting.

Before Channel 4 and S4C, the UK had three terrestrial TV services: BBC1, BBC2 and ITV. The Broadcasting Act 1980 began the process of adding a fourth, and Channel 4 was formally created, along with its Welsh Counterpart, S4C. The Welsh language channel S4C split its programming between original Welsh language news, magazine programmes and drama and shared some of the Channel 4 broadcasts. Channel 4 was extremely influential in shaping an 'alternative' TV landscape away from the 'official' BBC and the older-demographic-focused ITV.

The channel is crucial because it represents a pushing of boundaries. It would be the natural home for Davies to return to with *It's a Sin*; only the home of *Queer as Folk* would have been a suitable space for it. But beyond that, Channel 4 is a home of inclusivity – from its commitment to disability inclusion in hosting the Paralympics since 2010 and creating *The Last Leg* as a comedic companion, which then became a late-night staple in its own right. In terms of LGBTQ+ representation, too, Channel 4 has regularly hosted Pride-themed work. In 2022 the channel went all out with a month of programming from LGBTQ+, from *First Dates* to documentaries about the history of Pride, to a 'Pride finale' party hosted by comedian Joe Lycett. That show, which included an array of mini documentaries, a 'twat signal' pointed at Vladimir Putin and a drag queen doing poppers in the background of a shot, was as queer and inclusive as it's probably possible to get on TV. *Queer as Folk* remains an iconic part of that legacy twenty years on.

The title of the show comes from the Northern expression 'there's nowt as queer as folk', and plays on the (to this point) largely insulting term for gay people. Originally it had been called *Queer as Fuck*, but even Channel 4 drew the line at that (and certainly American buyers would have). This drive for Davies to 'write gay' came following a personal crisis, after accidentally overdosing on recreational drugs in 1997.[12] A plot line that would ultimately make it into the lives of the Manchester gay friends in *Queer as Folk.*

The show centres on the iconic duo of Stuart Alan Jones (Aidan Gillian) and Vince Tyler (Craig Kelly). Stuart is a high-flying advertising executive (though it's never entirely clear exactly what he does). Vince manages a supermarket. Stuart is good-looking (and knows it), confident and sexually free. Vince is more reserved, less confident and hopelessly in love with his best friend.

Meanwhile, Nathan (Charlie Hunnam), aged fifteen, bursts onto Canal Street and into Stuart and Vince's lives. While the main plot centres on this trio, there's also an array of friends and family around Stuart and Vince, showing both the domestic home-life realities of gay men in the 1990s, often seen in the harsh light of homophobia, and the backdrop of Canal Street in 1999 and the gay men who brought it to life.

Queer as Folk, although on the surface a realistic-adjacent depiction of gay city life in the 1990s, is also meant as a fantasy, with the three central characters – Stuart, Vince and Nathan – as gay archetypes. In a snapshot, they're supposed to represent the whole 'world' of queer life. Given that the series is shorter (British TV drama tends to be, in contrast to its American counterparts), there isn't time to give deep back stories to the characters. Instead, the characters give a sense of the world that gay men at this time and in this place represent.

Stuart and Vince and 'types of gay man'

Firstly, there is Stuart, who is out there, over the top, camp and the slutty one. But 'slutty' in Stuart's world is reclaimed, not shamed. Stuart is also doing something radical for 1999: proudly defying heteronormative standards of how to live a life. Repeatedly, particularly in stories about queer characters, gay men are rendered acceptable and palatable if they mimic traditional families in acceptable ways. Stuart Alan Jones says a resolute 'no way' to that and is unapologetic for it. Yet Stuart was sex-positive before it was popularised as a term. He has sex without apology; he is without inhibitions.

Next, we have Vince, who is the gay nerd (as discussed in Coda:

'Nerds'), a subsection of the community that should be celebrated in *Queer as Folk*. It is not surprising that gay nerd Davies wrote a gay nerd as a protagonist, but he was a rarity when it was written. In a community largely (on the surface, at least) obsessed with drinking, going out and sex *à la* Stuart, being a Vince was refreshing. Being a Vince in a world of Stuarts still feels anarchistic, even today. Vince shows you can be both: you can be gay, go to clubs and bars, have sex (or at least try to) and be a nerd. All of his 'connections' to men come when they share his nerdy passions, or he can connect to them through a love of TV, or similar. Even when he's set up with a woman from work, he declares in a parallel universe he'd just met his wife – because they bonded over TV.

Of course, Vince raises questions about whether the gay community *should* be dominated by pubs and clubs and drink and sex. The question is: is he *really* happy doing both, or does he just want to find a man to watch *Doctor Who* with? His character asks whether there are adequate spaces for all kinds of queer men, and the answer is, probably no. But there's space to be both.

The ongoing references to Vince being 'good-looking, actually' are also important. Gay culture is notoriously image-obsessed, and as in the friendship group, when everyone focuses on Stuart, there's an expectation that only the 'Stuarts' will have dating success. Of course, the truth is that Vince is perfectly nice-looking and, in essence, just a nice ordinary bloke (with all respect to Craig Kelly, who does look like a man you'd describe as 'nice looking'). Vince isn't gym-honed or Brad Pitt-looking (insert relevant cultural reference there). Still, his inclusion is vital to illustrate that you can't tell a gay man just by looking at him. Case in point, everyone at work thinks he's straight. Similarly, Vince is a total nerd, he loves *Doctor Who*, and that representation was also important, even if he was the butt of jokes. Because of the nerdy nature of *Doctor Who*, gays saw a place for them in the community too.

One-dimensional characters?

Linked to this too is the question of 'one-dimensional characters'. At the time, the response to the character portrayals in *Queer as Folk* was mixed from gay commentators. Some felt that the portrayal was too stereo-typical or even too narrow as a definition of what the gay experience should be. Again, the comparison to *Sex and the City* is apt, obvious, even. Just as straight women were deciding if they were a 'Carrie' or 'Samantha', gay men could decide if they were a 'Stuart' or a 'Vince' – while acknowledging that these archetypes would never fit completely snugly. *Queer as Folk* has more realistic living situations than *Sex and the City*, with Davies as ever incorporating working-class people authentically into his narratives. However, it's still 'aspirational' TV.

Queer as Folk explores many different minority characters, although it is the white, middle-class, twenty-something, homosexual man whose experiences are portrayed in the most positive light. The representation of lesbianism is not as positive, as Russell T Davies creates lesbian characters that just want to have babies, settle down and be responsible, as opposed to the portrayal of excitement and rebellion that the male characters enjoy in their lives. As much as *Queer as Folk* was clearly designed as a look at gay male life, it is a frustration that the lesbian characters fall on the side of stereotypical narratives that were no better than more 'straight' shows at the time. It also feels like a slightly missed opportunity to represent the broader community.

In addition, *Queer as Folk* speaks to the high standards queer narratives are held to – expected to be all things to all people. *Sex and the City*, or other cultural juggernauts like *Friends*, weren't all things to everyone. They didn't 'accurately represent' the demographics in their shows, either – they, too, were fiction, and aspirational fiction at that. But because queer media was so limited still, when Davies was writing *Queer as Folk*, there was a mentality of needing to serve an entire community with one show. This is always a complex issue, as while multi-faceted gay characters shouldn't be too much to ask for, Davies was breaking new ground. Previously, gay characters were essentially 'token' characters rather than the show's focus. Except for the first wave of the TV version of *Tales of the City*, nobody had ever included this many gay characters in one narrative. So, while they couldn't possibly represent everyone, and indeed, they may be 'archetypes', their very existence was a huge step and extremely influential.

What *Queer as Folk* does, and what has made it endure in some respects, is offer a view of a particular time and place. Through the show, we get a snapshot of a particular element of gay Manchester at the turn of the millennium. We get a capturing of the post-AIDS, Gen-X party moment. Was this everyone's experience? Of course not, even those of the same age in Manchester would not all have had the same experience. But it is a broad, encompassing experience of that era – the partying, the casual sex, even the drug culture. Also, the universal theme of queer friendships is at the heart of the stories in the show.

'Problematic' themes

Aspects of the show naturally look 'dated' to a present-day reading. Some elements, like mobile phones or dial-up internet, have quaintly dated. Other elements pose a more 'problematic' reading, with hindsight. There's a mix of things at play here – rarely is a TV show truly 'timeless' and *Queer as Folk* was written as a snapshot of a particular time and place. Meanwhile too, times change, from the language used around the LGBTQ+ community to the types of behaviour seen as acceptable.

There are things that have always been 'unacceptable' or at least regarded as 'questionable' behaviour. Just because they're included in a TV show doesn't mean they're 'ok'. Fiction isn't necessarily a moral guide, and in no way did *Queer as Folk* position itself as a guide for good queer living. Nor was it a documentary, or entirely fiction. Audiences familiar with the gay scene in Manchester or elsewhere at this time likely saw many familiar elements and characters. But at the same time, nobody was positing Stuart Jones as an ideal model by which to live one's life (as much fun as it might look on TV).

One good example of this is drug use in the show. Drugs are omnipresent across the series – from the very start, with Stuart popping an unknown pill in the first episode. Then, after bringing Harvey home from a night out in the third episode, Phil overdoses and dies.

Harvey is never punished for his crimes, which may be to do with the attitudes towards gay people in 1999; thus, *Queer as Folk* reflected that. Although views towards the gay community were becoming more progressive at that time, it wasn't until post-*Queer as Folk* that gay experiences started receiving more positive coverage on TV and in reality. The effect was cumulative, from soaps like *Brookside* having the first gay character a decade earlier in 1985 and *EastEnders* following suit four years later. There had also been progress in other dramas, significantly the adaptation of Armistead Maupin's iconic queer novel series *Tales of the City*, which aired in 1993. British drama *This Life* (1996–7) also included a gay character (Warren) in its central cast. In *This Life*, much like *Queer as Folk*, the characters led exciting lives of the kind that couldn't be described as 'sensible'. They, despite being predominantly a heterosexual group of friends, also made many questionable life choices as well as choices that would not be deemed acceptable today.

However, the death of a gay character in a TV show is often at least historically problematic. The TV trope known as 'bury your gays', whereby a gay character would only be part of the show if, ultimately, they were killed off (as a kind of historic moral lesson), is one that has haunted TV and film. However, this is not to be misunderstood as 'any gay person dies on screen'. Instead, it is the 'convenient' killing off of the gay character, so as not to have to give airtime to a gay plotline, or as some kind of moral message about being queer. It's also used to lose one queer character in a largely heterosexual cast. So, while there is a death in *Queer as Folk*, and while that death is of a gay man, it does not fit the 'bury your gays' stereotype. As a large portion of the characters in *Queer as Folk* is gay, as is writer Russell T Davies, this is not the case here and is merely a characteristic of the drama genre that we expect to see on TV. In the TV trope known as 'bury your gays', the queer characters are killed because they can't be allowed to live happy, normal lives as it would be seen as morally questionable. However, when Davies kills a gay character, it isn't in direct response to him being gay or to illustrate a moral point about gayness. It's simply part of the plot. Proving that these things are complex and nuanced, Davies uses the death of a character to explore the negative implications of the choices made by some members of the gay community (drink, drugs, risky sexual situations).

Phil's mum comments on this when she corners Vince and asks him, 'Would a woman have run away?', referring to the fact that the man who gave Phil the drugs left him dead on the kitchen floor. Vince argues it has 'nothing to do with him being gay'. And she disagrees. While this scene *is* talking about wider community attitudes and the dangers of drugs, it also has AIDS parallels. The idea is that going home with women wouldn't have killed Phil, but going home with men could have. That AIDS wasn't the cause of Phil's death almost doesn't matter at this point – what matters is that because of AIDS, Phil's mum has learned to prepare herself for her son's early death and has asked herself these questions many times before it happens. It also shows another side of that period, and something Davies would revisit in *It's a Sin*, namely, the complicated relationship of parents to the sons who died too young. It's not about Phil's mum, any more than it will be about Ritchie's in *It's a Sin*. Still, their part in the story is acknowledged, and their grief and struggles are acknowledged, and that's vital.

Phil's death is an important comment on drug culture in the gay club scene. But that doesn't mean it can't be a metaphor for AIDS. Just as Davies chooses not to reflect directly on AIDS, it doesn't mean the threads of it aren't still woven into the story. Like any gay man who remembers that era, AIDS is difficult to avoid, even when directly trying to avoid it (an element explored in Coda: 'AIDS' in parallel with Davies's work on *It's a Sin*).

Of course, there is Nathan's overarching – and central – plot. When he meets Stuart, he is underage, not just for the age of consent for gay men (then twenty-one) but also for straight people (sixteen in the UK). Both facts are commented upon; Stuart is aware that he is underage, but he pursues the sexual relationship anyway. None of these characters are being posited as moral role models. There is, of course, an element of 'this would be different now'. It's unlikely that Davies would get the storyline cleared today. TV programmers have become more conservative, but there would also be a sense today of including the morality of the situation in the narrative.

That said, while 'of its time' is not necessarily a defence, the show is indeed of its time. If we asked the 'Nathans' of the time, or indeed an average sixteen-year-old, who was then going out clubbing – they'd say that sneaking in underage had been a rite of passage. While times might have changed and ID and door policies (might) be stricter in some places now, it is still a part of teenage life. As is sexual experimentation, and while Stuart isn't absolved of that – Nathan looks his age – underage sex is also something that happens, and something that happens for gay men. The way this happens now has shifted with app culture; in the late 1990s, going out to a club and 'pulling' was the way to meet men.

The relationship between Nathan and Stuart also comments on how the community used to function – younger guys would find older ones to 'show them the ropes', for want of a better description. Does that stray into 'problematic' territory? Of course it does. Does *Queer as Folk* show that too? Yes. We also see elements of the 'community' looking out for Nathan – as much as Vince complains he always gets stuck with Stuart's shags, he also keeps an eye on Nathan, driving him home and generally looking out for him. Vince's mum is a mum to everyone, including Nathan, giving him (Vince's) room to crash in and being conscious that if Nathan is telling the truth (he isn't), they should protect him from a homophobic family. While the relationship is problematic, viewed through current standards, there's an element of reflecting the times the show is set in and things being more nuanced than just Stuart taking advantage of a teenager.

In 'Shame/Pride Dichotomies in *Queer as Folk*', Sally Munt writes that *Queer as Folk* was 'castigated by the ITC for failing to "provide educational backup to the series on subjects such as safe-sex, and young people and sexuality".[13] *Queer as Folk* is a celebration of homosexuality, so its focus isn't necessarily on homosexual issues. The issues the show does cover – underage sex, drug abuse (the third and fourth episodes), and bullying and coming out – are often an afterthought and are not dwelled on. When Phil dies from an overdose in the third episode, he isn't found for several days. The show does not focus on loneliness and peer pressure to do drugs. Phil's mother only implies it, but blames his death on being gay and sleeping around. The lack of educational backup for the issues the show explores could have potentially been pretty damaging, as it doesn't provide its viewers with help or support on issues they might be combatting themselves. However, this is not a documentary or an educational film; it is drama, and the lessons are inherent in the story. It is not the responsibility of the writer to safeguard or even second-guess every viewer's response. This is why we see warnings before programmes or references to support lines after shows with traumatic and triggering content. The responsibility lies with the broadcaster, so in this case Channel 4, not Davies.

In 'Queer Cosmopolitanism: Place, Politics, Citizenship and *Queer as Folk*', David Alderson writes that 'the character of Stuart embodies this internationally recognisable queer lifestyle'.[14] Stuart has many sexual partners throughout the show, many of whom he meets in clubs. In 1999, this would have been the primary way gay men met each other, this was the 'recognisable queer lifestyle' of that day, and Stuart was the iconic gay character who embodied this on TV.

A commentator in the *Daily Mail* called for censorship in the wider press and media, somewhat predictably, of course, for a newspaper with a track record of homophobia (as well as racism, sexism, and all-round discriminatory reporting). Beck's Brewery sponsored the first four episodes, but then withdrew its sponsorship halfway through the series. Following a backlash from the gay community, Beck's offered to sponsor the second series. The producers refused this request.

Munt writes that there were three main complaints received for *Queer as Folk*. The first was, as quoted by Munt, 'the explicit and graphic nature of the sexual encounter involving an underage character', which I have already mentioned as being very controversial. The second complaint was 'that the phrase "fucking bastard cunts" had exceeded suitable boundaries'. This language is much less likely to receive complaints now, as viewers' tolerance for bad language has increased, and the dreaded 'c-word' is no longer banished from TV. Thirdly the show received complaints as 'the portrayal of troilism (three-way sex) had exceeded acceptable boundaries'.[15]

Of course, an outraged headline sells more papers/gets more clicks than a review that says a show was great. As we see again with *It's a*

Sin decades later, queer sex offers an opportunity for media which already looks to villainise LGBTQ+ people to publish scandalised, often exaggerated, headlines. Even with *Doctor Who*, where Davies was accused of making the TARDIS queer (as I explore in Chapter Three: 'Gay aliens?'), when the TARDIS was always pretty queer.

Perhaps *Queer as Folk* wasn't universally acclaimed when it first aired, but maybe that's because it wasn't a show for the mainstream. It was a show for the queer people who needed it.

Nathan's importance

Nathan offers what would later become a staple in queer coming-of-age dramas – the coming-out narrative. He doesn't so much as come out of the closet as hurtle out of it and straight into Stuart. He has his first gay club experience, his first sexual encounter, and weirdly, his first encounter with a lesbian and her baby, all in one night. While Nathan's isn't what would become typical of coming-out narratives of today's Young Adult novels and Teen movies, it is perhaps a little more authentic, at least for British teens. As discussed in this chapter, the British experience, particularly in the 1990s, of sneaking off to a club, trying out drinks (and sometimes drugs), and experimenting sexually, was not that unusual. Indeed Nathan's 'straight' friends in school talk about drinking and messing around with girls sexually at parties, and what Nathan does isn't that different.

The vital thing in some ways about Nathan is that he doesn't struggle with his sexuality. In classic coming-out narratives, we see a protagonist struggle with his sexuality. While that's valid and a lived experience for many, it's also refreshing to have a joyous 'arrival' rather than a reluctant, angst-ridden coming out. Nathan knows who he is and thinks he's ready to throw himself into gay life, so he does.

Not that his coming-out journey is without struggle entirely. We see him struggle in school with being 'out', and we watch him witness a fellow pupil get beaten up while the bullies cry 'fag' at him. We also see him come out to his best friend, Donna, with no drama; she supports him emotionally and practically. Donna is his rock – even when he doesn't appreciate it – and she protects him when he doesn't want it. In short, she's the woman every young gay man needs. A theme in much of Davies's writing is to recognise the women in queer communities who do the work. We see it later in *It's a Sin*, and across *Cucumber, Banana* and *Tofu*. We know Davies writes about strong women. He's particularly mindful of their place in the queer community. Donna later eases the way for Nathan, and in a 1990s British school setting where 'gay' would have been the favourite insult, she makes life easier for him.

Looking retrospectively at Nathan and his experience, we're reminded of what 'coming out' was like pre-internet. Whether it's his stack of porn magazines hidden in the wardrobe or having to go to Canal Street to encounter another gay man, the experience was lived in analogue. But that aside, perhaps part of the reason for the nature of Nathan's coming out, his subsequent actions, his relationship with Stuart, which is all a bit messy and dangerous, is because there were no roadmaps for queer young people pre-internet. Today Nathan would likely take online quizzes, stumble onto gay porn, or find a Reddit or TikTok that would lead him to his sexuality. Through those platforms (delete as applicable for age), he'd likely connect with other people who would educate him, allow him to meet friends, and, crucially, connect with queer people his age. Because the internet has democratised things, there are now more opportunities to connect with other queer people for people of his age.

In a slightly meta-reference, Nathan is finding his way without a TV show like *Queer as Folk* to guide him through coming out and everything that follows. As already mentioned, at that time, the show became a coded reference; if someone had seen it, it was a 'clue' to their sexuality, along with countless other pop culture references, through which queer people have figured each other out. Today, the Nathans of the world can walk into a bookshop, or turn on numerous streaming services, watch programmes, see films and read books about queer people. Outside of porn and the odd, usually terrible, gay arthouse film, queer representation was almost non-existent for Nathan. So that's why Nathan, too, is important in the show; he represents the generation that would grow up with things differently because of him.

Nathan isn't a role model; let's get that clear. However, there are two groups which probably define themselves as in the *Queer as Folk* generation. The first group are people, now around twenty-eight to thirty years old, the 'Vince and Stuart' generation, who saw their lives reflected in real time. These people were, to a degree, doing with *Queer as Folk* what straight people at the time were doing with *Sex and the City*, seeing a glossy version of their lives on screen and possibly defining themselves in terms of the characters. These guys (and girls) were already out, living the life, and of course, had waited a long time to watch a TV show about them. The other group were the Nathans, primarily watching the show on smuggled VHS, quietly in their bedrooms, seeing for the first time something like what they thought they might want, or hadn't even entertained before.

It's perhaps impossible for the generation after that to entertain that Nathan is partly very *Nathan* because of the culture he grew up in. A vacuum existed then, where nobody taught him how to be gay until he stumbled out into a gay bar and found Stuart and Vince. Generations after, found Stuart and Nathan on TV and in everything that followed. But that meta-element of the types of gay men we see in the show can also be explained by the fact that we didn't have other gay men in life or on TV to model them after.

Community and friendship

Besides all the sex, *Queer as Folk* is a story of friendship and community. Vince and Stuart are at the heart of it, but their network of friends and allies is much broader. We see this in the slightly idealised version of the Manchester gay scene. The group of friends is the kind of 'chosen family' many queer people aspire to have and dream of having. Being a *very* British take on that (in contrast to the American version of the show, or shows like *The L Word* (2004–9) and *Looking* (2004–6) that would come along later), it feels surprisingly 'real' despite being a fantasy.

It helps that the backdrop *is* real – Davies knew the Manchester/Canal Street scene well in that era and replicated it in the show. But the general pub/club scene of the late 1990s in any major town or city for twenty- to thirty-year-olds is also apparent in the show, as is the network of 'pub friends' and 'work mates' for that generation of people. Bearing in mind this was largely pre-internet, contacts were developed through the people you saw down the pub, mates and work friends. Once again, retrospectively, the show feels like a time capsule moment. It also illustrates that particular type of friendship and the dynamics of the friendship group.

We see the friends looking out for each other and feeling a sense of community. The way any of them periodically stop to speak to a friend/former hook-up on Canal Street in those scenes is meant to invoke that sense of the queer community at that time. There is a sense of community around the bars and clubs. But Davies also uses the narrative to posit the question of how superficial that community might be. When Phil dies, and it takes days for his 'community' to realise he's gone, his body lying on the floor of his kitchen undiscovered and so far unmissed, the show highlights the limitations of that community. However, the community is also one that consists of strong friendships, like that between Stuart and Vince, and a friendship that looks out for Nathan (or at least tries to). Davies seems then to be showing us both sides – successes and failures – of the community he's depicting. Of course, it's really a moment captured – as a year later, two years, or ten years, the Canal Street 'community' will be altered once again. Flawed and ever-changing as it is, Davies gives us his version of that community.

The show also gives us allies and inter-generational gay men: for example, Vince's mum Hazel, who appears in the pub without Vince knowing when she's just having a night out. At this point in the story, Hazel seems to have embraced the gay scene even more than her son. She appears wearing a feather-boa, dancing with drag queens, and Vince is only slightly embarrassed. While Hazel is an embarrassing force of nature, she's also an ally. She's a mum, not just to Vince but to the group. We know that if something happens to any of them – mainly Stuart – she will do everything she can to help. She's the mum some of them don't have anymore, and she takes her role seriously. We see her look out for Nathan, too, in that manner, balancing a no-nonsense approach with being a caring mum.

The fact that Vince and his mum are also working class is important. A lot of queer characters on TV tended, particularly in earlier depictions, to be of the urban middle-class types. For example, Will in *Will & Grace* is a New York lawyer, or the urban middle-class mix of characters in *Tales of the City*. This working-class influence is important, partly for telling working-class stories on TV more broadly – something Davies, as a big fan of *Coronation Street*, was passionate about (and trivia-wise a fun fact is that Craig Kelly, who played Vince, also starred in *Coronation Street*). Also, because historically many cultural representations of queerness came from more middle-class backgrounds. Looking to earlier literary representations like those of Oscar Wilde (albeit coded) or Evelyn Waugh in *Brideshead Revisited* or more recent works by Alan Hollinghurst, these authors' works were more middle-class depictions, mostly the result of reflecting their creators' backgrounds. Davies in *Queer as Folk* was a forerunner in integrating a more diverse class spectrum in his depictions of queer characters. Because both queer characters and working-class characters were then underrepresented on TV, it felt important to Davies that Vince was both. It is crucial to note Hazel lives in a run-down terrace house with a lodger after Vince leaves and that she's seen after a night out putting together Christmas crackers to earn money. It's not only important to show that kind of background to a gay man – not everyone is a 'Stuart' with his loft apartment – but also for other viewers, who might live in a similar environment, to show that one of their parents can be a 'Hazel'.

Her lodger, Bernard, is also relevant. He is played brilliantly by Andy Devine, who would go on to soap fame in *Emmerdale*. He's important on several levels. Firstly, he is another working-class gay man. Vince also helps with this representation; despite having a slightly aspirational lifestyle, he still works in a supermarket and seems happy. We don't know what, if anything Bernard does; he helps Hazel with her Christmas crackers and rents a room rather than having his own place, so we assume he's not well off. What's also important is that he's an older gay man.

We don't see many – in fact, no other – men over about forty years in *Queer as Folk*. While obviously, the focus is on the turning-thirty demographic of Vince and Stuart, there's a critical element as to why this is. We are missing older men in the show because many of them have recently died. While the show has been critiqued for lack of dialogue on AIDS, it's there; it's woven into the fabric of the show, if you know what you're looking for. (See Coda: 'AIDS'.) We have no 'elders' in the story; Vince and Stuart are the 'elders' because so many of the generations directly above them, in particular, have simply not survived. They died of AIDS not long before the events of *Queer as Folk* took place. For others, that shift, the seismic impact on their community, affected how they engaged with it. They perhaps shifted away from the 'scene'; they took themselves away from big cities like Manchester. After such immeasurable loss, their lives changed. So, the presence of only one older gay character is very important.

Phil's death is one of the most moving moments in the series. It's shocking, too, and in what would become characteristic Russell T Davies style, it demonstrates that you must not get attached to anyone because they'll die the minute you do. Phil is a pleasant, charming presence in the backdrop to Stuart and Vince's adventures; as Vince says after he dies, 'We were pub friends.' We see that Phil meant more to them than they thought or perhaps realised.

At Phil's funeral, Stuart seems detached, unemotional and self-involved; in other words, Stuart. He uses it as an opportunity to cruise; he exploits the situation for some marketing copy for work. But he also does the most moving thing in the whole series; he clears out the stuff in Phil's house he wouldn't want Phil's mum to see. Stuart takes Vince to Phil's house and tells him to clear the porn. It's a small, somewhat ridiculous gesture (they do keep the porn for themselves, too, it seems), but it's also moving. While Vince protests that Phil's mum knows he is gay and doesn't care, Stuart retorts that she still doesn't need to see his porn. He's right, of course, and Stuart is sweetly protecting the friend he protested not to be close to, even after death. It's an act of community solidarity. At the same time, while Stuart isn't close to his own family (as seen in the second series); he understands Phil and wants to protect his memory for his mum. Having seen Phil's mum's suffering, Vince also realises this is important. They're both aware of this small thing they can do for a friend, even in death; it's one of the most moving community aspects of the show.

The group of friends, too, might be superficial on some levels, but they are also important; they are an oasis in a straight society. While the extended group that Stuart and Vince see might revolve around drinking, sex and drugs, and long hours in the clubs and pubs, they also represent something important – being yourself. For the rest of the week after Phil's funeral, all of that group are, to a degree, not being themselves. Even Stuart, who is as out, proud, and as uniquely Stuart as possible, is a different version of himself at work. As much as we all 'mask' in life, queer people do it more. We know that at first, Vince isn't out at work, and we see him performing heterosexuality continually, exhaustingly, in work environments and social settings. Even beyond that, in day-to-day life, this was a time when still appearing straight in most places was the ideal. However, for the time the group is with each other – be that on Canal Street or watching Princess Diana's funeral in the flat – they can be themselves. It's an expression of shared minority experience that only with one another can they 'unmask' fully and be themselves. The pubs and clubs of the 1990s were primarily the places to do that. So, while it might seem like just a show about drinking and fucking, it means something more significant.

Stuart and Vince – unrequited love but a deeper queer friendship

Of course, Stuart and Vince and their friendship are at the heart of it all. Showing a gay male friendship was a very important element of the show. While Vince's unrequited love for Stuart is an aspect of the drama, and we perhaps end up 'shipping' them, ultimately, that's not the point of their friendship. (Shipping, or shippers, in fandom circles is short for 'relationshippers', a term that originated in *X-Files* fandom around wanting the central characters to get together. It's now a broad fandom term for desiring a romantic or sexual relationship between characters.) It's probably a good thing the show is only ten episodes long because that doesn't give the story time to 'give in' and show them getting together. Instead, we get a snapshot of an authentic and very, very queer relationship.

Stuart and Vince's relationship shows the kind of friendship queer people have – it's different in dynamics and, to some degree, importance compared to friendships between straight people. For queer people, friendships look different, partly because they often don't conform to the heterosexual norms. Also, Stuart and Vince are joyous; honest and loving, and in the context of a queer friendship group, this is something to be aspired to. For many viewers, especially those isolated from queer communities, the idea of finding their Stuart or Vince, not as a romantic partner but as a friendship, was just as important as the idea of finding a partner one day. Particularly in a pre-social media age, finding people 'like you' could feel like a distant dream. Queer kids and young adults back then dreamt of finding their 'Stuart' or 'Vince'. In TV, too, it was aspirational; on straight TV, we had *Friends* and other US sitcoms to show us how we 'should' do our twenties, what our friends should look like, that we should have such a group around us. Queer people often watched shows like *Friends*, with no solid queer representation, wondering, 'Where are my friends then?' And *Queer as Folk* showed them.

Moving against the mainstream

Queer as Folk sat on the borders of queer life more broadly than other contemporary TV. It was provocative in firmly sticking to its queer lane. It wasn't queer TV for straight people in the vein of *Will & Grace*, which was broadcast around the same time. There wasn't the token gay character like in a soap, who is gay but not too gay. It was pure, unapologetically queer for queer audiences. It didn't care if straight people didn't want to see rimming on Friday night TV; it didn't care if they wanted a nice romcom ending; instead, it gave them hedonistic and self-destructive nights out. It was going against the mainstream, heteronormative 'safe' bet of what gay men should be.

Did *Queer as Folk* perfectly represent the nuances of queer life? No. Was it a considerable stride forward? Without a doubt.

For a start, someone has to go first. Someone has to burst through onto the scene and kick the doors down. By that point, doors had been cracked open. We can definitely say that in British TV *Queer as*

Folk kicked those doors open. It's easy to criticise the first to do it with, 'Well, it could be better' or, 'You could have done…', but getting it made at all was an achievement. Also, as much as the point has been laboured, it was a British series of only ten episodes. There's only so much you can do with that in terms of storytelling. Therefore, what it achieves in the broader sense is more important than the nuances of content.

The adventures of Stuart and Vince might firmly be a late 1990s moment, but actually, their impact crosses two decades. For one generation, they will forever be a formative TV moment that perhaps propelled British culture into the next stage of (queer) life. For others, they illustrate a quirky historical moment that influenced not just the shows that share their name and origins but far more.

Awards, longevity and spin-offs

Notably, of course, *Queer as Folk* was remade in the US, where it ran from 3 December 2000 to 7 August 2005. The series was produced for Showtime by Cowlip Productions and it was set in Pittsburgh, Pennsylvania (with much of the series being shot in Toronto). The show was significantly, culturally important for American TV. It quickly became the number-one show on the Showtime roster.

And whilst not as graphic as the UK version, the sex scenes marked a huge step forward in American TV, with queer sex being depicted for the first time (and, yes, there was rimming there too). There were also frank depictions of casual sex and drug use, just like in the original series. There were understandable fears that there would be a backlash, particularly from conservative factions of American society. Perhaps they simply didn't choose to watch a show with *queer* in the title. Perhaps they didn't venture beyond the FOX network. Either way, the backlash was limited.

Queer as Folk in the US was a solid hit for Showtime, and many of the cast and writers have continued to flourish, proving too that a 'gay' show isn't the career-killer it once was. The show, while not a mainstream hit, had a strong fan following and, much like the UK version, was formative for many. More importantly, it forms part of the general massive upswing in queer TV across the last two decades.

At the same time, while the British show was originally an outlier, many US dramas already had queer-centred storylines, whether that was 'straight' shows like *Grey's Anatomy* being able to have queer characters without it being an 'issue' based storyline, or other queer dramas, starting with *The L Word*. As time went on, we saw queer-led programmes from Teen dramas like *Love, Victor* (2020–2) or mainstream hits like *Schitt's Creek* (2015–20). The latter broke down further barriers by ending with a happy queer wedding. Still, it wouldn't have gotten its mainstream success had it not been for the subversiveness of *Queer as Folk*.

When *Queer as Folk* first aired in 1999, it offered a shameless education on rimming, unrequited love, and the sort of sexual positions the likes of which had never before been seen on TV, and it brought the hedonistic joys of a pre-Grindr world to mainstream viewing. When there has never been a 'gay series' before, how do you create a story that is able to relate to the lives of hundreds of thousands of men and women? But *Queer as Folk* wasn't trying to be a 'message' or even to be the revolution it became: it didn't need to. Simply being, queer, folk, on TV, was enough.

Coda

Nerds

Nerds rule the world in Russell T Davies's universe, and honestly, who are we to argue?

Davies gives us Vince, the *Doctor Who*-obsessed nerd, and Ianto, who is more at home organising the coffee than running around with guns but still manages to save the world. There's overlap with the women that Davies celebrates. Bethany, in *Years and Years*, uses her love of technology to think about the world critically. Martha Jones is a doctor and an infinitely sensible companion to the Doctor. Quiet, sweet Colin is the accidental hero of *It's a Sin*. Davies keeps the less-than-cool characters at the heart of the narrative and shows what they can do. He also integrates the beautifully nerdy into the narrative.

Vince

Vince in *Queer as Folk* is the ultimate nerdy guy. But what's excellent about Vince is that nobody tries to change him. On paper, it seems weird that Vince and Stuart are friends – the gregarious, cool kid and the nerd. Of course, it's a classic tale of introverts adopted by extroverts that many a nerdy kid will be familiar with. Also, Stuart doesn't mind Vince's nerdy behaviour; he leans into it, embraces it and likes it about him.

This is shown in the final episode of the first series, where we know that Stuart loves nerdy Vince for everything he is, while Cameron doesn't. How do we know this? Because Stuart can list all the Doctor Whos, except for Paul McGann. Paul McGann doesn't count. The speed at which Stuart does it, despite having little interest in an old sci-fi show, indicates Vince's importance to him. Their little shared in-joke, clearly borne of Vince repeating 'Paul McGann doesn't count,' adds to that. Stuart doesn't care about *Doctor Who*, but he cares about Vince. Or, more likely, he's grown to care about *Who* because he cares about Vince. Cameron's dismissal of the all-important question, 'How many Doctors can you name?' is a dismissal of Vince and everything necessary to who he is.

Similarly, we see this with the gift of K-9 (the Fourth Doctor's robot dog companion). As much as Stuart is in part trying to 'one up' Cameron here, he's also demonstrating (with a robot dog) that he knows Vince. He shows that he embraces Vince's nerdy side. Also, this is the act of a gift genuinely tailored to what Vince loves, however weird/extravagant, a genuine gesture of love from his best friend. It's a lovely feeling, too, to love the things that make the people you love who they are. While Stuart might have less than zero interest in *Doctor Who*, he doesn't mock it; he embraces it in Vince because he cares about him.

All across *Queer as Folk*, we get Vince's love of *Doctor Who* integrated into his character, dropped into conversation, even in the background of his house. It's a simple thing, and, of course, clearly a projection of Davies's love of *Who*, and one that became a lovely throwback once he took over the show. But it's more than that. How often are nerds the real protagonists? We root for Vince more than Stuart. He's the quiet, sweet underdog we want to win. More than that, Vince's nerdy predilections aren't mocked in the show. Take later series like *The Big Bang Theory*, where the fact that the group was made up of nerds was the joke (and about the only joke) of the entire series. Vince as a character isn't a joke because he's a nerd; it's part of who he is.

Also, despite everything else, it's Vince that Stuart wants to be with at the end of the day – as his best friend, as someone he loves in all love's complexities. Nerds do win out in *Queer as Folk*. In addition, the show illustrates that the unremarkable nerdy boy who works in a supermarket can also be the protagonist of a TV show, which is a wonderfully powerful thing.

Nerds rule the world...

Elsewhere, too, Davies likes to tell the stories of the nerds and out-siders and give them agency. One example is Thorpe in *A Very English Scandal*, who, despite having power and influence, is also a slightly oddball, nerdy kind of politician, unlike the others Davies has created elsewhere.

In *It's a Sin*, too, we get sweet Colin, who is quietly passionate about tailoring, and later, photocopying. When asked where he wants to be in ten years, he replies that he wants to know everything. What a simple, pure aim that is, to know everything about his chosen profession. Colin is happy learning, it doesn't matter that it's not glamorous, and the tragedy of his short life is that he had such simple aims and pleasures. He was happy to desire knowledge, and he never got to fulfil what he wanted. He's essential, like Vince is, to the nerdy gays, showing there's not just one way to be gay. We see him curled up with a comic book after lying to his mum about going out to the pub. Colin goes out with his friends, but he's equally happy being at home reading a comic. None of it makes him any less part of the queer community. In a community that tends to exclude those who don't want to do the standard 'gay' things (drink, drugs, casual sex), showing a group of friends accepting Colin, who enjoys reading his comic book at home, is essential. It shows that the Colins of the community can find their chosen families. And when the friends mourn Colin, it's because he is by far our hero of the story, even over Ritchie.

In *Years and Years*, where Bethany quietly becomes the central voice of reason and cleverness in the story, even when we're worried for her, even when we doubt her choices, we can't doubt that the girl who loved to learn about tech became the woman who helped save her family and helped them to do good. While there's a moral lesson from Bethany's experience integrating tech into her body, there's value in showing the younger generation leading the older characters in tech-nology, while also being something of a victim of it, too. The value isn't through being 'cool', it's through learning and understanding the technology. Much like Colin, all Bethany wants is to learn. When she gets the chip integrated into her mind, she is excited about the knowledge, the world she can see all at once. We see inside her head like it's a computer, and for many a 'nerd' viewer, it is what they've dreamed of. Imagine all that knowledge in your mind: accessible, available, to learn from. Bethany experiences this; she sees things, she absorbs them, and learns from them. Whether it's Aunt Edith and the radiation poisoning – she figures out how long she has left – or seeing what her dad did to Viktor – helping her mum put that right – or bringing down Vivienne Rook, Bethany uses knowledge. While Edith is more practical – protests, infiltration, even rocket launchers – Bethany uses knowledge for good and to help good win out. It's the ultimate nerd move: defeating everyone else via information.

Ianto Jones: 'coffee boy' and ultimate nerd

Ianto Jones doesn't change because he starts dating a man. He continues to be the same old Ianto Jones, teased by colleagues, efficient at his jobs, helping Torchwood save the world. He doesn't change how he dresses, sounds, or acts. The only change is who he is having sex with/dating/loves. That's just as important as seeing all kinds of queer characters – from the outrageously camp or butch end of the stereotype for different genders. Having queer characters whose personality isn't altered by their relationships is essential. Ianto continues to wear smart suits and be Welsh. He doesn't suddenly become uber-camp, change his clothing or start shouting 'yasss queen' to Jack (maybe in private). He remains himself.

Why was Ianto Jones so important to fans?

In part, because he was the 'everyman'; he was 'coffee boy' who got the guy. He was the sweet, quiet geek who saved the world several times and just went home again afterwards. He was the way in for many people, maybe for the quiet nerds who rarely see themselves as heroes without being made fun of. That was always the essence of *Doctor Who*, after all. Still, unlike the Doctor, Ianto was a human, someone fans could see in themselves, much like the companions, but again maybe here we have that '*Doctor Who* for grown-ups' element at play. Companions grow up to be the Ianto Joneses of the world. Even if he was the 'coffee boy' and the 'admin' of Torchwood, he had a lot of sway; he did heroic things. He was the person fans could see themselves being.

For fans, too, Ianto was a nice guy, as was the actor who brought him to life. Gareth David-Lloyd has remained loyal to the fandom; he continues to work on audio dramas and attend conferences. Fans have equally supported him – from watching his band play gigs in various south Wales venues to supporting him on stage when he's performed, to, of course, watching his other TV roles. Although Gareth is straight, his respect for Ianto as a queer character has meant a lot to fans. The endless love and mutual respect that exists means that for many fans, Ianto Jones endures.

Ianto Jones's story didn't have a happy ending. Fans didn't get the happy *Torchwood* they so badly wanted and, dare we say, deserved. However, that doesn't mean that Ianto wasn't hugely formative, influential and meaningful to many fans. He might have been the first queer person they saw, the first gay kiss on screen, or just the 'coffee boy' who saved the world. Either way, he meant a great deal to fans. We might roll our eyes at the 'shrine' to him in Cardiff Bay, but who are we to scoff at a depth of feeling and a character that meant something deeply to many people?

The Doctor – ultimate nerd (and very, very queer)

Of course, the ultimate of nerds is the Doctor, which shows that nerds will inherit the Earth or maybe the universe. In *Doctor Who*, the quiet nerds are often the heroes of Davies's stories. He makes a point of finding the hero of each story and giving them power, whether it's the quiet 'Sisters of Plenitude' cat-nuns in 'New Earth' or Midshipman Frame in 'Voyage of the Damned'. This plays into the classic underdog trope, of course, but the heroes the Doctor finds are often those who wouldn't usually be recognised as 'cool' or the ones to save the Earth. Instead, they are the unassuming ones with niche knowledge to help the Doctor save the day.

Of course, the companions fulfil this role time and time again. In particular, Davies gives us the woefully underrated Martha

Jones, who is training to be a doctor and doesn't need another one to save her. She is her own person; she is strong, but she is also fiercely intelligent and obviously a bit of a nerd too. Davies shows us the clever people – but not in a naturally gifted way, the ones who worked for it – and tells us they're the heroes of the world. Ianto Jones is another one of those in the Whoniverse. He's 'coffee boy' but so much more; he knows everything that goes on in Torchwood, and, therefore, ends up being the one who can save them time and time again. So, too, can Sarah Jane when we welcome her back in 'School Reunion'. She paid attention when she was with the Doctor all those years ago, and she took that and built on the knowledge so that she's ok to go off and rival the Doctor in saving the world. Davies's nerds are about wanting to learn and use knowledge as a force for good, and all his companions take that from their time in the TARDIS (even Captain Jack, as distracted as he often is).

Of course, the Doctor is the ultimate nerd. The Doctor is at their best when they're using cleverness and facts to win the day. Over time and space and 900-plus years, they could have collected anything, but they chose to collect knowledge. The Doctor, too, uses knowledge and being a nerd to save the world. They aren't the strongest or the fastest person but the smartest – and not from being naturally intelligent, but from collecting information, which is the nerd's favourite pastime. The Doctor is an illustration that the love of knowledge, sometimes seemingly esoteric knowledge, is cool. The Doctor amasses lots of information, seemingly 'useless' to others, or chooses to pass on the knowledge that perhaps nobody else cares about. Information that comes in useful when it matters. In the Doctor, we have the ultimate nerd saving the world, repeatedly.

But, too, for all those who were ever mocked for being that nerd, the Doctor makes it cool. They look cool but don't follow the crowd; they have friends but are unconcerned with being popular. They choose to embrace who they are, whatever that might look or sound like, and however 'different' it makes them. That's a vital lesson. Davies didn't invent that aspect of the Doctor. It's always been the case, but he does lean into that message and reinforces it repeatedly with both Nine and

Ten. They both marvel at the universe as they travel it, always learning from the humans and other species they encounter on the way.

Nerds do indeed rule the world, and Davies's universe. Quite right too, as the Tenth Doctor would say.

Chapter Three

Gay aliens?
Doctor Who

When most people think of Russell T Davies, two shows immediately come to mind: *Queer as Folk* and *Doctor Who*; poles apart in many ways, but equally influential on the fans that love them. Equally, for Davies, they occupy particular areas of his passions that have shaped his career. While *Who* is not per se a queer narrative, Davies certainly writes a queer 'Whoniverse'.

'New *Who*' offered viewers what they never had seen as kids. Davies didn't invent *Who*, but he did, to a degree, reinvent it. One significant element he added was to put a more overtly queer slant on *Who* that wasn't in the original.

There are multiple elements of *Who*, old and new, that are queer, not gay. They encapsulate the often rebellious, out of sync with the dominant culture, subversive elements of queerness in its morality and world (universe) view, also in the embodied sense of fun and campness. There has always been a queer camp aesthetic to *Who* – it's in the campy monsters, the over-the-top Doctor's outfits – it's high camp sci-fi. All of this gives it a queer aesthetic or feeling. After all, before queer stories were readily available, queer viewers found a 'home' in stories that weren't overtly queer but gave them the feeling of belonging.

Who embodies that: the idea of the outsiders, irrespective of whether the Doctor or the companions, being the ones who quietly save the world, feel in line with queer experience. So, too, does the Doctor choose their family – they pick the world's misfits and allow them to be themselves. The TARDIS is a queer safe space where you will find a home wherever you are. Add to that the eccentric fashion of the Doctor and even the companions, with notes of queer culture. It's no surprise that young queer fans like Davies were drawn to the world of the Doctor, even if the queerness wasn't explicitly represented when he was watching it as a child. This is something he would bring to it, too, as an adult.

Despite these best efforts, the world (or universe) in which *Who* previously existed was a difficult one to be queer in. However, queer content and queerness are not always the same thing. Particularly before the time of recent legalisation regarding homosexuality and during the days of Section 28 of the Local Government Act 1988 (a law that prohibited the 'promotion' of homosexuality in schools and other environments) and beyond, queerness was only found in a 'coded' sense on TV and other media. Sometimes there were softly queer-coded characters, those known to be queer without saying it. Other times a show or story is queer by aesthetic and feel even if the themes are not overtly queer. This was – and is – the case with *Who*.

Pre-Davies queer *Who*

When *Doctor Who* was in its original form – being a 1960s BBC programme aimed at children – queer topics were not something that could readily be examined. Indeed, the show began in 1963 before homosexuality was decriminalised (this took place in 1967 in England and Wales and in 1980 in Scotland). But that said, elements of queerness were worked in. Writer Ian Briggs revealed many years after the production of 'The Curse of Fenric' (1989) that the story's Dr Judson was intended to be – like the man he was based on, Alan Turing – struggling with his homosexuality. However, this was cut in 1988. Briggs, instead, reworked his writing plans such that Turing's frustration at being unable to express his true sexual identity was converted into Judson's frustrations about his disability. Elsewhere, *Who* writer Rona Munro, has revealed that in 'Survival' (1989) there was a lesbian subtext intended in the relationship between Ace and

Karra. (This is a widely accepted fan reading of that relationship, too, along with fan fiction on the subject.) This raises the possibility of Ace being the first queer companion on screen. Munro would further acknowledge this in interviews, indicating that the costume for Karra impeded the affection between the two characters.

In the original incarnation, the queerness inherent in the show peeked. It was the kind of queerness that drew fans even before they had a name for it. Valiantly, too, the original team had champions of queerness who incorporated queerness into the work, slowly drip-feeding some representation through. Much like the life that *Torchwood* would take on post-TV, the audio dramas and novelisations were a place to break new ground. Until, of course, in the mid-2000s, *Who* came back and slowly surely got a bit queerer (and a bit more Welsh) in the process.

The new Whoniverse
Doctor Who left TV screens in 1989 and, apart from the 1996 film, and a special for Comic Relief in 1999, while it lived on in re-runs and VHS and DVD, there was a younger generation who, unless they had parents who showed them the original, had never known *Who* on TV. The first new episode of *Doctor Who* in sixteen years, 'Rose', aired on 26 March 2005 and was watched by 10.8 million viewers and received favourable critical reception. This was a strong start for a BBC Saturday night show in the teatime slot. However, positivity was overshadowed by the announcement that Eccleston would leave after only one season. He's since spoken about his personal and professional struggles at this time. Despite all that was going on behind the scenes for him, Eccleston's Doctor is as iconic as any.

Shortly after, David Tennant, who had recently worked with Davies on *Casanova*, was announced as the Tenth Doctor. When the show returned for a Christmas special in which he was introduced ('The Christmas Invasion'), it felt like *Doctor Who* was firmly back, despite the initial teething problems. From then on, it became a part of the BBC Saturday night and Christmas schedule. Over the next five years, the Tennant/Davies partnership would take the show's success to the next level. Something clicked in their respective writing and performance styles which rarely happens on TV; when it does, it's like bottled lightning. Tennant would stay until 'The End of Time' in 2010, following forty-seven episodes as the Doctor. He announced his departure live on TV from the Royal Shakespeare Company stage door, where he was appearing in *Hamlet* during the summer break. Davies would leave with him, but during that time, they took the archived, campy TV show that Davies fought to bring back to life to become the highest-rated BBC show at the time, and a cultural phenomenon.

Queerness and the Doctor

While Davies didn't invent the Doctor, they are perhaps the queerest of the characters Davies has written. This isn't a new idea; the queerness of *Who* is woven into the space and time of the TARDIS. Any glance at the Doctors' past outfits certainly nods to a camp queer aesthetic (Only a queer character would wear celery with cricket jackets or that scarf.)

Doctor Who, as a series, is camp, in a singularly British way. That much is clear. A lot of the Doctor's queerness comes from that. But the Doctor as a *character* embodies so much queerness. When Davies took over the show, that quickly became apparent.

Even if the Ninth Doctor, as played by Christopher Eccleston, was more 'masculine' presenting than his successor, David Tennant, he still had an air of queerness about him. Inherent in that is a certain queerness. Nine is, we might argue, the most 'masc' of the Doctors. However, their physical presence isn't without nods to the queer community. After all, the leather jacket, big boots and close haircut are giving out either leather queen or lesbian vibes. But, also, the energy of being quite masculine, quite rough around the edges (and this is Eccleston's strength as an actor) but with a vulnerable, sensitive side, of course, queers our notion of masculinity. This queerness makes Eccleston perfect for the role and for bringing back the Doctor to our screens. Eccleston, as the Doctor, is like the bloke from the pub who is actually soft, caring and sensitive. They are everything blokey blokes wearing leather jackets and big boots aren't supposed to be – they are tender, kind, they'd cry for you, and with you, and they'd care for you. They care for the whole human race, after all. Sometimes queering is quite subtle. Nine is very queer in subverting our expectations of leading male characters on screen. Once again, we owe Eccleston more than he gets credit for in that.

Also, the Doctor is very queer as a character. After all, they are an alien who defies gender. Even before a woman played the Doctor, this disregard for gender was inherent in their character. A familiar trope to a lot of sci-fi audiences perhaps, with examples like Jadzia Dax from *Star Trek Deep Space Nine*, who had storylines that emphasised their gender defiance – making a political point through sci-fi and *Star Trek*, like *Who* often does through its characters. However, in mainstream drama, that is a rarer element. The Doctor has always defied categorisation of all kinds, including gender. So much so that they/them pronouns should probably be used for Doctors of all ages because, regardless of the gender of the actor playing the Doctor, the Doctor has no gender as humans understand it.

Davies's Doctors also embodied this. Eccleston, as mentioned above, brought a blend of masculinity and sensitivity to the role. It's fair to say, David Tennant, as the Tenth Doctor, brought all-out camp back to the role. Tennant's Doctor is wide-eyed and full of wonder at the world. However, within the unashamed excitement is a blurring of the traditional 'male' demeanour with something not-quite-feminine-not-quite-masculine. While again, the outfit Ten chose has more lesbian chic about it: trouser suit, Converse, chunky glasses. They embody more of a gender-fluid, non-binary presentation with it. After all, anyone could wear Ten's outfit and look cool.

Beyond the show, we only have to look at cosplaying fans for that. So many female-identifying fans cosplay Ten and look not just good but remarkably similar to Ten/Tennant. Cosplaying Ten doesn't have the same 'gender-bending' effect that some male-to-female cosplays have because Ten's outfit, overall look and demeanour defy gender already.

Ten brought a sense of gender neutrality and gender euphoria to the Doctor, the idea that while still played by a cis white male, there was also an element of subversive queerness to them. Tennant himself has always seemed, again while being cishet himself, comfortable in camp queerness. Ten leans into the 'brilliant' campness of it all and is allowed to be over the top, not 'masculine' just, them.

Ten also defies gender and attraction expectations in a couple of other ways. Firstly, Ten flirts with everyone. They're an equal opportunities flirt, be that with Shakespeare, Queen Elizabeth, or anyone else in time and space.

But the twist is that the Doctor isn't interested in anyone that way. The Doctor is asexual.

There are various ways this can be analysed across different Doctors. Still, in the Russell T Davies era, the Doctors (Nine and Ten) are distinctly asexual in their approach to love and romance. Asexuality is a lack of sexual attraction (or limited and very specific sexual attraction), and the Doctor embodies all of that. They are one of the few canonically asexual characters on TV, which is very important to the queer community as a whole. Generally, there is such limited asexual representation in our culture and having such a culturally significant asexual character is extremely important. Davies doesn't necessarily invent the asexuality of the Doctor. Much like their campness, it had always been there. However, he leans into it and queers it further.

How is the Doctor asexual?
What does it mean for the Doctor to be asexual?

Non-asexual audiences (allosexuals) have probably never noticed the Doctor's asexuality or dismissed it as 'well, that's just how the Doctor is'. They're right. However, the way the Doctor behaves is distinctly asexual.

First and foremost, across the Davies era specifically, the Doctor doesn't have sexual relationships. That might sound obvious for a kids' show, but in reality, how often are (heterosexual) sexual/romantic relationships a plot in kids' TV? The answer is: fairly often. Handled in the right way, there's nothing wrong with that. Crucially, the Doctor is essentially our 'romantic lead', yet they never have romantic or sexual relationships. Nor is it hinted that they ever have or will.

An important distinction here is that asexual people are capable of romantic love. (Those who don't experience romantic attraction are known as aromantics. Sometimes there is a crossover of these identities, but not always.) The Doctor is capable of romantic love without it being sexual, and this often happens to Ten. We see Ten love deeply and fully but in very distinct, very queer ways, either romantically or platonically.

We see, of course, that the Doctor loves Rose. But we also see Rose *fancies* the Doctor; she's sexually attracted to them. From the moment they change from Nine to Ten, we know she's attracted to them. Cassandra even says so in the episode 'New Earth' when she comments, 'you've been looking'. Yet while Rose (and others) flirt with Ten, the feeling isn't reciprocated in the same way. That's not to say that Ten doesn't feel for companions, friends, and even people in passing. They do, and deeply, as is the Doctor's way. They also feel deeply on a platonic, even possibly romantic, level for Rose, Donna and Martha. Martha also illustrates how the Doctor is out of step with the rest of humanity. Martha loves the Doctor, but the Doctor will never love Martha back in the way she wants. On one level, it can be read as the Doctor still having feelings for Rose. While to the large degree, the love goes deeper in that the Doctor *doesn't* feel romantic and sexual attraction like humans, like Martha does for them. In that way, the Doctor's experience is a very asexual one.

Martha feels very alien to the Doctor. Ten can understand affection and love, but not the kind of attraction Martha feels. It's a plot which looks like a funny 'the alien man doesn't get it' one to allosexuals. On one level, of course, that interpretation is true. But to asexual audiences, the Doctor, here, looks like a character who finally gets it. Because the Doctor isn't repelling Martha's advances because they don't like her, they are repelling them because they simply don't know *how* to experience what she does. For asexual people, that's exactly what life is like, not understanding how the rest of the world experiences sexual (and sometimes romantic) attraction. It's the sheer obliviousness that the Doctor has to Martha's advances.

But what's also important to the Doctor as an asexual representation, is that they are still a fully rounded character without this being part of their life. Think about how almost every other TV character's sexual attraction at some point plays into their story. If it doesn't, then their reaction is portrayed as a character flaw. Because the Doctor is an alien, and because they don't function entirely on a human wavelength anyway, they're 'allowed' to be asexual. They're allowed to just be themselves. That's something asexual people long for; an acceptance of that, of not being like everyone else.

It might be an accidental piece of representation, but it's an important one. In rebooting the franchise, it could be argued that Davies felt he had to bow to pressure to 'sex it up' a bit. Given, too, a handsome young Doctor in Ten, along with a variety of attractive female companions, there may have been a conversation or two about making it 'sexier', making it appeal to 'today's youth' (and their parents) and making the Doctor suddenly interested in 'that sort of thing'. On the one hand, this change of emphasis is a disservice to the Doctor's character, who has always been absent from that kind of relationship. But also, considering the bigger picture, it would have denied a generation of asexual fans a piece of vital representation.

What we also get as a replacement of the more traditional romantic and sexual misadventures, is a character who values platonic relationships and curates a chosen family across time and space. These are two very queer notions. In queer culture, a 'queer platonic relationship' is a relationship that is somewhere beyond a friendship, something not romantic or sexual. It's a bond that is placed with as much value as romance or sex in a person's life. The Doctor, and their relationships with the companions, mirror this kind of bond. The Doctor, after all, would sacrifice just about anything for their companion. They keep them close and support them in what they want to do. They are the best of friends, and more. That, too, is what Rose becomes to the Doctor, in keeping with the asexual thread of Ten in particular; the Doctor can say, 'I love you' (even if not out loud) because there *is* love there, a particular deep kind of love that arguably transcends the romantic love Rose feels, it's a queer platonic bond, and it runs incredibly deep.

Queerness and the TARDIS

The Doctor clearly creates the very queer notion of 'chosen family' in the companions and others they collect along the way. One wonderful moment that visually illustrates this is when all the companions fly the

TARDIS in 'Journey's End', an episode which presents a small snippet of all the people the Doctor has touched and, at the core, a chosen family they have curated. The Doctor, too, emulates queer life in their exile from home. The Doctor has left Gallifrey and is viewed as a black sheep, an exile, someone who can never return (for many complex reasons depending on what timeline of the show you follow). The Doctor no longer has the blood family of the Time Lords. They are considered 'not like' the other Time Lords. They 'do things wrong' and have 'affection for the wrong people' (humans). It is a very queer narrative – kicked out of home (Gallifrey) and finding a community (Earth) that accepts you, finding friends that accept you for you (the companions). Also, away from Gallifrey, the Doctor discovers who they are – they go through many incarnations, many styles(!), but keep discovering more and more about their true self when allowed to experiment, be who they are, and be around people who accept them. All in all, this makes it a very queer narrative and the Doctor a very queer character.

The other vital strand of the Doctor's queerness is their acceptance. Again, this is a thread that's always been in the show, possibly its central message. It's no surprise, maybe, that Davies leans into this. The Doctor has a very distinct 'come as you are' approach. Whether that's a purple two-headed alien or Captain Jack's sexual misadventures, the Doctor sees all and accepts all. The TARDIS is a space that accepts everyone, and the Doctor does too. They don't blink at same-sex couples any more than a cat-nun. This has long been a running thread in *Who*, but Davies makes sure to lean into that. With personal queerness also comes a queer outlook and acceptance.

The Doctor, arguably, is the queerest character Davies ever wrote. It's fitting, too, that *Doctor Who* inspired young Russell to be a writer. Or perhaps this is unsurprising. The show, and the Doctor, have always been queer; Davies just ensured that idea was cemented in the twenty-first century.

Beyond the Doctor, the Davies version of *Who* also indirectly leans towards several lessons in queerness, from an overarching focus on inclusivity and equality as a theme to themes of 'being yourself' and, more specifically, queer elements around exile and chosen family.

Firstly, the overarching themes of tolerance and acceptance in *Who* are very queer notions. While Davies didn't invent this side of *Who*, it has been a strong theme since the start, and he does lean into it heavily. Davies steers us towards how 'brilliant' (in Ten's words) the human race, or any species, is in embracing that difference. It's important – and again, a very queer notion – that the Doctor sees difference as a positive. In 'The Christmas Invasion', the Doctor is intrigued by the Sycorax, sympathetic to their plight, and wants to help, rather than being repelled by their difference. It is key to the core beliefs and values of *Star Trek* that aliens by their actions are usually simply protecting their own homeland, or just curious about humans. There's a parallel to *Who* here, particularly the Davies take on *Who*. Just as *Star Trek* aims to gently educate human viewers about tolerance and acceptance through curiosity, *Who* uses its different slant on sci-fi to do similar.

There are other subtle inferences to queerness and difference in the 'bad guys' of the Davies era. The werewolf in 'Tooth and Claw' or the bat-teachers in 'School Reunion' all have that 'queerness' of being different, being marked out as 'alien' in a literal way, yet among the humans, which is a classic queer trope. That neither set out to harm, but ultimately do so because of their circumstance, can also be an analogy for queer people ending up ostracised, making bad decisions, and ending up in 'trouble'. That the Doctor approaches both of the 'threats' with initial compassion and an attempt to understand is also an extension of this attitude of inclusivity for the Doctor.

Across Davies's era, too, the lesson in acceptance for who you are is ever-present. Again, this is part of the fabric of *Who* which Davies brings to the fore. Whilst it's not directed *at* queer people (aside from Captain Jack), this idea of 'be who you are' is a broader queer attitude. This extends to race and to Martha. The Doctor accepts her even to the point to which he doesn't understand her fears about race when they travel in time ('The Shakespeare Code'). But still, the idea of 'queering' attitudes and acceptance prevails. Again, with class, the Doctor accepts Rose and Mickey, and Jackie, without judgement that they're working class and live in a council estate. It's never commented on, yet they are the heart of the series, and as working-class characters and representation for viewers, their acceptance was a big thing. Here we have the broader 'queering' at work again, subverting expectations and putting the idea of acceptance at the core.

This theme continues, too, with the Time Lords and Gallifrey. The Doctor is alienated from both their homeland of Gallifrey and alienated from their people, the Time Lords. This exile from their place of origin and blood family – seeking a home and friendships elsewhere – is a key theme in many queer people's lives also.

There are two threads of this: the Doctor and their companions. For the Doctor, they become an embodiment of queer people shunned or exiled from their homes or community. The Doctor is forced to wander time and space to find a new home, a new community, or a family because their own family does not accept them. The Doctor is different, too; their fascination with humans is seen as a negative by the other Time Lords and contributes to their exile (along with a general rebellious attitude). This, coupled with their affection for – and determination to help – humanity, is seen as strange affectation. That the Doctor is also a rebel, someone who sits outside of the norms of their people, even in their dress sense – not just the camp flamboyant sensibilities, but also mimicking humans – is again seen as strange, 'not how it's done' in their world. For this, the Doctor is rejected. They don't follow the traditional route. Therefore, they are destined to be forever outside the community they were born into – a very queer experience.

The way the Doctor chooses to rise from it, too, is very queer. They rebel, and they run away. Is the Doctor stealing a TARDIS and running away to Earth that different from Nathan in *Queer as Folk* running away to Canal Street? Not really. Both are running from the world that refuses to accept them as they are and running as far and fast as they can to find the people they instinctively feel will. The Doctor, as Nathan did, chooses to do all the things that their 'family' (the Time Lords) and community (Gallifrey) won't let them. The Doctor doesn't follow the directives on behaviour. Instead, they make friends with humans despite it being frowned upon, stand up for what they believe in, and protect others like them. All of that is such a queer way of being. Again, this is no different for the queer person who runs away to a new city, finds a queer community, builds a queer friendship group and stands up for queer rights. The Doctor is a one-alien gay rights parade. Quite right, too, as Ten would say.

Above all, the Doctor embraces their chosen family. The Doctor moves through time and space and picks up the people who need a home or a place to heal to become the best version of themselves. It's such a queer notion, and one that the Doctor under Davies leans into. The Doctor has a chosen family because they weren't accepted by their own. Equally, the Doctor chooses a family of people who needs them. They aren't queer for the most part, but the notion of having a chosen family is a queer one. The Doctor takes on the collection of misfits, the lonely or lost – from Rose, who didn't know how capable she was, to Donna, who thought her only 'success' might be to get married, and to Astrid, who only had a life as a waitress on a ship, all of them are given a home in passing, or for longer, with the Doctor. The doors to the TARDIS are always open for those who need them, and that mirrors what queer people have done for years, not just for other queer folks but for anyone who didn't fit into 'normal' society. That's a true queer ethos; finding a way to help those who find themselves on the outside. By helping anyone who needed that chosen family and safe space, the Doctor created the family they needed for themselves.

The best example can be found in 'The Stolen Earth', when we finally see the TARDIS flown as it should be by a huge group of people. That visual sticks because for years we've watched the Doctor run around in a frenzy flying the thing. We thought that was just how it had to be done. At that moment we learn it was because the Doctor had to fly solo, because they were exiled and alone. Now, their chosen family comes together to support them, to fly the TARDIS home. Where is home? Not Gallifrey, but Earth. The Doctor made a home somewhere other than where they were from because that home didn't welcome them. Now that new home, that chosen home with chosen family, is fighting with the Doctor because they are loved by those they've met there. It's the queer dream to find that family. *Doctor Who* might be a family-friendly sci-fi fantasy of a show. But what about the roots? They're deeply queer. What the Doctor stands for, too, is deeply moving and important to a queer audience.

Finally, the Doctor and *Doctor Who* are just very, very camp. The show itself has always exhibited that particular brand of camp British sci-fi – a bit over the top and ridiculous, but in a good way. Sci-fi is camp by nature; it's over the top and errs on the side of the fantastical, and that's why people love it. *Doctor Who* has always been such, and while the wobbly sets and men in plastic suits were toned down and levelled up for the reboot, Davies doesn't stray too far into 'serious' and 'worthy' sci-fi; the fun, the silliness is still there. Davies's *Doctor Who* is the embodiment of camp because camp is over the top, and is there anything more dramatically over the top than a Dalek?

But what about the Doctor? The Doctor is campness embodied, too. To be camp is to be non-conformist in attitude but playful with it. That's the Doctor; that's *Doctor Who*. It's a rebellion with style and not taking things too seriously – whether it's the feminising of the Doctor in Ten while still being masculine; the playful flirting that made its way in, including with Captain Jack, of course; or the Doctor's flair for drama. After all, why just 'do' a thing when you can do it with a flourish?

Whoniverse and legacy

Who is nothing short of a cultural icon. Bringing it back greatly benefited the actors and writers involved, some of whose careers skyrocketed afterwards. But above all, it benefited the kids who got to love the adventures of a Time Lord again. Of course, it would be part of Davies's life forever, too, as he said before it started in 2004 to *The Times*:

> Absolutely, this thing will follow me for the rest of my life. But the marvellous thing about writing *Doctor Who* is that I know when I die there are magazines that will report my death.[16]

Davies also opened the door for a truly queer TARDIS, and that's exciting. Davies gave the world of *Doctor Who* back to us. This was something that a whole generation never thought they would have again. He proved that the campy British sci-fi drama has a place in the contemporary world and that the UK (in particular, Wales) can do sci-fi on a global scale.

For many writers, directors and producers, *Who* has been a staple of British TV, a place to develop their craft and from which to go on to other things. Across the show, the forum it provided for producing ambitious TV on a BBC budget has been a hothouse of British TV talent. Davies isn't solely responsible, but he's got a hand in a show with a new generation of home-grown, and specifically Welsh-grown, TV talent. The role of *Who* in rejuvenating the Welsh TV and film sector has also been vital. The commitment Davies has shown to nurturing Welsh talent and showcasing Welsh locations is a crucial part of Wales's creative industries and a legacy to be celebrated. Included are all the Welsh actors – both in principal roles and supporting artists – who were part of those shows and will continue to be. All the apprenticeships are run by places like Ffilm Cymru or Screen Alliance Wales. The opportunities for trainees at home in Wales wouldn't have existed had it not been for that mad time traveller with a blue box. It all comes back to Davies (along with Tranter and others), and this matters a lot to Wales and the industry.

It's a remarkable achievement to have brought back such a special and important show and made a success of it to the extent that nearly twenty years later, it's still on the air, going strong. There's a whole web of influence around that: from showing the world that Billie Piper is not just a 1990s pop singer but is one of the finest actors of her generation, to David Tennant giving millennials an iconic Converse-and-tight-suits look and to bringing the world's focus to Cardiff as a filming location/tourist destination. At the same time, a new generation was yelling 'exterminate!' in the playground (though that might just be their parents). Kids' TV matters to the kids who watch it, the adults they grow into and those who watch it with them. The inter-generational nature of *Who* is unique; the question of 'which Doctor is your Doctor' defines many people's experiences of childhood or fandom, and it's a hugely formative experience in either case.

The fandom around *Who* exploded in the mid-2000s. For the first time, it felt like a space for women and queer folks in a way it hadn't been previously. That's not to say that there were no queer or female fans before this, just that the space was dominated by a particular kind of cis white man. The cis white men, of course, are still loud in that space, but the leadership of a queer man and the time and attention he gave to female characters opened the fandom to those sides as well. For many, *Who* is the first fandom which had a lasting impact. Whether a good or bad experience, this fandom is also fairly formative. Blogs, and later social media platforms, came to the fore in fandom spaces; there was a space to share fan art and fan fiction and connect with Whovians who were perhaps more in the demographic of new *Who* fans than the older generation of *Who* fans. So, fandom space was carved out for those new to the show, and a new kind of fandom was born. And offline, as discussed with *Torchwood*, Cardiff became a hub (pun intended) for fans to gather. They travelled to watch the filming, visit locations and take pictures in cosplay. They came to meet up with other fans. Cardiff became the place to be for *Who* nerds. Some even moved there or studied at the university for that reason. Either way, Cardiff became important in the TV landscape, and in the *Doctor Who* fandom landscape and, by association, was on the map. This might well be, in some respects, a very specific nerd map. Still, we know that Davies honours nerds, a mark of a deep accolade for his achievements.

Doctor Who matters to the people who watch it. Not just the beautiful fans who create fan art and fan fiction (the act of writing stories based on existing media to share with fellow fans) and talk about it online, but the ones who are at home, week in and week out, watching, the fans who have a little TARDIS on their desk at work or a Doctor action figure on a shelf. The families who still shout *Allons-y!* at each other and don't think about why. The friends who only have to mention Rose's goodbye and start crying. It's the chats over cups of tea and pints of beer about the best and worst of *Doctor Who*. For eighteen years now, that has meant so much to the fans. A new generation of kids, teens and twenty-somethings got to 'grow up' at various stages, with Nine and Ten being their Doctor. That stuff matters. It's only TV, but it matters. Someone thought they could be a bit clever and still be the hero. Clever TV characters, making being clever, or a bit nerdy, cool, are important, whether that was Lisa Simpson from the 1990s, Mr Spock or Wesley Crusher in *Star Trek*, or Willow in *Buffy*. Those TV characters were not the cool kids. They made clever and passion cool and they made these things matter to viewers, especially young ones. So with *Who*, they were inspired. Someone somewhere thought there was good in the universe if the Doctor could exist. Someone somewhere made a friend because they had a TARDIS on their desk at work. The universe feels a bit less lonely knowing the Doctor is out there. Russell T Davies gave us that back.

Coda

Welshness

There is an inescapable Welshness to Davies's writing. He's probably equally known for his Welshness as he is for his gayness (with occasional overlap). While Manchester has probably featured more heavily than Wales as a location in Davies's work, the thread of Welshness in his work is extremely important.

One of the other similarities between Davies's inclusion of Welsh characters or references into his work to how he integrates queerness is the occasional 'incidental' nature in which he does that. While *Torchwood*, for example, integrated Welshness into its identity, equally, there is an array of somewhat randomly interspersed Welsh characters and actors across his work.

Hearing Welsh accents on TV

It seems a minor point, perhaps, for the more broadly represented areas of the country or, more specifically, London-centric media, but hearing regional accents of all kinds on screen is essential. This is particularly so for people from Wales, whose accents have often been the butt of jokes. This isn't limited to Wales in terms of Davies's work; he has an array of accents across his characters (with the notable exception of the Tenth Doctor not keeping David Tennant's Scottish accent). But for Welsh people, hearing Welsh accents, incidentally, on-screen is essential. Generally, Welsh actors are conditioned to believe they will only work if they can work in RP (received pronunciation) accents and hide their 'real' accent and any other signs of where they're from.

Again, this is not limited to Welshness, but includes an array of regional or class-linked accents. However, the fact that Davies also embraces Welshness as an identity is essential. So, when Welsh characters pop up in his work, they are simply Welsh with whatever accent they have, and this feels enormously refreshing.

Wales on TV

Davies has, of course, integrated Welsh characters and narratives in other ways beyond the biggest of all, *Doctor Who*. *Mine All Mine* is the most obvious. This is by far the most 'Welsh' of Davies's work to date. In this quirky Welsh comedy, Davies revisited his roots in Swansea and integrated a crowd of Welsh actors. In the cast – led by Griff Rhys Jones, but including Joanna Page, Siwan Morris and Lynn Hunter (latterly of *Cucumber* as well) – Welsh audiences saw an array of well-known actors from Welsh TV and stage, perhaps less so beyond it. The humour, and the storyline, is peculiarly and brilliantly Welsh. Perhaps it was too niche to expand beyond that audience (although it was moderately successful). Living up to a Davies tradition of featuring actors multiple times, *Mine All Mine* also features Gareth David-Lloyd. In this his name is Yanto Jones, fulfilling the other time-honoured Davies tradition of re-using character names, in this case, in *Torchwood*. Or perhaps Yanto soft-mutated his name and moved to Cardiff to fight aliens? Maybe. The idea of a Davies-Welsh-Multiverse isn't so far-fetched; after all, he did discover a rift in space and time through Cardiff.

The impact on Wales

When people think of Davies's Welsh stories, most will think of that rift in space and time, that mix of 'incidental Welsh' dropped into *Who* and *Torchwood*. When *Doctor Who* was rebooted, Cardiff was its filming home. Davies quickly integrated the 'real' Wales into the Whoniverse with the first series episode 'Boom Town'. This was the first time Cardiff had been part of *Who*, but not the last. In the episode, in the early twenty-first century, we see the setup for what would eventually be the building blocks of *Torchwood* – the rift in space and time running through Cardiff and, indeed, Captain Jack himself and the link he has to the place.

We see Cardiff playing itself for the first time in this episode. Much of 'Boom Town' was filmed on Cardiff Bay. One scene in particular was filmed in front of the Millennium Centre, at the time a relatively newly opened venue and one that is now intrinsically linked with Cardiff and immediately recognisable – possibly partly from its prominence in *Who* and *Torchwood*. We see several sweeping shots of Cardiff Bay, which would of course become a familiar sight in *Torchwood* episodes. In this episode of *Who* we see specifically the restaurant (Bellini's) that the Doctor has dinner in with villain Margaret. We also catch glimpses of what will become the entrance to Torchwood Cardiff (and later Ianto's shrine). In a nice nod to the location, we also see the Doctor reading the local paper, the *Western Mail*. Davies stated that he wanted to incorporate Welsh culture as the series is made in Wales and contains a lot of Welsh crew members.[17] In a behind-the-scenes segment for the BBC's official website, director Joe Ahearne also comments that he wanted to show how beautiful the area could be.[18] Aherne calls it the 'Welsh tourist board episode' of *Who*.

Ahearne is right, too, because *Who* gave a massive boost to Welsh tourism and was a means of putting Cardiff on the map. It's hard to understate the impact on Cardiff, particularly of the Russell T Davies era of *Who*. The first two series of *Torchwood* were filmed and set in Cardiff, and the series was conscious of portraying the city as a modern urban centre, and avoiding Welsh stereotypes in portrayals of the city and country.

Welsh identity is integral to *Torchwood*. There was a certain playful irony at work here, in that for several years *Doctor Who* had been doing its best to disguise Cardiff in its filming – even when prominent landmarks were on display. Cardiff in *Who* had become, much like Canadian cities Montreal and Vancouver – stand-ins for every other city in the world – now Cardiff was allowed to play itself. This change for *Torchwood* was indicated from the off, with the prominence of the Wales Millennium Centre and 'Torchwood Tower' in the promotional materials, and would be cemented by the inclusion of Cardiff locations in 'real time', across the series.

It begins with those prominent set pieces that come to define *Torchwood*. Anyone from Cardiff with a particular nerdy predilection, or from elsewhere with a similarly nerdy disposition, may well refer to the large silver sculpture outside the Wales Millennium Centre theatre in Cardiff Bay as 'Torchwood'. It's not this author's proudest moment. However, until researching this book, I had no idea about the providence of the artwork that is, in fact, 'Torchwood'. Is it a slight to artist William Pye who designed the piece as part of Cardiff Bay's regeneration (pun somewhat unintended)? Or perhaps it is a boost, as the work has been seen more times than it would have been in more countries, thanks to a strange little sci-fi show. Either way, the imposing twenty-one-metre-high sculpture is made of stainless steel; it's flat on one side, curved on another, and has a constant flow of water running down it. According to Pye's description, it was meant as part of a 'reclaiming' of the space from a dry dock to a meeting place. It's certainly become the latter, especially with people meeting on the 'magic step' that leads to Torchwood HQ.

Filming in Cardiff captured imaginations, and the comprehensive 'Doctor Who Locations' website that had already meticulously catalogued *Doctor Who* to this point, could now add *Torchwood* to that. It includes everything from the South Wales Traffic Management Centre to Cardiff Castle. Of course, much of the filming of *Torchwood* employed the same smoke and mirrors as *Doctor Who*; the hospital where Gwen stalks Weevils is in fact Cardiff Metropolitan University's old school of management building. In places, *Torchwood*'s navigating of Cardiff is somewhat fictional, like when Jack Bauer races around Los Angeles in *24* he often takes routes that are impossible, or at the very least would land him in a traffic jam.

Despite this, much of Cardiff was able to play itself. This included the hub of Torchwood, the fake 'Tourist Information' entrance to Torchwood Cardiff, situated in Mermaid Quay, and the site still of Ianto's shrine (discussed later in this chapter). Also, the Millennium Centre and Norwegian Church feature heavily in many bay-centric shots. Likewise, the areas around Mount Stuart Square in the bay, with its Victorian-style buildings, are also often used as backdrops. More niche, perhaps, the back of the Waterguard pub in the bay (which now overlooks the BBC studios and, previously, the Doctor Who Experience), was the setting for 'Boeshane Village' in which young Jack in the fifty-first century was raised – with the help of a bit of sand and clever camera angles. More iconic buildings include: the castle (where Gwen watches the attempted destruction of the city) and the St David's Hotel (Owen's apartment, maybe Torchwood paid its staff too much?). Whilst every location wasn't precisely geographically correct – several car chases would definitely have got caught in rush-hour traffic – the locations felt like a love letter to the city.

As did other aspects of the show, like Gwen, Rhys and Ianto (along with others) being allowed to speak in Welsh accents. This is a massive thing for Welsh actors and audiences, as explained above. So few stories, aside from those about miners, get set in Wales. Often, Welsh actors have to hide their accents. *Torchwood* was unapologetic 'Torchwood Cardiff', and the characters, both central characters and guest actors, were from Cardiff. This not only offered a boon for local actors, in high-profile work (another element sorely lacking), but many could also now celebrate being 'Cardiff' in a show about 'Cardiff'. The show doesn't open with the cast singing 'Mae Hen Wlad Fy Nhadau' and wearing a rugby shirt (though actually, Rhys wears a rugby shirt at least once), yet *Torchwood* is as Welsh as Cardiff city centre on match days and is not afraid to show it.

Torchwood had a huge fan following and was part of a 'golden age' of the BBC in Cardiff. Fans would gather at outdoor shootings for both *Torchwood* and *Doctor Who*, often travelling and staying over in Cardiff when there were rumoured filming blocks. For the most part, this was welcome – *Torchwood*, in particular, was a fairly 'cult' level hit, and the fans were what kept it alive and helped maintain the BBC's interest in it. As Jean Seaton, professor of media history at Westminster University and the official historian of the BBC, noted on the impact:

> One of the interesting things about Davies's Doctor Who is that it's made in Wales. The BBC has invested in Wales and this is one of its success stories. It is the product of creative

autonomy in a creative economy created by public subsidy. Queer as Folk was made in Manchester. Davies is an innovator and has harnessed the creative power of the provinces. He recognises an energy there that is very often ignored.[19]

As *Torchwood* was set in Cardiff and because of the ongoing *Who* influence, fans began gravitating towards the city for filming tourism. This isn't a new phenomenon. Major cities like London or New York have many 'film locations' tours, for both the actual locations used in films and fictional ones. But this was unusual for Cardiff. A few 'unofficial' tours sprung up, along with fans just following self-guided tours using online information. Locals would see fans posing outside the 'Torchwood' hub entrance in Roald Dahl Plas outside the Millennium Centre. Or fans would stage photoshoot recreations – sometimes in full cosplay. They would also visit other key locations. Of course, most visiting fans were also *Doctor Who* fans, so visited key locations from that, too. But it was the Cardiff-ness of the *Torchwood* locations that in fandom circles put the city on the map. Even today, in certain circles, mention you're from Cardiff and *Torchwood* will come up in conversation, often accompanied by, 'I visited there once.' The idea of Cardiff as a must-see city was also helped by the Doctor Who Experience, which periodically had elements of *Torchwood* content, and also got in on the walking tours act for a time. There were plans for a *Torchwood* exhibition for a while, but it never materialised.

However, it was the fans who kept the show alive. There were also various unofficial conventions ('The Hub' was the main one) as well as a handful of academic conferences with *Torchwood* papers. Strangely, no big *Torchwood* convention was ever held in Cardiff, which seems like a missed opportunity.

The ongoing impact of *Who* and *Torchwood* has become an enormous part of the Welsh capital's tourism identity. While the filming of *Who* continues in the surrounding areas, albeit with less fanfare and attention than in the original Davies era, this focus on Cardiff as a filming hub is essential. What was also important was that Davies integrated Cardiff into the narrative.

Davies subtly (and not so subtly) incorporated Welshness across his series, and this did a lot for Wales and Welsh writing. It encouraged writers coming up behind Davies to own their identity, not to hide it. The parallels to how he handles queer characters are clear, and that this may seem reductive to some indicates how Welsh identities are treated in the media. But even the subtle visibility of Welsh characters in his stories lets both actors and writers know it's ok to put that part of themselves in the story, and it doesn't have to be the punchline (or they can make it the punchline and own it as they do their Welshness). He was also conscious of putting Welsh actors in shows with a more national and international platform than they previously would have had – many actors can be well known in the Welsh language TV landscape and/or the theatre landscape but not graduate from bit parts in national level shows. In his characteristic way of working with actors he liked across multiple shows, Davies gave many Welsh actors a bigger platform and opportunity. Some, like Gareth David-Lloyd, even got their own dedicated fanbase alongside a career boost.

This, coupled with the tourism and attention boost that *Who* and *Torchwood* gave Cardiff and Wales and Davies's tenure on *Who*, was extremely important for Welsh identity on screen. Davies didn't single-handedly revitalise the film industry or tourism in the area, but his impact was massive and is still felt today. From Bad Wolf studios being born out of (and, of course, taking the name from) that era, and a multitude of big-budget, high-profile shows being under their wing (including *His Dark Materials*), to other high-profile BBC shows being filmed in Cardiff, like *Sherlock* (under successor Steven Moffat's guidance, and his own production company, Hartswood Films), the impact on Cardiff's growth for filming was significant, as was the symbiotic relationship with tourism.

Putting Cardiff front and centre – both in the stories it featured in and in talking about it in all the wrap-around information on *Who* – had a noticeable impact. Along with the prominence, the ability to show what the Welsh capital (and beyond) could do, there's a softer, more meaningful side, too, and that is the fans. The fans of *Who* are dedicated and passionate, and many made the 'pilgrimage' to Cardiff at some point to visit where their show was filmed. It's a lovely thing to think that through writing in Wales, through showcasing it, the country has blossomed. Cardiff is now part of fans' memories of their show. The world over, having conversations about Cardiff and hearing people say, 'I love *Doctor Who*', and knowing there's a bringing together of Welshness, with something people are so passionate about, is on both sides a wonderful thing. And if you think about it, that really is Davies in a nutshell.

Chapter Four

Doctor Who for grown-ups: *Torchwood*

Despite it being labelled as such, by press and fans alike, Davies has often referenced being told he's 'not allowed' to call *Torchwood* '*Doctor Who* for grown-ups'. In October 2005, BBC3 Controller, Stuart Murphy, invited Davies to create a post-watershed *Doctor Who* spin-off because of the popularity of the new *Who* with parents. *Torchwood* was named after an anagrammatic title used to prevent leaks of *Doctor Who* in the first Russell T Davies series (often used on filming location signs and other communications). The show also includes elements of a previously abandoned project by Davies called *Excalibur*. It centres on fifty-first-century time-traveller Captain Jack Harkness (first seen in the Steven Moffat-written episodes 'The Empty Child' and 'The Doctor Dances' (season 1, episodes 9 and 10). In *Torchwood*, Jack is part of the quasi-governmental organisation (also included in other *Who* episodes, notably originating in the Queen Victoria episode 'Tooth and Claw' and later 'Army of Ghosts' and 'Doomsday' in series 2). Torchwood Cardiff in the narrative is a breakaway organisation from the original Torchwood. The series began production in 2006, and on transmission was one of the most successful BBC3 shows to date.

Torchwood follows the exploits of the Cardiff breakaway team of alien hunters. The initial main cast of the series alongside Barrowman consisted of Gareth David-Lloyd, Burn Gorman, Naoko Mori and Eve Myles. In its first two series, the show used a time rift in Cardiff – as set up in *Doctor Who* – as its primary plot generator, which accounted for the unusual preponderance of alien beings in Cardiff. In the third and fourth series, Torchwood operated as fugitives. Gorman and Mori's characters were written out at the end of Series Two. In the following series, Kai Owen was promoted to the regular cast, while Gareth David-Lloyd was written out with the death of Ianto. Added to the core Welsh cast were American actors Mekhi Phifer, Alexa Havins and Bill Pullman.

Sexy aliens?

Torchwood is defiantly sex-positive. The rift in space and time in Cardiff must have a specific effect on sex drive, given the time the Torchwood Cardiff team dedicates to that part of their lives. Was the show an example of a bit of boundary-pushing on Davies's part? Maybe. But it was also an incredibly sexually fluid, sex-positive show and very queer in the broader sense.

We think of Captain Jack as the heart (or other organs) of this culture, but the fluidity and promiscuity (used here in a positive connotation) apply to the whole team. In 'Everything Changes', Owen Harper seduces a woman and her boyfriend using alien technology. Gwen Cooper has a boyfriend, but she reciprocates the advances of a sex-driven alien in a woman's body in 'Day One', albeit under the influences of alien-enhanced pheromones. Later in that episode, when the possessed woman attempts to absorb the orgasmic energy of various men at a sperm bank, one of them briefly protests that he's gay. Toshiko exhibits bisexual behaviour: she is interested in her teammate, Owen, but in 'Greeks Bearing Gifts', she has a sexual relationship with 'Mary'.

As much as it's fun to watch and discuss the sexual misadventures of Team Torchwood, there's also an important side to this – positive depictions of sex and sexuality. Historically, TV has not been great at this, particularly with queer characters, and it is something that Davies has integrated across his work. *Queer as Folk* and *Torchwood* have this in common: an amount of sex that has been criticised as gratuitous but serves to normalise conversation around sex and sexuality. Or perhaps, even (for the pearl clutchers of the world, or the *Daily Mail*), it is just, entertaining. This is because in part, the sex in *Torchwood* is a collection of enthralling asides in the ongoing battle to save the world. It's the message that human interest and sex and romance make the world go around. Assuming an adult audience, here Davies balances expressions of sexuality with saving the world – the way he does this is perhaps a more light-hearted version of how, for example, later in *Years and Years*, Russell Tovey's character, Daniel, has sex while a nuclear explosion happens. Humans seek connection at the worst of times, sexual desires don't necessarily stop for nuclear explosions. In *Torchwood*, surviving a Weevil attack makes people horny, and nobody is here to judge that.

Captain Jack

Starting in 2013, Jack's sexuality made him the subject of an internet meme highlighting the ethics of sexual encounters with nonhuman characters. Known as the Harkness Test, the meme spread rapidly and was applied to other fandoms such as Pokémon and My Little Pony. It is a hypothetical test which seeks to determine whether it's permissible to have sex with someone (or something). The criteria are, 'Does it have appropriate intelligence to consent?', 'Can it communicate that consent?' and 'Is it of an appropriate age to consent?' The modelling after Jack is based on the fact that while he would (and does) have sex with just about any species he encounters, he does so under a moral code.

Phil Wickham, in his book *Understanding TV Texts*, notes that Captain Jack explicitly 'brings to the fore' his 'brazen bisexuality', which is 'something we have to come to expect [from Russell T Davies] as viewers of his work'.[20]

Commenting on the show's postmodern attitude towards bisexuality, or what Russell T Davies calls 'omnisexuality', Glyn Davis and Gary Needham say about Jack: 'His character brushes against definitions of queer sexuality in that he resists any sort of classification based on sexual orientation.' They also comment on the impact of Jack's storylines, including his gay time-travel romance 'Captain Jack Harkness' and the idea of the time-travelled Jack and his impact on forbidden gay attraction in what they call 'post-Brokeback television'.[21]

But the man is more than a meme. Captain Jack is important to so many viewers. Despite some problematic elements of character and connection with the actor, he remains a really important part of many people's coming-out journey, acceptance of their sexuality, or simply seeing themselves on screen.

Captain Jack is sexually fluid, to the extreme. Even in *Who*, we see the (child-friendly) version of this. Jack's sexuality and slightly wild past were introduced (in more family-friendly terms) in *Doctor Who*, and one of the joys of *Torchwood* was the ability to reference his other 'adventures' in more detail. In 'They Keep Killing Suzie', Jack claims to have had a sexual relationship with twin brothers, both acrobats. However, it is unclear whether he is speaking sincerely or simply trying to distract Gwen from asking difficult questions. However, in the second series, Jack remarks to Owen while they are in police custody in the episode 'Dead Man Walking', that when you have been alive as long as he has, 'you don't make any more up', implying that the many past relationships he refers to are genuine. Other relationships described or alluded to (both in the TV series and other media) include ex-girlfriends Estelle Cole, Duchess Eleanor, Stella Courtney and Lucia Moretti, ex-boyfriend Angelo Colasanto, as well as an unnamed ex-wife.

In 'Captain Jack Harkness', a sub-plot of the episode revolves around Jack's namesake's sexual orientation. His uneasy behaviour and his dismay at having convinced his girlfriend that they were in love, combined with his flirtatious interaction with Jack, suggested he was gay and trapped in an unwanted heterosexual relationship, unable to come out in his era. At the episode's climax, at a dance and knowing he would die the next day, the two Jacks danced and kissed, before they had to part, to the amazement of the 1940s guests all around them.

Discussing whether his character could ever find 'the one', John Barrowman asserted that Jack 'likes everybody, and his love for each person is different'. Barrowman believes that Jack does harbour romantic feelings towards the Doctor but 'would never take that beyond infatuation' and 'would never let the Doctor know'.[22] Yet in the same article Barrowman also talks about the platonic and paternal love for everyone in his team (as well as referencing 'fancying' the Doctor's companion Martha Jones).

The second series of *Torchwood* introduced Jack's ex-lover Captain John (played by James Masters, known for his role as Spike in *Buffy the Vampire Slayer*). Chris Chibnall introduced John to act as a 'proper nemesis, somebody to really test [Jack], to push him, and to reveal something about Jack's character'. The inclusion of his character allowed for a peek into what might have been, as Chibnall also comments: 'you see the way Jack could have gone, and probably did, for a little while,' which underlines how 'Jack, in his experiences with the Doctor and Torchwood, made a very conscious decision to move away from that behaviour.'[23]

Representation mattered

Captain Jack was a revelation for many. He was a 'love the one you're with' kind of guy, and a 'flirt with everyone' kind of guy. But he was important for several reasons.

Firstly, he was pansexual (omnisexual, polyamorous, too, probably). It's fair to say that neither gender nor species put Captain Jack off. Moreover, he saw both as a challenge. Captain Jack Harkness was one of the first mainstream pansexual characters on TV. A few years later, we have the brilliant David Rose on *Schitt's Creek* (2015–20), who declared he loved 'the wine not the label', but before there was David Rose, there was Captain Jack, who barely stopped long enough to ask the wine its name, never mind origin, before flirting with it. Captain Jack moved through time and space and flirted with every species along the way. But he never apologised, was never embarrassed and certainly was never ashamed of his sexual orientation. Pansexual representation on TV was crucial as it was so rarely seen (and still is, comparatively), so this was important.

In addition, John Barrowman himself was an out-and-proud gay man. Indeed, during his tenure as Captain Jack, he married his long-term partner Scott in a ceremony in Cardiff (between shows and while appearing in pantomime at the New Theatre). Barrowman had been working in theatre for around twenty years when he was cast as Jack, and had been out within that world, and much like Jack, there was little to keep Barrowman in the closet. His larger-than-life personality aside, it was vitally important that Barrowman was an out gay man, so we had an action hero who was gay in real life on British TV. That fact was huge for the mid-2000s. This was still relatively unheard of. Also, Barrowman was outspoken in his views on gay rights, his support of queer charities, and of course, being unapologetically himself.

Captain Jack did a lot of good and was an immensely fun and important addition to the queer canon, but does his character do more harm than good as a cliché 'slutty bisexual'? Some might argue that Captain Jack further perpetuated the trope of 'bisexual' meaning to want to have casual sex with anyone. We could then ask, what's wrong with that?

As with Stuart Jones in *Queer as Folk* and even Ritchie in *It's a Sin*, Davies's sexually permissive characters are very real. As much as Captain Jack is an immortal alien with what we can only assume is a uniform fetish, he's also, as the popular phrase goes, 'living his best life'. Because, while there are genuine reasons to do away with the stereotype of 'slutty bisexuals', there are equally valid reasons to endorse sex-positive attitudes. In all that Captain Jack did, we have no reason to believe he either misled people or coerced them into sex and that it was generally a 'good time had by all' experience (particularly for Jack). One aspect that supports this in a strange, unexpected way is the Doctor's attitude to Jack. The Doctor simply laughs and thinks, 'it's just Jack'. They are flattered by the flirting but not interested themselves (see Chapter Three: 'Gay aliens?', for more on the Doctor's sexuality and its importance). The crucial thing is that the Doctor doesn't judge Jack for it. As in much of life, we could all do with being a bit more like the Doctor, accepting Jack for who he is, and acknowledging that, for some people being a 'slutty bisexual' is no bad thing.

The move from *Who* to *Torchwood* was important, too, because people need queer role models, and while Captain Jack does some questionable things, or at least makes questionable romantic and sexual choices, he is a role model. He's a man who tries to save the world over and over again. He's a man who dies to save the world and his friends (obviously he knows he'll live, but the point still stands). We don't have many queer superheroes. A few like Supergirl and Captain Marvel and others from the Marvel cinematic universe creep through into mainstream culture, but they're still a minority, and we certainly didn't have any when *Torchwood* was made. To have an action hero who is also a queer man is to say to all the queer young people and adults, 'you can have an action hero who is like you'. That's vital.

Just to have a leading man who was queer was huge. Not in a show *about* his queerness but in a show where it wasn't hidden. He was allowed to kiss boys if he wanted to while saving the world. We hadn't seen this before. More importantly, he had the seal of approval from the Doctor.

Captain Jack and… Captain Jack?

The episode 'Captain Jack Harkness' is a fan favourite. However, some academics took issue with the depiction of Jack/Jack. In *Queer TV*, Glyn Davis and Gary Needham discuss Jack's role in *Torchwood* as what they term a 'post-gay' romantic hero. They comment that it is via Jack that the show is able to 'mine its queerness'. Discussing Jack's brief romance with his namesake, the real Captain Jack (Matt Rippy), Davis and Needham have also noted that:

> The Captain Jacks both share the same name and are quite similar in physical appearance, thus literalising the homo-ness of the situation. Through the time-travel device this points to a narcissistic self-fascination, the old cliché that homosexuality is the love for sameness.[24]

That moment with Captain Jack was pivotal for so many. The episode, 'Captain Jack Harkness', is a sweet, if ultimately tragic, romcom. Remember that, when this aired, such things were still a rarity on TV. Representation on TV was still lacking; this was pre-shows like *Modern Family* or *Schitt's Creek*, which normalised gay romance and relationships within the plot lines. Queer stories around this time were still the reserve for queer shows like *Queer as Folk* (US) or *The L Word*. We didn't yet have many Teen queer TV shows like *Heartstopper* (2022–) and *Love, Victor* (2020–2). Hence, those queer fans who had been growing up with *Doctor Who* and transitioned to *Torchwood* as young teens or twenty-somethings perhaps got their first queer TV romance in the form of Captain Jack and Captain Jack.

It could be argued that this is an example of *Torchwood* hitting another 'tragic gays' trope. The fact that this story doesn't let either of the Jacks find happiness feels forgivable in the name of drama. It feels like the *Titanic* of *Torchwood*, like Lady Mary in *Downton* losing Matthew. In short, it feels authentic to the story. It's also a valuable 'know your history' moment. Neither Captain Jack could have the life they want in the era the original Jack lives in, and that's a tragedy we should know and be mindful of and tell stories about, while also celebrating their love. That's what that episode does. It is also a glorious romantic movie crammed into one episode.

The audience sees a dance and a passionate kiss to close, and so many queer young people would never have seen a pair of men romantically dancing on TV. It's hard to stress, particularly to younger audiences now, how important this would have been to many at that time, to see Captain Jack, the man who had grown to mean a lot, the action hero and cool guy, get to dance on TV with another man. Many adults, even the *Queer as Folk* generation, hadn't seen that either. For a minute or two on screen, while 'A Nightingale Sang in Berkley Square' rings out, there's a moment of queer romance magic.

As much as we could also argue that there is an element of the 'tragic gay' trope about it, too, largely, the Captain Jack storyline is charming, heart-warming and romantic. Although the episode ends on a sad note, overall, it's one of queer joy. It is an episode of TV dedicated largely to a gay love affair in a show that isn't 'about' being gay, something that feels very 'ahead of its time' (much like Captain Jack himself).

There's also a danger of over-analysing or judging queer TV too harshly. As addressed in the *Queer as Folk* and *It's a Sin* chapters, there's a tendency to ask queer TV to be all things to all people. Were the queer characters in *Torchwood* perfect? No. Were the storylines flawless? No. But we hold queer narratives to too high a standard in that respect – pick any other romantic plots from the same year in straight TV, and would it hold up to the same level of scrutiny? Probably not. Do we need to honour the neglect queer stories have been subject to, of course, but not at the expense of making them.

The Captain Jack/Captain Jack narrative was a satisfying piece of drama that had the bonus of queer visibility. Also, if we go back to the above academic analysis, it's a clever joke on the show itself. Who else could Captain Jack truly fall in love with, but himself? He's been framed as a man who is a narcissist, albeit a loveable one. He's vain and slightly self-involved, at least when seeking sexual satisfaction. Who could break that mould except, himself, Captain Jack?

Bury your gays?

Firstly, in *Torchwood*, Davies did 'bury your gays' – he buried Captain Jack outside Cardiff Castle, where he died and came back to life for 107 years ('Exit Wounds', Season 2, Episode 13). Perhaps a coincidence, but also one that can be read as an amusing commentary on the 'bury your gays' trope. Traditionally, this refers to the inclusion of a queer character who will later be killed off. In literature, this used to be a means of passing censorship; a queer relationship could be included if there was to follow a moral message about the impact of that character's actions. So, usually, the queer characters would die. As time went on, this continued into TV and film, especially where queer characters were tokenistic and expendable, and often they died first. Even as queer characters gained prominence, they were less likely to get a happy romantic ending and still fell foul of early deaths.

Captain Jack, in general, can be read as a neat defiance of this. He, of course, is in many ways a defiance of the way we see queer characters on screen, and this should be celebrated. His death-defying antics are of particular significance. Jack is, in that way, quite literally, the opposite of what we expect, in that he repeatedly defies death over and over. It feels like a sort of defiance of all those other queer characters who died. Jack is the one who simply wouldn't,

84

couldn't die, no matter how hard people tried. It's a great piece of subtle rebellion against the trend.

Coffee boy and true love? Ianto and Jack

In the bigger picture, Captain Jack allows Jack Harkness to become who he needs to be to follow through on his relationship with Ianto. That's important. He has to go through something to make him the version of Jack that could have feelings for Ianto and be a boyfriend to him.

There's much in the Jack and Ianto relationship that's important. Firstly, their attitude to each other and sex is progressive and sex-positive. They embrace both non-monogamy, at least at first; it's casual that nobody is putting labels on things, and there's a half-joke about getting Gwen, their colleague and friend in Torchwood, involved at one point. Monogamy, after all, seems a very twenty-first-century notion to fifty-first-century Jack. Beyond that, too, they don't label things or each other. While that might feel frustrating to some who want to codify their relationship in a traditional heteronormative way, it's also refreshing to see a queer relationship on its own terms. A slight nod by Davies, too, that perhaps queer relationships don't have to follow a heterosexual model.

The fact that they don't need labels is a strong, important state-ment. Ianto dating Jack doesn't become an angst-filled reflection on sexuality and a traumatising coming out. Instead, they just date. As much as coming out stories are needed and important, the ease with which Ianto moves to date a man without fanfare or soul searching is refreshing, and just as important as those stories. Similarly, just like Jack doesn't ascribe to twenty-first-century labels, we see Ianto eschewing them. When finally challenged on his relationship with Jack by his sister, he talks about it just being about loving Jack, and for Ianto, that's enough.

We might read Ianto as demisexual – a sexual orientation whereby the person needs a connection to another person to feel attraction. Demisexual people can only feel sexual attraction once a bond is formed. Many demisexual people also label themselves as 'gay', 'straight' or 'bisexual', but it is the demisexuality that dictates their attraction. For Ianto, perhaps he never realised he could be attracted to men until Jack, because he'd never formed a bond with one that elicited that. Demisexuality and other labels on the asexual spectrum, are woefully underrepresented, and so the reading of Ianto as part of that community is also incredibly important to that community.

Much like the Doctor, who provides asexual representation, Ianto's demisexual representation is just as important as the queer represen-tation in *Queer as Folk*. While neither may be intentional – this is not meant to be a slight to Davies, because the asexual community largely goes underrepresented – they mean a lot to a lot of people. Indeed, in recent years, conversations about aspec identities (asexual and aromantic identities – those who do not experience sexual or romantic attraction) have become more prominent, and people have begun retrospectively ascribing their experience to other characters like the Doctor or Ianto. Whether or not the characters were intended to be that way is largely moot – much like the queer-coded characters of previous generations, before it was permitted to depict them openly – if this interpretation helps people to see themselves on screen in character, it's positive and valid.

And Ianto ticks all those boxes. He says it out loud, 'it's not men it's just him,' which is pure demisexuality. Ianto has formed a bond with Jack, and he finds him attractive from that bond and ultimately falls in love with him. Previously, he'd been with a woman, where we can assume the same happened. But regardless of that, for many fans who also identify as demisexual, that was important. They were seeing their life experience reflected.

In the same way, watching Ianto's story also resonated with any person who had previously been with a woman then dated a man, and vice versa. The beauty of Ianto not labelling himself overtly is it gives everyone who sees their experience reflected in the show the chance to see themselves in that experience. Isn't that a beautiful and inclusive thing?

Or we can classify him as bisexual/pansexual, again, like Jack. In that respect, he's an important character for representing the community. Ianto Jones is a great example of sexual fluidity and acceptance. While his sexuality isn't the show's focus, there is no deep soul-searching or negativity around his shift to sleeping with, dating, loving Jack.

Everybody dies...

Of course, Ianto's love story is somewhat muted by what happens to him in 'Children of Earth', which unfortunately does fall into the 'bury your gays' trope. So many fans wish it wasn't this way on many levels. Firstly, obviously, on a dramatic level and out of love for the character. Secondly, out of love for Davies and what he has done for queer TV. This is unlike Phil in *Queer as Folk*, a side character whose death served both dramatic purpose and part of the larger conversation. It's not even like Colin or Ritchie in *It's a Sin*, whose deaths are unavoidably part of the central narrative. While Daniel's death in *Years and Years* gets close to this trope, there are dramatic, political and conversational reasons and justifications for it. Ianto's demise unfortunately looks more like that now-clichéd example of Tara in *Buffy* – killed because while she was there, the romantic plot lacked drama, or killed just to create drama. Davies is known for killing off characters suddenly, unexpectedly and mercilessly. We saw that in the first episode of *Torchwood* when Suzie was killed (and later when she was killed several times more). But Ianto's death feels different. The deaths across *Torchwood*, even the deaths across *Who* (especially across *Who*), feel earned, dramatically, and like they have a purpose. Ianto's death lacks that.

What exactly happened to Ianto Jones? Just as Jack and Ianto's relationship develops, Ianto dies in 'Children of Earth'. At the moment of death, it's dramatic, poetic, and, yes, moving. But was it necessary? Arguably not. Arguably, a show that was doing so well at giving rounded, interesting, queer characters whose queerness wasn't the centre of the story didn't have to go down the 'bury your gays' route.

It hurt, and fans made their feelings known at the time, and continue to do so. After Ianto dies, and during Jack's cameo in 'The End of Time' (2010), the Doctor sets Jack up with a new romantic interest, Alonso

Frame (Russell Tovey), who was last seen in 'Voyage of the Damned' (2007). Some fans resented this pairing, and compared it to the situation on *Buffy* where Willow, following the (equally untimely) death of her girlfriend Tara, was swiftly paired off with another love interest. This fuelled the negative reading of Ianto's death and the feeling that it fulfils the trope of 'bury your gays'.

Of course, Ianto lived on in fan culture, not only with the 'shrine' to him in Cardiff Bay. CitySeeker tourism website describes the shrine as 'one of Cardiff's best-kept secrets, also one of the weirdest places to visit in the Welsh capital'.[25] While to outside eyes it might be, it also represents an important moment for fans, who were outraged when Ianto died. The public outcry that followed sparked an enormous online campaign, a charity fundraiser in his name (which raised more than £10,000 for *Children in Need*) and then the shrine in Cardiff's Mermaid Quay. While in the show Ianto died in London, fans used the fake entrance to Torchwood Cardiff in the Bay as a place to create a memorial. After the episode in which he died aired, fans fixed notes and flowers to the wall in Cardiff Bay where the Torchwood entrance had been filmed. Over time, the 'shrine' grew and grew with fan art and letters and all manner of fan ephemera attached to it. It became something of a place of pilgrimage to fans, who had often travelled to Cardiff to visit filming locations, and this became a way to remember a favourite character.

Fans, love of the show (and Ianto) and ongoing life

Ianto died in 2009; at the time of writing, the Ianto shrine is, if not exactly, going 'strong', still going. It's now weather-beaten and faded, but fans still periodically add to it (usually on the anniversary of his death). This links to the significance of Jack and Ianto's relationship and the fan engagement with the show through various fan practices, chiefly fan fiction, where the fans sought to 'fix' what Davies had got so wrong.

In the time-honoured tradition of 'fixing' what is wrong with a series, fan fiction (along with fan art) is rife among *Torchwood* fans, and much of it has centred on 'what could have been'. Given that the show was almost like fan fiction to begin with – 'what would happen if

Captain Jack were given humans and adventures of his own' – it's easy to see how the show captured the imagination of fans.

Kristina Busse, in *Framing Fan Fiction: Literary and Social Practices in Fan Fiction Communities* argues that fan fiction is a fragment of a broader fandom discourse. She writes that 'much of the text's meaning can be tied in with a specific place, time, and community',[26] underlining the importance of the context in which the authors write their stories in influencing the stories they tell. Busse's argument is exemplified by the development of fan fiction in *Torchwood* fandom after its third season, once the relationship between Ianto and Jack became canon (became 'real' on the show). This was a point at which the fan community became much more focused and engaged with this idea of 'shipping' the characters by associating the fan fiction around it. Fans feel that their fan fiction community is a vital part of their fandom experience. Fan fiction often forms a formative part of growing up and coming out for many young people. On a fundamental level, it continues to be an important part of life for many as they grow older. For example, when they decide that Merlin and Arthur in the BBC's *Merlin* is gay because there aren't enough gay narratives on TV, or when they decide to have the Doctor's companions fall in love with each other, run off, and save the world instead of waiting for them. For many a *Torchwood* fan, who had perhaps been in their late teens when *Who* was rebooted, *Torchwood* would have been their first queer fandom experience, a queer awakening maybe, a chance to read and write queer stories in fandom settings – a multitude of exciting formative, and, indeed, pretty queer things.

The elephant in the room is that fan fiction often involves a lot of sexual content. Fan fiction can range from non-sexual to highly explicit. Both within the *Torchwood* fandom and beyond, fan fiction varies from the continued adventures of the characters, to romance, to the sexually explicit, and everything in between. Fan fiction doesn't *have* to be about romance or sex, indeed many stories also continue the style of the show they're a response to, and don't focus on relationships. However, it has long been a tradition of fan fiction to reflect the relationships unseen on screen, whether that was 'shippers' of Mulder and Scully in *The X-Files* writing the relationship they wanted to see between the two agents, or whether it's the more adventurously divergent-from-the-source-material explicit adventures of, say, Captain America and Groot in the Marvel cinematic universe – a story completely out of the range of possibility and ridiculous in every sense (imagine the splinters).

Traditionally, too, fan fiction has been a space in which to write the queer stories that don't get seen on screen. So, whether that is, say, creating a queer *Merlin*, as mentioned above, as they were never likely to be written as queer, or fixing 'queerbaiting' in shows – where a programme or film will tease a potential queer romance only to never deliver. Some examples of this from around the same time as *Torchwood* include the BBC's *Sherlock* in which the relationship between Sherlock and John hinted more and more at something greater than friendship, but never took that leap, or *Supernatural* where the hinting of a potentially queer relationship between Dean Winchester and Castiel, the angel, was teased right up until the final episode, where it was never delivered. Fan fiction 'fixes' these narratives over and over again.

In the case of Ianto/Jack (and other 'queerships'), when *Torchwood* began, fan fiction was about imagined possibilities. Fan fiction ran the gamut between Gwen/Jack and Ianto/Jack, with fairly standard fandom divisions around which 'ship' (relationship) should become canon (part of the show). As we might expect from *Torchwood* fans, too, there's a good deal of fun and silliness in keeping with the show's irreverent attitude. Also in the mix, again as we might expect, is the more explicit end of what's implied on the show, things that can't be shown on the BBC. Given that the relationship became canon, the relationship within fan fiction was different, where fans were 'fixing' the narrative, at least at first. Instead, they were building on the existing stories, expanding upon them and taking Jack and Ianto on their own adventures. In a similar way to other shows like *911 Lonestar*, where the central queer characters are in a relationship, or *Schitt's Creek*, where the queer romance is the central plot, *Torchwood* allowed for fan fiction to build on what's there, rather than have to imagine another alternative version where fans get what they want.

However, after Ianto's death, Ianto/Jack quickly became the dominant theme in fan fiction, in what had looked like something *Torchwood* fans might avoid – fixing the queer narrative. Instead, a storyline that had for two seasons been a joyful 'will they, won't they' narrative turned into an established relationship, and so the fan fiction now became a 'fix it' narrative, along with most other screen queer relationships. For *Torchwood* fans, their fan fiction was more important than the *Doctor Who* version, where an imaginary alternative has the Doctor running off with Rose, making right what they *almost* had.

Cultural impact and ongoing life

In retrospect, it's hard to encapsulate how 'everywhere' *Who* and *Torchwood* were in this era. Fans rarely get such a 'buy-in' from the channel that owns their show, but the BBC saw the popularity of *Who* and, subsequently, *Torchwood* and ran with it. There were companion programmes. *Torchwood Declassified* was a 'making-of' programme similar to *Doctor Who Confidential*. From *Torchwood*'s inception, there was a substantial online presence for the series (in line with the BBC's digital 'push' around this time across its shows). This included an animated web series alongside the fourth series.

Torchwood marked a cultural moment at the BBC, and the multi-layered tie-ins, and fan appetite for them, meant the world of *Torchwood* expanded well beyond the show. Various tie-in media were produced, including audio dramas, novels and comic strips. For a long time, *Doctor Who* fans have loved tie-in media, and since the show's reboot, such media has proven a great promotional tool and, frankly, money maker for the BBC. Most *Doctor Who* merchandise was produced under the BBC Worldwide brand, which meant it could be 'for profit' outside the corporation's main arm, and the same could apply to *Torchwood*.

Despite a slightly fractious final relationship and a slightly disconnected fandom after *Children of Earth*, the ever-plucky 'Torchwood Cardiff' crew, endure. As mentioned above, the impact of fans, fandom and, of course, fan fiction knows no bounds, and particularly Jack and Ianto endure there. Much like the darker years of *Who* pre-Russell T Davies, *Torchwood* finds a way to endure. With both tie-in books and tie-in audio drama, the adventures continue.

The ongoing Big Finish investment in *Torchwood* shows fans' enduring great love of the series. In continuing the *Torchwood* that fans loved, there is a sense of *some* righting the wrongs too. The 'original' camp, silly, grown-up *Doctor Who* – because as much as the BBC didn't want it called that, it was what fans wanted – worked. Had the show kept to the original format – thirteen episodes of chasing aliens around Cardiff with breaks for innuendo and sexual dalliances, fans would likely have remained happy. Even with an unresolved 'happily ever after' for Ianto and Jack, one more season of that would have been welcome. The inherent problem wasn't the 'bury your gays' moment; it was the shift in what *Torchwood* became. It was no longer camp, funny men in suits running around the corridors of Cardiff Met University (as per 'Everything Changes'), it became a slick, over-produced, and trying-to-be-American sci-fi. The lesson for Davies and the BBC was that you could take *Torchwood* out of *Doctor Who*, but you can't take *Doctor Who* out of *Torchwood*.

Coda

Women

Among the many things that Russell T Davies has gifted TV over the years, one of the most significant is brilliant women. At the heart of his stories, the women are often the heroes, or at least the ones talking sense.

Of course, there are exceptions. Emma Thompson's Vivienne Rook in *Years and Years* is a notable one, as is Harriet Jones (the Prime Minister) in *Doctor Who*. She begins well but is turned. (Maybe the lesson is not to trust female politicians in Davies's world, which would make sense for a gay man who grew up under Thatcher, who is the unseen politician villain of *It's a Sin*.) However, these exceptions aside, even within the politicians, Davies gives us a collection of complex women full of agency.

We see, of course, another incarnation of the strong woman character in Jill in *It's a Sin*, as explored later in the section on her. But she's important to cite here because of how she can be compared to Hazel, to Bob's mum in *Bob & Rose*, and the women of *Cucumber* and *Banana*. From when he first started writing for TV, women who support the queer community have all been woven into Davies's work. Jill, of course, strikes a chord because she's based on a real person and because of the fraught, emotional circumstances in which she exists. Jill is also full of life and agency. She's a young, vibrant woman taking on the role of a mother yet still retaining who she is. This is key to what Davies creates: rounded, but not perfect women.

We see women as caregivers but not in a clichéd or lazy way, as is often the route of TV portrayals. Davies highlights the importance of their role as mothers or caregivers without reducing that to being all they can do. In *Queer as Folk*, women are in the background, but they're a vital part of the story. The mothers of *Queer as Folk* illustrate this, in particular Hazel. Hazel doesn't just take care of her son, Vince, but all of his chosen family. However, she's not an apron-wearing traditional housewife. Hazel is a Canal Street drinking (and karaoke-singing) independent woman. We are never told where Vince's dad is, but when we meet Hazel, we get the sense that Hazel has had to manage on her own for a while. Hazel is a gift of a character – a rounded, older female character who is funny, has agency and is central to the story. As another example of one of Davies's vital women in queer narratives, we are given Monica Gossage (played by Penelope Wilton) in *Bob & Rose,* busy organising protests against homophobia.

We see great mums again and again in Davies's work. They are often fierce working-class women who are a force to be reckoned with. Jackie Tyler, as Rose's mum in *Doctor Who*, is an excellent example. In *Doctor Who*, we see exactly where Rose gets her good qualities from, yet Jackie is her own woman. The working-class women seen across Davies's work aren't there just to be examples of either negative versions of working-class characters or to show suffering and struggle (especially for women), which is so often the case in TV portrayals. Davies is a big fan of soaps as mentioned before, and British soaps tend to centre primarily on working-class characters and are renowned for using strong female characters. Davies's working-class mothers reflect that. Before Davies came along, how often had working-class kids seen their parents' lives reflected in characters like Hazel in *Queer as Folk*, who makes up Christmas crackers to earn cash?

Moreover, how often had working-class queer kids seen that? Never, until *Queer as Folk* aired. This was still unusual when *It's a Sin* aired. We have the scene where Colin's mum is shown as a working-class valleys mum, and the family eats their tea (not dinner, tea) on trays in the living room. By and large, queer people on TV still seem to come only from middle-class families. This is in part skewed by the American queer TV we see. Recent examples include *Looking* or *The L Word,* which use queer-centric metropolitan elite middle-class families. We see this also in comedy favourites like *Modern Family* and *Schitt's*

Creek, where the family background is distinctly middle class. There are some more contemporary American exceptions like *One Day at a Time* or *Love, Victor* that include blue-collar families with queer kids. Earlier queer characters, like Warren in the previously mentioned *This Life*, were largely separated from family and living in a middle-class environment, or like Will in *Will & Grace*, who lived a distinctly middle-class experience. Vince, working in a supermarket in *Queer as Folk*, with a mum who made Christmas crackers at the kitchen table to earn money and took in a lodger, is not sharing the experience of gay characters we had previously seen on TV. Mostly, gay characters seem to end up fully formed living a *Tales of the City* existence. They tend to be university educated and in middle-class jobs. Having Vince from *Queer as Folk* and Colin from *It's a Sin* showing their links to their working-class roots, with working-class mums, still feels like a revelation; queer people can have backgrounds that look like that.

Seeing working-class mums look after their queer kids is hugely important for people from that background; especially, too, in terms of regional identities, as so many TV stories are largely American-centric or London-centric. Seeing Welsh or northern English working-class identities on TV is really central. 'You can't be what you can't see,' as the saying goes, and simply seeing queer people from the same background as you on TV, with their mums accepting them, is a massively hopeful thing. This isn't saying that working-class communities are statistically more or less homophobic. It's that outside of soaps, we don't see them on TV in a positive light as often. It's about showing that working-class stories are valid, they exist and are part of drama. Showing accepting parents, in this case, mums, is validating for those audiences.

Muriel Deacon in *Years and Years* is an example of an extraordinary matriarch. Having a grandma rather than a mother as the head of the family is an interesting dynamic, but it works. She is both formidable and fair. Choosing her daughter-in-law over her son after he cheats on her, siding with her and taking her in at the same time as kicking her son, Stephen, out and chastising him in the process, is one of her greatest moments. Despite tensions between the two, Muriel chooses Celeste and her granddaughters over Stephen. It's a great moment of women choosing women and women supporting women. Davies's great women and great women's parts aren't just about 'good' people. Muriel isn't above selfishness; she chooses to pay for her eye surgery over leaving an inheritance. In a way that makes the audience say, 'good for her'. After all, she is largely unselfish, for she allows the family to live in the house and supports them through all their mistakes. A good woman is a complex one, perhaps just one who doesn't conform.

Muriel is not above calling out the wrongs, even within her own family, even when she is at fault too. Muriel isn't a hero of the piece; she's not a villain, but she's an interesting person. In the same show, Celeste isn't just a 'wronged' woman; she's a person with agency and purpose of her own rather than just a foil to Stephen's story. This is an example of what Davies manages to do across all his women. Even when, by the necessity of the story, they are a side note, they are rounded humans. But they're also flawed. Muriel isn't always right; she displays moments of prejudice from generations past, she's rude to Celeste and others, and she makes selfish choices. But for those things, she's authentic and interesting as a woman.

Despite being negative characters, Harriet Jones and Vivienne Rook, the politicians mentioned above, are fascinating women. Harriet Jones starts as a brilliant person – the kind of politician and the kind of woman you'd want around. She's introduced as the MP for Flydale North, trapped in the Cabinet room in 'Aliens of London', and she helps the Doctor save the day. Nine tells Rose that Harriet is destined to be Prime Minister; the next time we see her, she is precisely that. We see her change as Prime Minister, and the Doctor turns on her when she deliberately kills the retreating Sycorax. The Doctor brings her down with six words: 'Don't you think she looks tired?'

It's a hell of a line, a comment on politics (as discussed in Coda: 'Politics') but also on women in the public eye. Those words wouldn't have worked on a male Prime Minister, and the Doctor is not above using human foibles and flaws against them for the greater good. Does it make it a good comment? Or even an acceptable one? Would it be made towards a male politician? The answer to all these things is likely, no. It's also a line that passed in 2004 and probably wouldn't today. It's a line that's, for better or worse, quoted in memes about our subsequent female Prime Ministers and politicians (or at least transient ones as the years 2019–23 have seen), proving that, like the Doctor, humans perhaps have flawed standards when it comes to bringing down corrupt women. It's a commentary on how we view women in power, too – only as good as they look, still, to a degree. However, Harriet Jones wielded power. Of course, *Who* fans were also aware that Harriet Jones was labelled 'a modern-day Thatcher' by a journalist called none other than…Vivienne Rook.

The same Vivienne Rook who we come across in another of Davies's stories? Surely not? You can never be too sure in Davies's world. After all, a journalist-turned-politician later on in *Years and Years* is what we get (although played by different actors). Given the crossover in commentary on women in politics and power, it's worth believing that maybe she was Vivienne Rook. Vivienne Rook, too, is an interesting and important female character for Davies. She's an exaggerated, larger-than-life character. Sure, she's a politician, but she's also an actual human, even if she is a despicable one. Or, is she? She's the villain of the piece, a woman who audiences will at some point no doubt say 'but…' about. That's the beauty of Davies's female characters, they manage to be more than one thing.

Of course, they also deliberately divide people, like Rook does. It's a time-honoured tradition that you can't please all (or even the majority) of *Doctor Who* fans, so of course, there was a backlash, and it is inevitable, too, that women, actors and characters, get the backlash. Even the really 'good' characters like Jill in *It's a Sin* saw a backlash because the story didn't 'serve' them (see Chapter Eight: 'Know your history' for more on this). However, the heart of this seems to be in creating women worthy of conversation; and in creating women worthy of conversation, Davies hasn't stuck to simply creating 'good' women.

In *It's a Sin*, we see this in its rawest form. While Colin's mother is caring and lovely and embraces her son and his chosen family, Ritchie's family is the opposite. In particular, Ritchie's mother creates tension and shows us the very worst of a mother to a queer child. Davies handles this with sensitivity, also, unflinchingly. She does not accept Ritchie; she takes him away from his friends and keeps his friends away from him. This in direct contrast to Colin's mother, who is there throughout everything with him. Ritchie's mum keeps Ritchie hidden away; she continues to deny who he is, denying him dignity even in death. She isn't there when he dies; she leaves him to die alone. On one level, it could happen to anyone; you could accidentally step away at the crucial moment. But in Ritchie's mum's case, we don't think that's true; she's been in denial about who her son is and what is happening to him. She is ashamed of him, and we see that in his death. What's worse is she denies him the people who would have been there, who would have cared. Jill sat with countless men like him; she cared for him through the worst of everything. But his mum cannot or does not. It's a brilliantly complex performance from Keeley Hawes and reminds us that complicated, interesting women are not always 'good' women.

Davies gives us this time and time again, from the larger-than-life politicians and countless *Doctor Who* villains, he makes women interesting. He also casts older women and gives them interesting roles. This was notable in 1999 with Hazel in *Queer as Folk*. It should not be something of note in 2021 with *It's a Sin*, yet it is. Davies's women are, by and large rounded, interesting whole humans, a remarkable thing across TV. This extends down to more minor roles, like Susan Brown as Mrs Bowen in *It's a Sin*, a colleague of Colin in the tailors, who plays a small but notable part. Again, she's not an all-out likeable woman; she's stern at first, seemingly an 'old school' woman of the workplace keeping Colin in check. She later seems kinder, but ultimately, also plays into Colin being fired. This type of character in Davies's work is not two-dimensional, even in such smaller parts. She's also allowed to be an older actress, playing an older character, much like Anne Reid in *Years and Years*. Davies allows older women to play their age. This is still a rarity on TV. Much like they're allowed to be unlikeable, too, this contributes to us seeing a rounded array of women in Davies's universe.

Davies give us complex, exciting women who he isn't afraid to make unlikeable. But of course, Davies also gives us incredible women, women to celebrate, to emulate. Donna Noble, Rose Tyler and Martha

Jones (yes, all companions of the Doctor) are brilliant, intelligent women who are more than a match for the Doctor. These women were hugely important in fully bringing the show into the twenty-first century. It's not that all the previous companions were badly written women; they were largely underwritten and at times one-dimensional. Some of the older companions were great, interesting and rounded characters; like Sarah Jane Smith (originally a companion to the Third and Fourth Doctor, who Davies brought back with her own show). These companions gave children intelligent, funny and brilliant female role models, and we do have to remember *Who* is ultimately a children's show. Most importantly, perhaps, for the original version of *Who*, they were women having adventures, showing young girls that they could too, which is something Davies continues to do in his version of *Who*.

Rose Tyler thinks she's unimportant; she just works in a shop as she sees it, but she saves the world. Martha Jones is confident, knows she's intelligent, and is a medical student, but she also knows to put herself first and not give everything up for someone else (even someone who is a clever, ancient alien). Donna Noble finds out she's more than a failed attempt at love, more than what her mum judges her for. Of course, the tragedy of Donna is that she will never remember any of it. Donna is important as an older woman who has seen some of life and is a role model for those other *Who* viewers.

One particular element of Davies's women is that they aren't cookie-cutter actresses. Of course, British TV has always fared better in this respect than its American counterparts. In *Who*, there was always a danger that the companions come from a young and beautiful production line that many TV shows are guilty of, especially when casting young 'sidekick' style roles. Davies's *Who* (along with Classic *Who*) generally sought diversity in the actors cast as companions. In New *Who*, further diversity in terms of race and age has been central to casting. That may be with the first Black companion to the Doctor in Martha Jones (Mickey, played by Noel Clarke, is also Black but might not be considered a proper 'companion' as his role was more a supporting one). In casting both Catherine Tate as Donna, and bringing back Elisabeth Sladen as Sarah Jane Smith, companions in the *Who* era also offered an array of age ranges. It shouldn't be a revolutionary, or even comment-worthy element, that female actors in their forties and sixties (at the time) are cast, but in an industry that favours youth, particularly in the sort of supporting role that the companions take, it is noteworthy that diversity particularly among the women, was a conscious effort. Did this go far enough in terms of broader diversity? Probably not, but it was, firstly, something that future show runners built on, and, secondly, something Davies intended to continue based on the initial casting during his second stint as showrunner.

Davies brought back Elisabeth Sladen as Sarah Jane Smith in the season two episode 'School Reunion' (she would later return in 'The Stolen Earth' and 'Journey's End' as well). Sarah Jane had been an iconic character of the original *Who* and was undoubtedly one of the best female characters of New *Who*. In *The Sarah Jane Adventures*, she was the fantastic mum who went on adventures. That's what Sarah Jane did. Sarah Jane was also an unmarried woman who borrowed the modern phrase 'living her best life'. Sarah Jane was a Classic *Who* companion with New *Who* sensibilities; she got out of the TARDIS, took everything she learned and did good with it – right up to the end. Davies didn't create Sarah Jane, but in giving her new life and voice in the twenty-first century, he cemented her as one of the Whoniverse's most significant characters.

Sadly, Elisabeth Sladen died in 2011, leaving the fifth series of *The Sarah Jane Adventures* unfinished. The BBC aired the final episodes with a tribute at the end to Sladen. But in 2020, a mini-episode, 'Farewell, Sarah Jane', aired online featuring a memorial to Sarah Jane, suggesting she'd been killed while preventing an alien invasion. This was a fitting tribute and farewell to an actress, and the story written by Davies, giving Sarah Jane back to a generation of *Who* fans, introducing her to a new generation, and creating an opportunity for such a farewell to a well-loved actress might just be the most incredible legacy of the women of *Who*.

Chapter Five

Other queer stories: *Bob & Rose* and *Cucumber*

The story that often gets overlooked in the trajectory of Davies's career is *Bob & Rose*. Chronologically, it sits alongside *Queer as Folk*. Thematically too, it sits alongside Vince, Stuart and others, given it's another Manchester-set queer drama. It's also perhaps aligned with *Cucumber*, *Banana* and *Tofu* in that it didn't get the recognition it deserved. On a practical level, history was not on Davies's side here; the first episode aired on 10 September 2001. Given the events of 11 September that year, the TV schedules and world attention were elsewhere by the time the remaining five episodes aired. In an era of pre-streaming, even catchup, once it was gone, it was gone, and it simply passed many people by. The world's attention was not on entertainment in those weeks, the press coverage and attention were swallowed in a news cycle.

Bob is a schoolteacher, who doesn't quite fit into the gay 'scene' of Manchester. He longs for a real relationship and a chance to settle down. After an unsuccessful date, he meets Rose while waiting for a taxi. Rose is similarly disenchanted by her romantic life, and by her reliable yet dull boyfriend. She falls hard for Bob, not realising he's gay. The episodes follow their on-again-off-again love affair. In classic romcom style, an interfering friend (Holly, played by Jessica Hynes) is in love with Bob. Meanwhile, Bob and Rose fumble through their relationship, Bob confessing that them having sex was his first time with a woman, and as confused as he is by it he wants to do it again. The series manages a positive conclusion for everyone – from Holly learning from her mistakes to Rose's boyfriend getting his own dream date. Bob and Rose too, end up happy.

Alongside the comedy and romcom sensibilities, Davies weaves in commentary on the gay 'scene' and its emphasis on physical acts over emotional connection, as well as differing standards for straight men, gay men and women. He also weaves in activism and gay rights statements, making even the sweet, charming and funny romance still have political clout.

Politics and controversy

Thematically, too, with *Bob & Rose* there is overlap with *Cucumber*, *Banana* and *Tofu* in that it just wasn't the 'type' of gay story people wanted, or dare we say, were ready for. Today, perhaps, Bob's sexual fluidity would resonate more strongly with, in particular, a younger generation who recognise that sexual attraction is a spectrum of experience. Davies, too, in writing, might have a better language now for Bob; he might be demisexual or pansexual. We might just have a more nuanced way to approach his character. As it stands, at that stage the story seemed ahead of its time and not one that queer or straight audiences quite knew what to do with.

The storyline, involving a gay man falling in love with a woman, is loosely based on events in real life of a friend of Russell T Davies. However, the 'Bob' character in the script states categorically that he is not bisexual: 'I was born gay, I'll die gay, and I'll have a gay gravestone.' He says he was attracted to Rose as a person, not as a gender choice. He says he will 'always look at men', but Rose is the only woman for him.

Like *Queer as Folk*, *Bob & Rose* contributed to the contemporary political debate around LGBTQ+ rights. It included a sub-plot involving the fictional pressure group Parents Against Homophobia (PAH), which is led by Bob's mum in the series Monica (Penelope Wilton). She is a passionate gay rights activist, seen campaigning against Section 28. In the fourth episode we see a culmination of that, with Monica and Bob leading a rally and handcuffing themselves to a bus as a protest to the bus company's donation to the Conservative party. The scene directly parallels protests against the transport company, Stagecoach, concerning founder Brian Souter's financial and political support of Section 28. At one point, Davies intended to explicitly name Stagecoach in the script, and was inspired by earlier protests undertaken by the LGBTQ+ rights pressure group OutRage!

There's a lot in *Bob & Rose* to celebrate, simply because it exists as a queer TV narrative. A romcom in the year 2001 addressing the diversity and complexity of sexual attraction? Brilliant. The fact that the character of Bob is an incredibly positive, but also extremely normal, depiction of a gay man is also important. Davies had done the hedonism of *Queer as Folk* with all its Canal Street excess. In Bob, we get an anti-Stuart, a refreshingly normal man who is just going about his life being gay. The show got some criticism for not being as outlandish as *Queer as Folk*, but there's an argument here for subtle subversion. The fact that Bob is quietly gay, a more 'acceptable' face of queerness, is ok. Not every queer drama has to be confrontational and show explicit rimming scenes. Also, Davies is clever; he doesn't desexualise Bob. We know he's having sex (off-screen, it's ITV, after all), from moments of dialogue and carefully structured scenes, or even just a simple act of picking a condom out of a bowl. This was still a big deal in 2001 – the simple existence of a sexual gay man, without it being a morality tale, without him dropping dead by the end of the series. That was in its own way just as subversive as a rimming scene.

The show was successfully pitched to ITV and Red Productions, and *Jonathan Creek* star Alan Davies was approached to play Bob. Russell T Davies's stance on 'gay actors for gay roles' would become a topic of press attention when *It's a Sin* was released, and retrospectively the casting for both *Queer as Folk* and *Bob & Rose* with straight actors would come under retrospective scrutiny. There are two elements at play here; firstly, the pool of 'out' gay actors willing to play gay roles in the 1990s was small, times being less permissive. Also, if taking a 'risk' on a 'gay' drama, networks might want a familiar household name to sell it. In this instance, they thought of Alan Davies, known for loveable detective Jonathan Creek in the show of the same name, which had made him hugely popular with TV viewers who would likely tune in to see him, even as a gay man. Despite Russell T Davies now being very vocal about casting gay actors in gay roles, we can see why he chose Alan Davies for this role at this juncture. To put it bluntly, a non-threatening, popular actor would get audiences watching. This show wasn't *Queer as Folk*. It wasn't designed to shock or provoke; it was a cosy, romcom gay drama, also designed for straight people to watch. If they cast a familiar face of an actor – gay or not – people would watch.

Is this a sad state of affairs? Maybe. Is it perhaps an era that TV had to pass through to get to where it is today? Probably. When *Queer as Folk* was cast, there weren't many queer actors willing to sign up for something so subversive. Even a few years later, when *Bob & Rose* was being cast, any kind of 'everyman' actor of the 'cosy' sort that Bob needed to be, who was gay, wasn't about to risk that status and the roles that came with it, to do that role. Playing Bob, for most of the suitable queer actors, would likely have been a 'coming out' for them, and it's understandable, if sad, that this was the case. But also in casting straight actor Alan Davies, the show got made, and this guaranteed that such a story of queer experience made it onto more TV screens than it probably would have if it had involved an 'outing' controversy. There are positives and negatives to the historical and contemporary conversation around gay actors for gay roles, which come up repeatedly in Davies's work. In the case of *Bob & Rose*, were it made today, a queer actor would likely jump at the chance of playing Bob. In 2001, it was better that it was made with a straight actor than not made at all. In one amusing caveat to this story, Davies didn't object to any of the 'gay' content (and why should he) but did, as an Arsenal supporter, object to Bob being a Manchester United supporter.

Identity and acceptance

The storyline of *Bob & Rose* caused an uproar among some gay rights activists who felt that the series's premise made it appear as if being gay was a choice or a phase. This, then, generated a strong counter-reaction by bisexuals who called the criticism unfair.

Bob & Rose, despite the slight controversies and a perhaps lacklustre reception, compared with *Queer as Folk*, is one of Davies's finest pieces of writing. It's subtle, nuanced and full of love. It wasn't *Queer as Folk*, which was perhaps its problem at the time – people naturally tend to want more of the same. What *Bob & Rose* contains, too, is a far more sophisticated understanding of sexuality than 2001 audiences were perhaps ready for.

Davies certainly didn't invent the 'gay man turned straight' genre. In a broader sense, this used to be a key trope of gay literature; men (and women) could be depicted as gay if ultimately at the end they 'did right' and 'turned straight'. Or moreover that to 'get away with the gay', our protagonist had to return to straightness (or at least pretend to) by the end of the story. In film, *The Object of My Affection* (1988) and *The Next Best Thing* (2000) carried this theme. However, Davies was attempting something new in *Bob & Rose*, showing how such things could be very human. Rather than failing at being gay and fitting in, Bob was just being human. The queer community talks a lot about 'love is love', and the idea of being able to love whoever you wish is (rightly) at the heart of a lot of the message. It's a shame that the story Davies wove into *Bob & Rose* wasn't taken in that spirit by a wider audience.

It also says something about the wider state of the queer community, in that the idea of accepting something outside of the arbitrary boxes and labels often takes a lot of hard work. The resistance to *Queer as Folk* not 'accurately showing' all of the queer community, or even later, *It's a Sin* not showing 'all of AIDS' is an ongoing theme in queer cultural work. There is so little representation (still) that we expect every work to do all the work. So, *Bob & Rose* should have been a fun, quirky romcom that told of one particular experience; instead, it felt forced to represent all things to all queer people and got 'called out' for not doing that.

Interestingly then, the characters of Bob and Rose were ahead of their time. While there's an argument for, say, *Queer as Folk*, being of its time, and any (British) remake being unnecessary, there is a question: what if we remade *Bob & Rose* today? Could Davies reframe it for a contemporary audience? Could we have that nuanced conversation today with Bob being able to represent a group of people who don't fit those neat labels?

Bob & Rose is also 'of its time' in the same way that *Queer as Folk* was, just in a different way. We could say that it is a *Will & Grace* of British TV, a palatable queer story that straight audiences will warm to. Like *Will & Grace*, it comes from a place not just of slightly unimaginative titling but of a gay man writing a story that lets straight audiences in and shows queer audiences that they're seen. *Will & Grace* did this by balancing the occasionally stereotypical gay men with a real understanding of gay life. Some might say it was muted and watered down in content for the sitcom audience, but it worked and paved the way for more. It's hard to imagine *Modern Family* or *Schitt's Creek* hitting our screens without *Will & Grace* coming first. And so, too, *Bob & Rose* does something similar; its roots are the same as those for *Queer as Folk*, but it shows another way to tell queer stories. It might be queer stories for an ITV drama – rather than the subversive, seeking-to-shock, late-night Channel 4 – but it has its heart in the right place. It's still told by a gay man who knows the lived experience of the character Bob. It's still a story designed to show there are many ways to be queer and tell that story.

While there was a sense with *Queer as Folk* that this was the 'blueprint' for queer stories – the young, hedonistic, carefree Canal Street version of being gay – *Bob & Rose* shows a different side to still-young queer lives and the impact of what being queer looks like beyond Canal Street. While queer characters remained a staple of Davies's work across his other dramas, it wasn't until post-*Who* that he returned to fully fledged 'gay dramas' in *Cucumber*, *Banana* and *Tofu*. While on the surface, these shows are significantly different – they are sexually charged (hence the name), together they constituted another late-night-Channel 4 outing, full of dark themes and starkly honest reflections on queer life. However, with a step back, they can be compared to *Bob & Rose* in the way they offer an alternative to the 'standard' gay narrative we've come to expect.

The 'new *Queer as Folk*'?

Codenamed 'more gay men' initially, what would become *Cucumber*, *Banana* and *Tofu* was, as a collective, a spiritual successor to *Queer as Folk* and was to focus on middle-aged gay men in the Manchester gay scene.

Cucumber centres on the life of Henry Best, and the breakdown and aftermath of his relationship of nine years. It was broadcast on Channel 4 in 2015. It is accompanied by *Banana*, an E4 anthology series about younger characters across the LGBTQ+ spectrum who also intersect with the characters in the *Cucumber* storylines, while *Tofu*, an online documentary series, was made available via All 4, the Channel 4 video-on-demand service. The three names reference a urological scale that categorises the male erection by hardness from tofu to cucumber and are used to symbolise differences in sexual attitudes and behaviour between the two generations. Billed as a 'new *Queer as Folk*', these integrated queer stories were ahead of their time in format and content. In terms of format, the way Davies and Channel 4 played with length and online/traditional broadcast was ahead of its time by a good few years – pre-empting the way streaming and traditional broadcasting would start using online platforms and 'webisodes' to expand their content.

Cucumber was a self-contained series, which concluded dramatically after one series (and was designed as such). In contrast, *Banana* was set up with a more open-ended conclusion, to allow it to potentially continue. While *Banana* and *Tofu* are excellent examples of Davies's writing and queer storytelling, next we focus on *Cucumber* for how it fits into the puzzle pieces of Davies's stories on gay men.

In 2007, while Davies was developing ideas for *Cucumber*, here he explains to Benjamin Cook a pivotal scene in the premiere of *Cucumber*:

> I can imagine a man so enraged by something tiny – the fact that his boyfriend won't learn to swim – that he goes into a rage so great that, in one night, his entire life falls apart. It's not about learning to swim at all, of course; it's about how your mind can fix on something small and use it as a gateway to a whole world of anger and pain…If I write the Learn To Swim scene well – and it could be the spine of the whole drama – then I will say something about gay men, couples, communications, and anger.[27]

In 2011, the series was in production with American cable network Showtime and being distributed by BBC Worldwide. It was casting before Davies moved back to Manchester and it was then picked up by Channel 4 with producer Nicola Shindler and the Red Production Company. This marked the first collaboration with Channel 4 since *Queer as Folk* and his first with Shindler and Red since *Casanova*. The Head of Drama and former *Doctor Who* executive producer, Piers Wenger, convinced Davies to return to the channel.

In *Cucumber*, greater diversity is represented in the LGBTQ+ community. Freddie, Henry's flatmate, is bisexual, as is Henry's friend Cliff. While lesbian and transsexual characters are present, they are not prominent in the show, as their personal stories are portrayed in the accompanying show *Banana* (2015). The small amount of coverage lesbians receive in *Cucumber* is mainly positive. However, there is an odd negative remark, such as in the eighth episode when Henry's friend, Raymond, says, 'They have no allies in nature.' While meant as a good-natured joke, this obviously might not have landed for some audiences.

One way in which the 'recognisable queer lifestyle' has not changed between *Queer as Folk* and *Cucumber* is in who is represented as having this lifestyle. Plummer writes that 'gay cultures consistently get depicted as white, middle class, young and beautiful'.[28] *Queer as Folk's* depiction of gay culture is almost exclusively for this group of men. Bernard, Hazel's lodger, is an elderly gay man. Although he features on the show, he does not represent the ideal gay lifestyle that the younger characters embody. However, he is still white and middle class, demonstrating an image of the queer lifestyle in Manchester as one requiring money and one almost exclusively for white people. Despite *Cucumber* representing a wide range of ages, classes and ethnicities in its depiction of gay culture, it still focuses on this singular queer lifestyle in the form of Freddie. Freddie is white, beautiful, young and desired by half the other men portrayed in the show. Despite being poor and living in extremely low rent accommodation, Freddie displays the taste codes of a very well-educated middle-class person, making his desirability even higher.

In *Banana*, Davies insisted that a transgender actor be cast as Helen, a move that is still somewhat ahead of the curve. He altered the script to fit the eventual casting of Bethany Black, and the actor has been vocal in her praise for Davies in this. It has become a hot topic in discussion around casting, and authentic portrayals of trans and non-binary characters in recent years, and Davies was here setting a positive example of inclusion. Helen's episode also features Julie Hesmondhalgh, who of course played Hayley in *Coronation Street*, one of the first trans characters on British TV. Her casting was progressive for its time, but would not be seen as such today, so this moment also feels like a passing of the baton between Hesmondhalgh – the cisgender actress who portrayed the transwoman Hayley Cropper in *Coronation Street* between 1998 and 2014 – and Black and the wider trans community. Here Davies is acknowledging the strides made previously – Hayley's character was indeed a giant step for trans stories – showing how he and others should strive to do better in casting trans actors. (Hesmondhalgh herself has been vocal about the fact that today she would not accept the role, saying it should go to a trans performer. She worked closely with the trans community during her time in the soap.)

In terms of the storylines, the trio of programmes didn't have the same cultural impact as *Queer as Folk*, perhaps because programming has moved on positively, and representation with it. The more pressing question may become whether Davies's mode of representing queer life has become dated and whether the community/TV landscape no longer needs, or wants, a *Queer as Folk* equivalent. Or instead, has his approach evolved? The discussions around sex for Henry as a gay man are quietly revolutionary in themselves. The honesty, the revelation that not everyone who is gay (or indeed straight) enjoys or engages in sex in the same way, and the opening up of these conversations, is in its way as revolutionary and revelatory as *Queer as Folk* was in its discussions and depictions of sex.

In *Queer as Folk*, Canal Street is not just where the characters go out, but it is also where Stuart lives. This grounds Stuart's 'recognisable queer lifestyle' as he lives close to his 'shags' and is firmly embedded in the scene. In *Cucumber*, the Canal Street scene also focuses on young people, just as it did in *Queer as Folk*. In the first episode, when Lance and Henry go to a club on Canal Street, the experience goes badly, and they appear too old for it. This is clear as even though they go there to dance, they end up standing around and drinking all night, seemingly not to intrude on the young people's fun.

In the fifteen years between the two shows, the attitudes towards gay culture and its representation on TV had evolved a lot. Gay cultures had gained equality partly through how the media has portrayed them. Since *Queer as Folk*, 'gayness' had lost some of its radical quality as it has come to be more widely accepted in modern society, and this may explain why *Cucumber* didn't receive any complaints for its representations of sex. The 'recognisable queer lifestyle' had already changed with mobile technologies and social media being a more acceptable way to meet sexual partners and even boyfriends/girl-friends or husbands/wives. The lines between gay and straight cultures were becoming increasingly blurred, and with gay marriage in the UK being legalised the year before *Cucumber* appeared on Channel 4, in 2014, the gay community became more equally accepted in law by straight cultures, which affected its portrayal on TV.

There is also a contrast between the main character in *Cucumber* and those in *Queer as Folk*. Henry doesn't enjoy sex. This challenged the dominant stereotype of homosexuality in 2015, which is that gay men have sex all the time and are obsessed with it. In 'Gay Cultures/Straight Borders', Ken Plummer writes that in gay culture, 'anal intercourse turns out not to be that common at all'.[29] *Cucumber* also features a diverse range of homosexual characters who are Black, white, Asian, old and young, fat and slim. Times had come a long way since *Queer as Folk* when most characters were white and conventionally attractive. Gay life had also evolved since *Queer as Folk* in that the characters don't have to meet their sexual partners in a club like Stuart does, as Henry meets Leigh in a fast-food shop in the fourth episode of *Cucumber*. Henry and the world of *Cucumber* present a snapshot, just like the characters in *Queer as Folk* did, of gay life for some, in a particular time and place. But what Davies is able to show via Henry and what he goes through, offers not a continuation of *Queer as Folk* as was expected, but an alternative slice of gay life from another perspective. What Davies has done across his dramas in fact is offer a peppering of gay characters, all different, all experiencing different facets of gay life, illustrating there is no monolithic experience while highlighting some shared ones along the way.

In *Queer as Folk*, Stuart is very masculine and isn't camp in any way, although he is very open with his sexuality. Fifteen-year-old Nathan has a stereotypical gay 'look' and would generally be seen as a 'twink'. However, despite his appearance, he does not necessarily conform to this stereotype of gay men. His youthful, slightly feminine look, usually attributed to 'twinks', might merely be down to the fact that he is only fifteen and, therefore, still a boy. His bold dress sense clashes with his deep voice and creates conflict between the traditional ideas of feminine and masculine. Alexander, Stuart and Vince's friend, is very camp and displays many feminine qualities that used to be attributed to gay men on TV and in film. The idea that homosexuality is liminal, in that it sits on the boundaries of femininity and masculinity, has not necessarily gone away since *Queer as Folk*, as some of the characters in *Cucumber* also have a liminal quality. For example, Lance is feminine in his voice and style but has a very masculine body type.

Impact and reception

Cucumber much like *Queer as Folk* pushed boundaries on depicting explicit sex; episode one contained both full frontal nudity and a fairly explicit three-way. However, audiences were not particularly enraged by this. Ofcom weekly broadcasts from when the series aired in 2015, show that it received no complaints over the eight weeks it aired. This shows either that people had become more accepting of homosexuality on TV or that those who would be upset didn't watch it. Now that viewers have access to hundreds of channels and the internet, they can easily choose not to watch programmes that they might find upsetting.

The show was largely favourably reviewed, too, with much praise for Davies's wit and observations on contemporary gay life. In a 2015 article in the *Independent*, Ellen E. Jones stated: 'In Davies's hands, the tragi-comedy of middle-aged desperation is so sad, but so, very, very funny.' Jones also argued that the show's appeal was 'universal' rather than limited to a gay audience.[30]

One of the most interesting responses in categorising these shows came in 2015 from the *Guardian*. Sam Wollaston said:

> I'm not gay (there, I've said it). This/these show/s is/are, very. Gloriously, explicitly, triumphantly, cucumberly. Gay to the core. But I never once felt left out, or that this wasn't relevant to me (on the contrary, I felt a worrying connection with Henry). As you'd expect from Davies, it's also dead funny and – most of all – very, very human.[31]

There is something interesting, and even important, about the fact that the 'new *Queer as Folk*' actually feels less 'for' queer audiences and more *by* a queer writer; rather, it feels like a chronicle of life, or as Wollaston puts it, humanity. In this trio of shows, there's a broader slice of queer life, but also, of course, it shows a more contemporary life than *Queer as Folk* ever could. This is, possibly, an indication that times had changed, that queerness is not so much in its Canal Street bubble as it was in Stuart and Vince's era, but instead, it is now actually integrated into society. After all, the queerness in *Cucumber* takes place in the offices, in the broader lives of the characters. As viewers, like Wollaston say, you don't have to be queer to enjoy queer TV.

This is pivotal as the show is talked of as less successful than *Queer as Folk*, but Davies doesn't see it that way. Davies thinks fondly of the show and believes that it was maybe mistimed, that people weren't quite ready to face the story Henry goes through. As he told *Gay Times* in 2019:

> Do you know what, to be honest, I kind of think everything Henry went through in Cucumber – one day people will turn around and say, 'that's very true'. I think some people didn't get Henry, and that wasn't because there was anything wrong with the performance or the writing.

I think he's a gay man who's not quite understood yet
because we don't see many people like him [on screen]. We
see simpler versions of gay men. I stand by everything I
wrote in Cucumber. And so does Channel 4, in fact. Fuck
complaining, I won a BAFTA for it! People love to paint it
as a bit of a disaster but it actually did quite nicely. I'm very
proud of it.[32]

The dark, difficult subjects discussed in *Cucumber* are educationally
backed up in the show, much more often than the same subjects
in *Queer as Folk*. Safe sex is discussed among characters, and condoms
are used, and are often brought up in conversation. Lance and a minor
character, 'Old Woman', discuss suicide among young gay people,
touching on a highly overlooked subject in the portrayal of young
gay men on TV. This increase in educational backup between the two
series may be an indicator of how TV and its regulations have evolved
to care better for the audience.

What was the impact of these new queer stories from Davies? It was
perhaps not as seismic as the impact of *Queer as Folk*, but what could
be? That was the show that broke the mould that went where nobody
had gone, something that can never be replicated. Many critics and
viewers neglected that Davies wasn't trying to replicate that; he was
telling queer stories. Not every queer show or queer character can be
all things to all (queer) people.

Similarly, not every queer show has to be revolutionary. After all,
we don't ask every straight show to be (as is evidenced by the
amount of mediocre TV in existence). But *Cucumber*, *Banana* and
Tofu don't *have* to be the next *Queer as Folk*. They can just be queer
TV from the same writer.

Different queer stories

What did *Bob & Rose*, and *Cucumber* have in common? They were
queer stories that didn't find their audience. They were stories that
deserved a wider reception. *Cucumber* was similar to *Bob & Rose* in
that respect – not quite finding the broader audience but being praised

by those who did find it. It's interesting that they both represent two extremes of Davies's writing – the sweet romcom versus the sexually charged confrontational drama – and they are arguably among some of his best works. Taken together, they perhaps form a microcosm of Davies's queer writing.

In *Bob & Rose*, we get a gentle, sweet and authentic feeling of exploration of identity and love. It's new love, discovery and exploration filled with a lot of hope against the bleaker backdrop of the world. *Cucumber* is a harder, harsher depiction of that world; it's the end of a relationship and identity in crisis. They both work because of their authenticity and their coverage of things that perhaps nobody wants to talk about. By the time *Cucumber* was made, the trend was towards much more 'fluffy' and 'happy' queer stories. The need for happy queer stories is a very real, necessary one in queer drama. But so is the need for real honest portrayals of queer struggles. In *Cucumber*, the brutal hate-crime murder of Lance is shocking, difficult and deeply upsetting to watch, yet also a necessary story to tell. So, too, are the explicit sexual stories (and sexual struggles) of the queer community across *Cucumber* and *Banana*. This is what Davies does best – that balance of dark and light, and brutal honesty. As much as there is a need for those happy ending stories, if there is a wave of people doing that already, why should Davies play into that, and why not do what he's good at, which is a darker, more honest drama? Even in the case of *Bob & Rose* wrapped up in a romcom exterior.

Above: The cast of *Queer as Folk* in Manchester promoting HIV/AIDS awareness with the Terrence Higgins Trust. (L–R) Charlie Hunnam, Craig Kelly, Antony Cotton and Denise Black.

Below: The cast of *Bob & Rose*. (L–R) Alan Davies, Lesley Sharp, Daniel Ryan and Jessica Hynes.

Above: Russell T Davies, Christopher Eccleston and Billie Piper launch the reboot of *Doctor Who* in Cardiff.

Opposite top: David Tennant pictured filming *Doctor Who* in a Cardiff suburb.

Opposite right: Russell T Davies makes friends with a Cyberman while promoting *Doctor Who*.

Opposite far right: Russell T Davies promoting the paperback of *The Writer's Tale* – an account of his time working on *Doctor Who* which became an accidental writers' bible.

Above: Captain Jack Harkness (John Barrowman) and Ianto Jones (Gareth David-Lloyd) kiss in the *Torchwood* episode 'End of Days'.

Below: The 'shrine' to Ianto in Cardiff at the site of the fictional tourist information office from the TV show. The shrine is still there some ten years after the character's death.

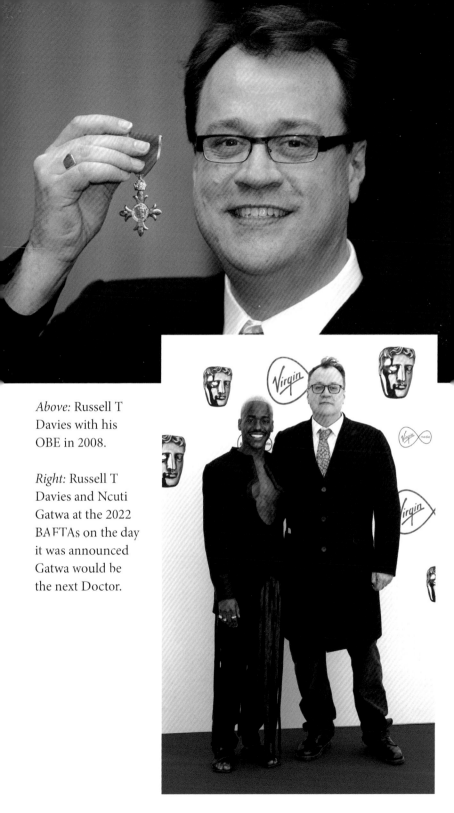

Above: Russell T Davies with his OBE in 2008.

Right: Russell T Davies and Ncuti Gatwa at the 2022 BAFTAs on the day it was announced Gatwa would be the next Doctor.

Above: Hugh Grant recreating Jeremy Thorpe's arrival at court in *A Very English Scandal.*

Below: Jeremy Thorpe exiting court in a scene that was recreated in the drama.

Above: Emma Thompson as Vivienne Rook giving another terrifying press conference in *Years and Years*.

Below: The cast of *Years and Years* at the *Radio Times* Television Festival at the BFI. (L–R) Rory Kinnear, T'Nia Miller, Anne Reid, Maxim Baldry, Russell T Davies, Ruth Madeley, director Simon Cellan Jones, Jade Alleyne, Lydia West, executive producer Nicola Shindler and Russell Tovey.

Above: The cast of *It's a Sin* after winning the New Drama award at the National Television Awards 2021. (L–R) Nathaniel Curtis, Jill Nalder (the real Jill), producer Phil Collinson, executive producer Nicola Shindler, Olly Alexander, Russell T Davies, David Carlyle, Shaun Dooley, casting director Andy Pryor.

Below: Olly Alexander (Ritchie Tozer) and Lydia West (Jill Baxter) in *It's a Sin.*

Coda

Politics

Politics without being overt

Even a cursory glance at Davies's shows betrays his queer politics. Davies uses his scripts to examine and debate significant issues such as sexuality and religion, especially from a homosexual or atheist perspective. He refrains from dependence on 'cheap, easy lines', which provide little profound insight, or at least he tries to.[33] Davies has never shied away from politics, both queer and governmental. Some of his work is obviously political, from *Years and Years* to *It's a Sin* to *A Very English Scandal*. But also, we see politics throughout his wider work, whether overtly as in these examples, or more subtly, in broader cultural politics, in his other shows.

Religion

Davies is an atheist and incorporates this into much of his sci-fi writing. His most notable commentaries on religion and atheism are *The Second Coming* from 2003 and his 2007 *Doctor Who* episode 'Gridlock'. In *The Second Coming* there's a more contemporary and realistic commentary on what the second coming might look like (one that would naturally look different in 2023 also). It's more focused on a love story that humanises the idea of a second coming rather than on religious references or iconography.

In contrast, 'Gridlock' takes a more proactive role in debating religion: the episode depicts the unity of the supporting cast in singing the Christian hymns 'Abide with Me' and 'The Old Rugged Cross' as a positive aspect of faith. Still, it depicts the Doctor as an atheistic hero through whom the show demonstrates faith as misguided because 'there is no higher authority'. He also includes this element as a bit of an undertone to some of his other writing. In 'Tooth and Claw' (2006), there is a sub-plot around the different beliefs of the Doctor and Queen Victoria, which he described as a conflict of 'Rational Man versus Head of the Church'.[34]

The general atheist view Davies has is subtly woven into *Who*, which lends itself to a universe without a higher power. Time Lords are sometimes framed as such, as a lesson in *not* positioning yourself rather than an actual messiah figure in the form of the Doctor. If anything, it is a warning about deities. *Who* gives us lessons on the multitudes of the universe, the fallibility of humans – and other species – and is the perfect vehicle for an atheist reading. However, Davies isn't heavy-handed in this, preferring instead to lean into the politics of *Who*.

Politics in the TARDIS

Doctor Who has always been political. Multiple articles across the New *Who* era cite the show's long political history, including in *SyFy Magazine*, which has been writing about *Who* for decades. In a 2020 article that focused on the backlash from the latest episodes in Chris Chibnall's era, the magazine looked back at Davies's era for examples. They said:

> Even in 2005, Christopher Eccleston's Doctor dealt with whether he (or anyone) has the right to sentence another being to death in 'Boom Town'. That episode managed to get the political themes while dealing with one of the farting Slitheen.[35]

The farting Slitheen aside, Brian Silliman is right that Davies's work was political from the off. This has long been embedded in *Who*. Silliman brings it back to the core message of *Who* saying:

> Every so often, you'll get reminded of the real world. It just so happens that we live in a real world where science

has become politics, and all seems lost. Everything seems
hopeless almost daily – that's why we need The Doctor.[36]

Davies also frequently commented on the media in *Who*, an early
example being 'The Long Game' (2005), where TV and control were
the subjects.

Beyond cultural commentary, the Doctor offers comment on society
and its breakdown. Davies digs deeper into the impact of war through
the Doctor's experiences in the Time War. He tells us that the Tenth
Doctor was a pacifist, still recovering from what they did in the Time
War, determined to be better. Davies's message was that guns solved
nothing and that we should extend peace to new species, not shoot
them down. Repeatedly, we see the Doctor reaching for whatever
alternative there is to violence. As much as the Time War through-line
was critiqued by some fans and some TV reviewers as convoluted, and
clearly political, it allowed Davies to make strong points on the impact
politically and personally of conflict. Also, of course, the Doctor was
always right; there was always another way.

Another element that runs through Davies's work is immigration
and inclusion. This comes naturally, for a left-leaning writer, one
whose identity leaves him somewhat on the outskirts. The backdrop
of Brexit can also be seen across *Who* and, of course, later *Years and
Years*, even *Scandal*. In *Who*, the broader philosophy is about accepting everyone. The Doctor is a literal alien who is accepted by humanity
and accepts all who cross their path.

One of his best pieces of political work is a lot closer to home, to
reality – the Tenth Doctor's words about Harriet Jones. When her
true colours are revealed, as she shoots down the retreating aliens,
the Doctor does something unusual, especially considering Ten's
war-scarred, staunch pacifist view; he takes it upon himself to enact
revenge, a sure sign that someone has crossed the line.

As already mentioned, fans know that Harriet Jones was called 'a
modern-day Thatcher' by a journalist called, none other than, Vivienne
Rook. Davies is known for recycling his names across series, but
the media figure turned Prime Minister in *Years and Years* might

share more than a name (despite obviously being played by different actors). Davies used *Who* as an astute political critique across the years he was in charge, pushing a show that has always been political, firmly into twenty-first-century politics (via several other centuries as well as dimensions, planets and an array of alien races).

Media critique

Not above critiquing the media, or indeed TV, the medium he loves, Davies often looks at how the media influences and controls people. This is a common theme across *Who* and other shows, especially *Years and Years*. But in both *Years* and *Scandal*, Davies looks deeper at how the media influences our world and what it has to say about politics.

In various ways, his work is seen as rooted in reality and sci-fi. We see the power of traditional media and a critique of it in *Scandal*. There's no denying where Davies is laying his allegiance in that show, with the media and the outcry associated with Thorpe and his 'scandal' being rooted in homophobia. The series highlights the power of the traditional broadcast and print media to create a scandal and reinforce it to create prejudices, and even to a degree, to create the 'characters' involved in the nation's minds. It's a powerful indication of the impact that the way stories are told has on public perception.

This, of course, is taken to the next level in *Years and Years* when we see this followed through to the imagined future conclusion. The grip media has on us in the present day is projected into the future. In truth, the reality will probably be even more frightening than Davies could imagine, but his version of 2019 and beyond, and how the media can shape, but also end up inside, our minds certainly doesn't feel far-fetched.

It's impossible to imagine how the media will evolve, but in *Years and Years*, Davies's repeated refrain on how the news 'used to be boring' has a double meaning. On the one hand, it illustrates the 'lull' that Stephen mentions in the show, that sometimes a generation is spoiled by living through a relatively slow political and social time. That much is true, but Davies is saying more subtly in *Years*, too, how the news had to become something more exciting, engaging the media machine to get attention. It is a self-fulfilling prophecy to fulfil a twenty-four-hour news cycle, and to do that, we had to find twenty-four hours' worth of news. As *Years* takes place in a version of the world where Trump exists, Trump is a product of that society. In Davies's imagined future, his success is more sustained, and what better illustration of the impact of the twenty-four-hour news machine in creating its fodder than the Trumps, or in Davies's mind, the Vivienne Rooks of the world? The news stopped being boring because the world became too shocking, but also because we created the 24/7 news culture. We formed the news that now fills the screens and our feeds with eventful happenings; that's also the warning Davies gives us.

Of course, *Years and Years* is a sci-fi reading of that future, but one that is deliberately, terrifyingly close to reality. In Rook, Davies gives us our version of Trump, or as she was somewhat styled, a more competent Nigel Farage. In fact, it's not really about Rook herself, but the machine of the media that allows her to exist; the one that created her. While we can brush off the 'Did we create this world?' or 'Did we create the news?' questions to a degree, we cannot shake off the fact that we didn't make the Rooks of this world. After all, as Muriel tells us in her speech, we are all responsible. If *Scandal* is Davies's indictment of the media and how it treats individuals caught up in it, *Years* is the indictment of the individuals that consume and enable it.

Davies is a child of the media caught between love and hate or even fear of love and hate. He uses media in his stories to make political points because there isn't a more powerful way to show issues than asking how a country chooses to talk about them. When his news-readers pop up again and again on *Who*, they show us a glimpse into the wider world and how humans view themselves, to allow the Doctor to comment on it. In *Years* and *Scandal*, we see the official view alongside the human view, and across all of those stories, it's as much a warning as it is commentary.

Politicians

Politicians never get off lightly with Davies. While we see Blair in John Simm's Master, there are traces of Thatcher across all of Davies's work. For a man of Davies's generation, Mrs Thatcher might be the greatest political enemy ingrained in his work. We see her unexpectedly embodied in Harriet Jones – and that's the trick, obviously – we think Harriet's one of the good guys at first. Indeed, she appears to be. Davies gives us a world with a female Prime Minister, and we rejoice. But of course, as in real life, it turns out dark. She, without a second thought, murders an alien race without remorse because of a perceived slight threat.

This contrasts with the Doctor, who sees the nuances of the situation and sees that the alien race is retreating and no longer poses a threat. To begin with, Jones sees the situation in black and white and erases the threat. Is it too much of a stretch, too literal, to see the alien race as a metaphor for gay people under Thatcher? An alien race who isn't really a threat but who is mercilessly left to die?

Indeed, we see that again in *Years and Years*, where we see Vivian Rook's government create 'Erstwhile' concentration camps for both refugees and people with the 'monkey flu' virus that starts to take hold in 2028 in the show. Now post 2020, we can see a clear parallel with a Conservative government's dealing with Covid. However, at the time of writing, Davies, who uses Monkey Flu as his virus, could be seen as making a clear analogy to AIDS. The government never did, but would they have, given a chance, shipped people with AIDS to a camp to die? Indeed, there is a form for it now. Given, in 2022, the rhetoric around Monkeypox and gay men, it was an accidentally prescient choice from Davies, as well. While the idea of right-wing politicians putting people in camps to die is tragically not a leap of the imagination of any kind, as recent years have taught us, it's hard not to look at Davies's writing and see the impact of AIDS and Thatcher on what he writes.

We see the overt culmination of that in *It's a Sin*. What's interesting here is that in the traditional sense, Davies isn't heavy-handed on the political side. Instead, he leaves it implied for the most part. He offers us the contrast; Ritchie is a Tory and Roscoe is dating one. Regardless, he makes his politics clear across the show.

Interestingly, his choice to emphasise Section 28 rather than AIDS inaction is subtly powerful; he's telling us that the denial of education and the removal of stories about queer people are more powerful. He's right. The denial of AIDS treatment and drugs was a crime, but the longer reach of Thatcher on queer communities was Section 28. The two went hand in hand – lack of education and awareness impacted the spread and awareness of AIDS. But inter-generationally, Section 28 has the longer reach. This is the reason Davies's queer work is so ground-breaking; the desert left in the wake of Section 28 means he is part of the generation playing catch-up and filling in the blanks. *Sin* is so powerful because of what Thatcher did, and generations were left without those stories.

But what, too, of the gay Tories? Or the gays who have sex with Tories? It's a great move on Davies's part to include Ritchie siding with Thatcher and Roscoe putting politics aside for material gain. After all, the idea that all gay men are left-wing socialists is a fairy tale. There are gay Tories, and while we might not be able to wrap our heads around the idea of 'turkeys voting for Christmas', it shows the many complex ways in which people interact with politics. Or perhaps it just shows a need for greater political education. Either way, Davies's willingness to muddy the issue reflects that the space where humans and politics intersect is a complicated one. Can we reconcile Ritchie voting for a woman who would gladly see him in jail, or worse? No, but can Ritchie as a character somehow reconcile this? Troublingly so, yes. Perhaps easier to understand is Roscoe, a Black son of immigrants, who sees a way into power and a way to subvert it. He is, quite literally, fucking the establishment, after all. He is exchanging sexual favours for personal advancement, which is a queer outlook, a provocative approach, and one we perhaps can't fault him for, on a personal level. It's also a great acknowledgement on Davies's part that however hard Thatcher tried, she couldn't entirely remove queerness from her vicinity.

And, of course, Davies makes his feelings for the Iron Lady clear when Roscoe pisses in her coffee pot. Actions do speak louder than words.

Queer politics

Queer as Folk is the primary vehicle for Davies's social commentary on queerness and advocacy for greater acceptance. The series examines an array of queer issues, including homophobia, coming out, internalised homophobia, queer and body image, sex-shaming and more – all inherently important queer issues. But none of these are delivered in a lecture format; they're embedded into the show's fabric. They are embedded into the stories, drama and humour – the mark of good writing. *Queer as Folk* often seems one of the least political of Davies's shows, but much like queerness, simply to exist was political. To talk about the community and show the issues faced was, and is, political.

But there are significant areas of gay politics at play in *Queer as Folk*. The series quietly advocates for the existence of queer spaces such as Canal Street, by demonstrating its importance to the characters and its importance in Nathan's journey – he needs the safe space, demonstrated by his standing up to the school bully at the end of the series. Tacitly, it asks for acceptance, or at least spaces to exist, and that's important. The show also demonstrates the dangers of homophobia without being an 'after-school special'. From Nathan's perspective, we see Vince's reluctance to be 'out' in the workplace and the dangers of being considered gay at school. In both cases, the political undercurrent concerns acceptance and a stand against bigotry.

Davies continued this with *Bob & Rose*, where family life and navigating 'coming out' (of sorts) take centre stage. It's a far more 'domestic' drama than perhaps the bright lights, big city of *Queer as Folk*, but it's quietly and, at times, more overtly political. We see Bob's mother and Bob actively campaigning for gay rights – something we don't see in *Queer as Folk*. We see this overt political statement alongside the domestic politics of the show's message on acceptance. In Davies's programming, overt and implicit politics are essential for queer politics.

As discussed in Chapter Seven: 'The future is a scary place', *Years and Years* is incredibly politically charged, and the queer politics of that show are subtle but ever-present. It works well against the overtly political elements discussed above to have queer politics quietly underneath. Their power and the emotional punch behind them are vital to the show.

In *Cucumber*, Davies reverts to the social politics of *Queer as Folk*. It's not about shouting about policies or politicians but *what* those policies and politicians have done to us all. In this respect, *Cucumber* truly is the successor to *Queer as Folk* in that we see the same generation of men decades later and we see what the world has done to them, while the younger generation have evolved in attitudes, politics and more – as is the way of the world. So we see in Henry the longer impact of AIDS, of growing up under Thatcher, and in his case, the personal, very real shame it brought upon him. We see the human impact of politics in Henry. When Lance is killed in a gay-bashing hate crime, it shows the impact of politics in stark action. Davies doesn't say this, doesn't make the links overt, but that's what *Cucumber* shows us. It shows us what happens when you grow up under Conservatism. It shows what happens to queer people when their identity is denied, shamed, and all but erased, by the powers that be. Given the time it came out, like his other drama of that time, it acts as a stark, but very specifically queer warning about the future.

Of course, the most political of Davies's queer shows is *It's a Sin*. Here, he stays away from the more overtly political *Years and Years* style; instead, the form loops back to what we see in *Bob & Rose* – community politics. It is impossible to write about AIDS without being political. Still, Davies knows his strengths and perhaps knows that the 'big hitters' of AIDS drama on TV – *Angels* in America (1994), *The Normal Heart* (1985), or even in recent years *Pose* (2018) – have said their piece on politics. Davies is also aware that these big American stories will inevitably be what his very British story is compared to. He does the sensible thing and concentrates on community action in the UK through Jill. All our activist knowledge is concentrated through Jill, and rightly so, considering Davies based her on the real activist Jill Nader. We see her researching when the boys are still largely oblivious; we, viewers, get the information from her.

Jill is so important, firstly, as a source of information for the viewer;

many who watched *It's a Sin*, particularly the younger generation, had little knowledge of the AIDS crisis. Jill is political from a viewer's point of view in that she enables political awareness. Using real-life activism to inspire is a meta technique; it is real-life activism. But the use of works of art and culture has long been at the heart of AIDS activism and education. Davies is, in a way, acknowledging this by using that same technique.

We also see politics in Jill's community work: not all politics is direct action or protests, and in her work for Gay Switchboard, in her visiting people with AIDS in hospital, she is political. Again, she is demonstrating politics to the viewers too. It is political to take on what the government did not, filling in where families neglected their children. Davies writes that into his script and challenges audiences to see that it is political.

Finally, we see politics in action, in a political demonstration, which is something we only see a handful of times across Davies's work. One of the only times we see it with a real-life event is when the characters protesting against pharmaceutical profiteering from AIDS get arrested. We see the homophobic responses of bystanders and police. This is the most directly political Davies gets. The show is direct, uncompromising and to the point; we see what they are protesting and the real-life consequences of it.

Above all, Davies is conscious of queer politics and the ever evolving need to be engaged and vigilant. In *It's a Sin*, he's cataloguing history, of course, but also commenting on the present. While he is memorialising and offering rage at the sins of the government past, we cannot escape the warning for the present implied within it. Davies is conscious of putting queer politics into the mix. As he told Nick Levine in 2019 at *Gay Times*:

> It's always a difficult time for us. Let's face it – Theresa May will be out of office soon, possibly very soon. We could end up with a Prime Minister who sets us right back. That could happen with the stroke of a pen any day now. So as a community, I think we have to be on our guard. Things aren't

too bad at the moment; we seem to have all the laws on our side, but just waiting for that to change. Just wait for a more conservative government to get into power, which seems to be where we're heading. So we shouldn't relax at all. We need to keep chipping away. The battle never really ends.[37]

This is the crux of Davies's queer politics – the battle never ends. Culture and stories will always be a means to resist.

Chapter Six

Queering history at the BBC: *A Very English Scandal*

What was Russell T Davies to do after commanding all of time and space in the TARDIS?

It's an unusual position for a writer to be in, facing an almost endless array of choices. *Who* was 'the big job' at the BBC (illustrated by the excitement/discussion of who Davies's successor would be) so the question of 'what next?' was a big one. In the *Who* years, Davies was everywhere, juggling show-running with writing and being the figurehead of the rebooted *Who* 'empire' (not to sound too Dalek-y about it).

Perhaps the logical step, or the one many writers in his position would have taken, was to be as un-*Who* as possible. Other writers might have gone dark and gritty, looking for the next crime drama or hard-hitting political take. Not for Davies, it seems; he remained, well, firmly himself.

There was a brief move to the US, for which he and Julie Gardner cannot be blamed. When American TV calls after years at the BBC, with its budgets and possibilities, you take it. Unfortunately, it didn't work out long-term, more for personal reasons in Davies's case. The sad illness of his partner Andrew meant that his life in the US was cut short. Davies took a break to care for Andrew, not returning fulltime to TV until after his death in 2018.

After his foray into American TV, Davies returned to the BBC with a variety of projects and to Channel 4 with more 'overtly queer' dramas. For the BBC, however, he seemed to take an historical approach to integrating queerness into his work, and what better way to do that than with a historical political scandal and a re-writing of Shakespeare? Fusing these two very different projects made up part of Davies's 'return to the BBC' post-*Who*. They offer a brilliantly juxtaposed look at queerness on TV.

The Thorpe Scandal

A Very English Scandal (2018) depicts the events of 1965, when MP Jeremy Thorpe (played by Hugh Grant), a Liberal MP, must contend with disgruntled ex-lover Norman Josiffe (played by Ben Whishaw), whom he met in 1961 and had a relationship with lasting for several years. The drama flashes back to when Thorpe met Norman, when the latter was a twenty-one-year-old stable boy in Oxfordshire, and wrote many letters to him, which Norman kept. So far, so Mills-and-Boon-esque. This could have been more *Bridgerton* than BBC drama in another writer's hands. The story becomes a mix of political scandal and an illustration of the lengths gay men would go to maintain 'respectability' in the eyes of the public. It also shows a subtle but crucial low-level support, even activism, on the part of minor players in the story, which until now has been both untold and hidden.

The end credits of Davies's drama note that Thorpe didn't hold another public office in his career. It also adds that he and Marion remained married until her death in March 2014 and he died nine months later. Thorpe's friend Peter Bessell remained in the United States until he died in 1985. Norman is still alive, owns eleven dogs, and does not have a National Insurance card.

A Very English Scandal

Here, the BBC handed over the keys to a very queer story – and an essential piece of LGBTQ+ history. It was a bold move on the BBC's behalf.

The story is told over three parts and was first broadcast on BBC1 between 20 May and 3 June 2018, directed by Stephen Frears, who is better known for his film work than for his TV offerings. Frears's films often depict real-life events – in particular, *The Queen* (2006) and *Philomena* (2013), and of course, *Florence Foster Jenkins* (2016), which also starred Hugh Grant. Frears has an affinity for stories based on real people, which made him a logical choice for this story. Davies was also reunited with long-time musical collaborator, Murray Gold, who composed the score.

The three-part drama feels like three different styles, or at least a story told in the classic 'three act play' structure. We get the setup, which could be a political play in the style of James Graham. We see Thorpe in the House of Commons, with his friends, doing his work as a politician. We see him outside of that space seducing Norman, who is at that point a stable hand. In the second part, we get an almost pure heist drama. Norman and Thorpe are estranged, and Thorpe, seriously or otherwise, keeps insisting he wants him dead. In a game of cat and mouse, while Norman's life slightly unravels and he baits Thorpe with the letters he wrote, we see what is at times a slightly farcical chase/heist. Finally, in the third part, we are given a classic courtroom drama, where the impact of the main characters' actions plays out. At this point, Davies muddies the waters with the question of who was right and who was wrong, and we see the complexities of their actions and the human element of the story.

While the political drama, in its literal form, is something of a departure for Davies, who typically hides his politics in plain sight, or on other planets, the story and the writing gel with his style exceptionally well. His focus on the people is the heart of this drama. While the movements of politics and Westminster are there, they aren't foregrounded in the same way as they might have been if James Graham had written it. Instead, the story becomes the human drama of Thorpe and Norman. Perhaps what's also initially shocking or jarring is how funny the drama is. It's an example of Davies's typical wit and humour. He finds the ridiculous in most situations, and this situation seems at first an odd one to be treated as if it were funny. But it is not, at least because Hugh Grant is given a gift of a role, one where he can marry his well-known comic timing with his lesser-known dramatic prowess. Also, when you step back, you see that the story is faintly ridiculous and funny in parts – and peculiarly English. Not least because a part of the scandal includes copious use of the word 'bunnies' said in an upper class English accent. In addition, the two men are charmingly odd and eccentric, which makes for amusing writing. The second episode, in particular, which almost doesn't know whether to be a heist drama or farce, captures the ridiculousness well. It shows a man sort of threatening to kill another man, not really meaning it, hiring incompetent help and ultimately failing. The fact that Blake Harrison of *The Inbetweeners* fame is given a little yellow car in which to enact his 'hit' falls firmly into an 'if you know, you know' perfectly executed visual gag.

Davies's script is witty, and both Grant and Whishaw have the perfect blend of comic timing and dry delivery to make it work. As with much of Davies's work, the humour is in the humanity of the characters. They are flawed men who are (repeatedly) getting it wrong. But the humour here once again belies the critical undertone of the piece. As Davies commented in 2018 to *Digital Spy* on reading John Preston's book *A Very English Scandal* (2016) and considering the drama:

> It suits my form of writing. I was reading it, thinking, 'That's how I write!' – the eccentricity and the savagery and the oddness and the humanity of it all; I like to think I write like that, so I very much felt myself chiming with it.[38]

The way the men are eccentrically funny forms part of that bigger picture of an important story lost somewhat to queer history, but also, here, there's an essential lesson in the flawed and often hurt humanity of queer stories.

Creating the drama

Casting is essential, too. Hugh Grant, the darling of 1990s romcoms, as the ambiguous in sexuality and morality Thorpe, was an exciting choice. Despite the conversations that came up later in Davies's career with *It's a Sin* on queer casting actors in queer roles, there is, perhaps, a case for Grant as Thorpe. On the one hand, this mirrors the reasoning behind choosing Alan Davies as Bob in *Bob & Rose* as a familiar and, indeed, heterosexual face for a gay character. There's also something interesting about any expectation we have of seeing Grant, as the 1990s romcom darling and the floppy-haired loveable, but wholesome, posh idiot, in the role of a scandalous politician and, he is, in TV terms, intriguing.

In terms of preparing for the role, Grant also managed to encompass both sides of Thorpe. He said to *Vanity Fair* in 2018:

> I talked to people who said, 'Jeremy would never hurt a fly; it is disgusting to even think he could have.' And I also spoke to people who said, 'Oh, he's a monster. Absolute monster.' He was capable of giving all those impressions.[39]

That Grant is no stranger to sexual scandal himself possibly helped him prepare. In 1995 he was arrested for 'lewd conduct' with a sex worker known as Divine. Being the 1990s, the tabloid press naturally seized on this story, and they planned to expose Grant (pardon the expression). Instead, what transpired was a 'scooping' of the press. Grant played them at their own game. He simply owned up. He admitted to all of it, was as open and honest as legality would allow, and of course the story didn't disappear completely, but it didn't have the power that the rabid tabloid press had wanted. Grant's career wasn't damaged, and he successfully undermined the power of the 'scandal'. Of course, as a straight man, he has the privilege that Thorpe did not, but the crossover in the experience and the contrast make for exciting, and surprisingly, fitting casting.

It must be noted that Grant wasn't doing a 'gay for awards' stunt. It is often an accusation (whether rooted in truth or not) that actors 'go gay' for acting kudos or awards – infamously Tom Hanks in AIDS drama *Philadelphia* (1993) was one such example, leading the community to feel exploited by straight actors using queer experiences to gain praise for 'bravery'. So actors like Jake Gyllenhaal and Heath Ledger in *Brokeback Mountain* (2005) or Sean Penn in *Milk* (2008) are often viewed as 'taking a risk' (partially in terms of being 'heartthrob' actors, but the same can be said for a younger Grant) in playing a queer role, in case they might alienate their female fanbase by playing gay. Reductive stereotype? Absolutely. Such has always been the Hollywood machine. However, Grant had long been subverting the film industry machine by making this point both in terms of speaking out against UK tabloid press, and outright taking a break from acting so he was not, like perhaps the younger actors, worried about associations or implications on his career.

Davies mentioned in an interview with *I News* in 2018 that he didn't believe Grant would take up the role. The actor had famously fallen 'out of love' with acting and hadn't worked for a while before that point. He'd also barely done any TV. Yet Davies recalled Grant carrying out far more research than even he had as the writer, working incredibly hard throughout. In terms of 'taking a gay role', Grant didn't need to reinvent or rejuvenate his career. After the success of his 1990s romcoms, he had the luxury of picking roles (or indeed not working roles) and therefore he periodically picked a 'curve ball' film. Films like *Florence Foster Jenkins* (2016) or *Paddington 2* are sufficient to remind an audience that he's a good actor. Of course, Grant had already done a 'gay film', perhaps the gold standard of gay films in the adaptation of E. M. Forster's *Maurice* (1987). This was before the hard stance on 'queer actors for queer roles' we'd see Davies make in *It's a Sin*.

To cast Whishaw as Norman is in keeping with Davies's stance on queer actors in queer roles. Whishaw has been quietly 'out' for many years and has performed several 'queer' roles including several on stage, like Mike Bartlett's *Cock*, Alexi Kaye Campbell's *The Pride* and Jez Butterworth's *Mojo*. On screen Whishaw played iconic queer (or at least queer-coded) role Sebastian Flyte in the remake of *Brideshead Revisited* (2008) and has recently played Adam Kay in the adaptation of Kay's book *This is Going to Hurt* (2022), which was also the writer/comedian's personal 'coming out'. Of course, Whishaw is more recently known for playing Paddington Bear, who while not queer, is an icon of inclusivity. In casting Whishaw, Davies's key argument for 'queer actors for queer roles' is based on the innate knowledge that being queer gives a performer some elements of experience. In *Scandal*, two scenes exemplify this and perhaps prove the 'rule' if it is to be a rule. When Norman takes the stand in the courtroom, he delivers a blistering speech about his experience as a gay man and with Thorpe. Moments later, we see him sobbing in the toilet. Shortly after that, he declares triumphantly to his friends: 'I was queer! I was myself.' These three scenes encapsulate queer experience: public defiance, private breakdown, pretending everything is ok. Even without the public court case, almost every queer person has experienced a version of those moments.

Telling historic gay stories – 'know your history'

Why the Thorpe scandal? While it's a good drama and a departure for Davies in the post-*Who* years, it's also hugely important in a 'know your history' sense. In an interview in 2018 with *We Are Cult Rocks*, Davies said it was 'the first time I'd heard the word homosexual on the news'.[40] A thought that is mirrored by the scene in the final episode where a character asks while watching the news coverage of the trial, 'are they allowed to say that on the telly'. The scandal, however, likely represents the first time many people had been exposed to such a 'gay' story in the mainstream press and in such detail. But this is also the reason it fell from history somewhat. As Davies told *IndieWire*, despite the story being big news at the time:

> I also think slightly it dropped out of history because it's a gay story. There's been a few straight scandals that keep being told again and again, because that's seen as more normal somehow, whereas a gay scandal is perhaps seen as more niche and not as likely to be told in the history lessons.[41]

There have been many instances of 'gay history' finally being told as stories, whether that's *Pride* (2014), which sought to tell 'untold stories', or more recent dramas like *When We Rise* (2017), the autobiography of queer activist, Cleve Jones. The stories we tell on TV tend to be those of liberation-era activists, or those involved in 'gay rights', or later AIDS, marriage equality or trans rights activism. These stories need to be told – and are told through the stories within *It's a Sin* which Davies himself would lean into later. But many men like Thorpe were living their lives and – in their way – campaigning and paving the way for future generations. This included those who operated in artistic or political circles, from Quentin Crisp to Christopher Isherwood. These men weren't invisible; they weren't inactive, but their way of being queer, even their 'activism' in the broader sense, often goes unnoticed and undocumented.

Was Thorpe's story the ideal one for progressing the status of gay men? Of course not. Is it part of an important, ongoing through-line in how we got to where we are today? Absolutely. We should show the good and the bad, the successful and less so moments in that history, to catalogue it fully.

Davies worried, too, that the more negative elements, along with the gay storyline, would mean a lack of interest, but perhaps the timing was right. As he said in *IndieWire* again: 'People were astonished that this story had been sitting underneath their noses for decades, and they hadn't heard about it, so weirdly, it had a significant effect.'[42]

While news moves on, and there are numerous political and sexual scandals to choose from in the interim (and indeed in the future), the fact that this one essentially got brushed away after the stories left untold says something about our lack of recognition for queer experiences. There's an element of 'but we won't speak about that' at play. It's a strange position to be in, asking to reclaim the 'scandals' of history, but it's essential.

Role in historical narratives

The Thorpe trial was necessary because it brought 'homosexuality' (as the parlance would have been then) into the public consciousness. While inroads were being made, we still had a 'turning a blind eye' mentality. We know the British media loves a politician caught with their pants down, even more so if there is an additional scandal. But the trial and subsequent media interest forced something else; an acknowledgement of gay people, their lives and how they are treated.

While we couldn't expect the *Daily Mail* to offer sympathetic coverage at the time, the trial – and subsequently this drama – did confront people who were oblivious to the reality of the closet for many gay men. Because of the conversation over whether Thorpe could come out, the power of the letters over him and his 'outing' is still relevant today. As are the judgements over who can and can't be themselves.

In episode three of the series, Normal declares, 'I was rude, I was vile, I was queer – I was myself.' That could be said for many now, but many are the 'Thorpe' of this scenario, still unable to be as queer and so 'themselves' as they'd like. But we also see in Norman that it is hard for him to be out, to be queer, to be himself. We see him crying in the toilets over it and struggling in life – it's not scripted, but we assume the mental health impact of his sexuality plays a very large part in his more significant struggles. We know Norman is a troubled man, and Davies's portrayal also gives us context as to why, and the context is a society that can't and won't accept men like him.

Saying homosexuality out loud

The court case and the drama are essential for their role in talking about gay men in public. As in the previous quote, it was the first time many people, like Davies, heard the word 'homosexuality' on TV, and this was a seismic shift in reporting and public consciousness. But what the case did, in its detailing of the affair between the men, was also force the wider public to confront elements of gay life they'd perhaps happily have remained ignorant to. As Davies said in an interview with *I News*:

> But it was also dark for those involved, because here was homosexuality – and the secrets of homosexuality – being spoken about in court and reported in the news. And really in detail. Norman Scott said he'd bit the pillow so he didn't cry out in pain when he was first penetrated. Saying that out loud was a huge thing.[43]

Why does it matter that the court case and the drama say this out loud? Because out of all the progress made, much of this remains hidden, and as long as we keep things hidden, we keep them 'wrong'. As Davies recalled in *I News* again:

> It would be easy to say that all these lying men in the papers made me feel like being gay was the most terrible thing. But school had already done that. In fact, it was kind of good to hear about this stuff – it was like a little chime at the back of my head. 'Well, it's not just me, then.' Obviously it was a story of darkness and murder and secrets and lies, but there's also plenty of that in the straight world![44]

The drama also shows the relatively recent struggles of gay men. If it is a living memory for Davies, it will be for many viewers, and even for those who do not remember it, the world of the drama is familiar enough to show how recently things were this bad. While it isn't that dark a drama – Davies delivers it with typical humour and humanity – the darkness at the edges is powerful, particularly for queer viewers.

One particularly poignant plot point to this end is the conversation with Lord Arran, whose brother was gay and committed suicide. He says, 'these deaths were murders, not suicides'. The deaths of queer people due to legislation and societal discrimination are tremendously influential, emotive and resonant today. Davies, at that moment, reminds us that this continues to be true now. We only have to look at the treatment of trans people in our society to understand that. We still lose far too many queer people to suicide, and what Davies, via Arran, reminds us there is that, yes, these are murders.

Davies, too, uses this drama to make a statement on homophobic violence. In a scene where Thorpe discusses his previous dalliances with his lawyer, who also confesses to being gay, he describes the times it goes wrong. As Thorpe talks, we see flashbacks of him meeting a wide variety of men. Then we see these encounters go wrong as he's attacked and beaten. For Thorpe's story, it's important; we have seen him lead a relatively charmed gay life up until now. We could be forgiven for thinking it's been easy for him. The drama is also central for the snapshot it offers of the broader gay community. Yes, there were men like Thorpe who got away with being gay to a point; yes, there were men like Norman who were able to be openly-ish queer. Yet it still came with a price and with dangers. The reality of 'gay bashing' is shown in this scene, with at least one of the men deliberately seeking out Thorpe for it. The broader danger of being a gay man at this time – and indeed today – is highlighted by the short scene.

Positive portrayals of gay men

For all its scandal, the story also has positive portrayals of gay men and allies. Thorpe himself, before the scandal, is doing very well at balancing being a gay man, being a public figure and progressing 'liberal' (in the general sense and his literal party sense) politics. We see from the opening scene that he's privately out to friends. He talks to his friend Peter Bessell (Alex Jennings) about his sexuality. They even have a frank conversation about sexuality, with Thorpe asking what percentage 'gay' Peter is. While Peter claims to be eighty per cent men versus twenty per cent women, Jeremy claims the opposite – eighty per cent gay. Perhaps they didn't have this exact conversation at this exact time, it's likely, as the conversation says, they might have been the first to say 'gay' in that context in the House of Commons. The point being, Jeremy Thorpe was living an 'out' life in the manner many gay men of that era did – out in some circles, if not in public life. It was working well for him. He had friends, like Peter, who supported him, and he could 'get away with' his 'lifestyle', as long as he was careful in his public life. Of course, all of this was supported, made possible by his wealth and privilege.

The stories of historical gay men are essential, particularly those that don't fall into the straightforward narratives of liberation. As Davies said in *IndieWire*:

> These heroes have been there for a long time before Stonewall came along, before gay rights were changed. People like Norman Scott were standing up and being proud for a long time in our history. People like Quentin Crisp, roundabout those years in the 1960s and 1970s – Quentin Crisp was a gorgeous brilliant icon, but he lived in Soho when he lived in the streets of London. He lived in artistic circles where it was maybe sort of easier. Norman Scott

didn't. Norman Scott worked on farms and lived outside of
London where it was harder, I think.[45]

But we see allies in the story, and Davies makes a point of integrating
them into the narrative. While Peter is central to this, in supporting
his friend before and after the scandal, we also get people like Gwen
Parry-Jones (Eve Myles) and Leo Abse providing an opportunity to
include Welsh elements of the narrative for Davies. The Abse family
were a particularly prominent family in south Wales through their legal
firm and their involvement in politics. They would certainly be in living memory for many viewers from that region. Gwen, who befriends
Nathan post-Thorpe, is a Welsh woman from Tal-Y-Bont. She's shown
as unfettered and unbothered by Nathan's past, saying, 'my husband
was in the army'. Here Eve Myles plays a sassy Welsh Gwen, not a
million miles from Gwen Cooper in *Torchwood* of course, which
might feel like a nice little in-joke for *Torchwood* fans.

While Gwen's story has a tragic end (she later commits suicide) and
plays a relatively minor part in Nathan's story, showing this inclusivity,
this allyship in historical dramas is essential. A version of the story
could have shown Nathan 'on the run' post the Thorpe affair, with
nobody supporting him, and in that version, these moments of small
allyship could have been written out. But Davies includes them as,
historically, while there has always been homophobia, there has
always been allyship too. We see this, too, in Leo Abse, the famous
lawyer, and MP, talking to Jeremy and Peter about his support of
decriminalising homosexuality. Abse worked for many years on this
bill, following the Wolfenden Report (1957), and in 1962 promoted a
Bill in Parliament. He continued campaigning on this and eventually
became the legislation's primary sponsor. Eventually in 1967, the Bill
was passed onto the statute book. Abse is a well-known Welsh figure
for his broader political work and the famous law firm (Leo Abse and
Cohen) he founded in Cardiff. But his inclusion here shows in parliament at this time there were voices of support for queer people. His
friendly manner to Jeremy (and Peter) in the drama, too, shows the
personal acts of solidarity and the friendship that also existed.

Of course, Davies is dramatising and cherry-picking the bits that best tell the story. But these inclusions are essential. In another writer's hands – and possibly if the story had been told earlier – the version of Thorpe's scandal could have been told differently. If we erase these friendships and moments of allyship, quite quickly we get a story of pure 'scandal' or Thorpe being 'found out' and 'brought down' for his 'sinful actions' and nothing more. This is why it matters that queer writers tell queer stories, particularly those from history. In dissecting Thorpe's story, Davies can do something meaningful; tell it from his perspective, to understand the humanity of it, the humanity of Thorpe himself. While he was reduced to tabloid headlines (and we do love a good political scandal regardless of sexuality), what Davies does is reclaim Thorpe's story both for its humanity and for knowing our gay history. Davies sought to get to the heart of Thorpe and Norman, as he states here telling *IndieWire*:

> [while much has already been written] none of them could ever quite tell you why these men did these things, what was going on in their hearts. And I thought that's what I'd been brought to this to do as a writer of stories and drama. It's my job to understand the hearts of men and to get inside why they do the wrong things at the wrong times and how they can live with themselves.[46]

While the Thorpe scandal is ultimately one of deceit, double-crossing, and, frankly, politics, it is also a story of two men, and Davies brings out their humanity. We understand beyond the headlines why they acted as they did, and the answer, in short, is that they lived in a world that wouldn't let them be who they are.

Reaction
Of course, in dealing with true stories, there is always a danger of getting them wrong or upsetting someone. In this case, Norman Scott, the only key player still living, wasn't enamoured with the portrayal on screen. In an interview with *Irish Times* in 2018, he said:

Artistic license is fine, but this isn't my story. And there's nothing funny about someone trying to kill you ... I'm portrayed as this poor, mincing, little gay person ... I also come across as a weakling, and I've never been a weakling.[47]

Davies is at pains to point out that due diligence was done in creating the story, and indeed as an adaptor of the book by Preston, we can't hold him accountable for the facts presented or the interpretation entirely. What he does say in *IndieWire* is:

Lawyers were studying every single word that I wrote to make it comply, but personally, I think I wrote those characters with a lot of truth in the end so that actually no lawyer could stand up and say, 'They never said that,' because I think they go, 'Of course they said that. Of course, they must have.'[48]

Davies also writes Thorpe and Scott with inherent sympathy. Here, we also see the importance of queer writers telling stories from a shared history. Davies recognises the pain of being in the closet, of the secrets hidden from the wider world. From the personal struggles, too, while the story doesn't dwell on any conflict Thorpe had with his sexuality, nor Scott, perhaps in their actions, it is plain to see Davies, too, thinks Thorpe is an important figure to remember. He says:

I think I could eulogise him. For all the wrong things he did, nonetheless as an icon of what those past days were and how they've improved, I think he's very important. I hope people now remember both Jeremy Thorpe and Norman Scott a bit more and recognise that in the constant struggle.[49]

The broader impact of this drama was more significant; it brought historical stories of gay history into the conversation.

Importance today

Scandal is an important chapter in queer history. It also has much to say about contemporary society. In part, it is a sad indictment of a lack of progress, but it is also an indication that lessons from history are critical. As with all of Davies's dramas, it contains a subtle political undercurrent about the present day. Firstly, given the timing of the 2018 airing, the consistent pro-immigration and pro-European undertones were not subtle, but they were warranted.

Beyond that, what the drama does well is weave in the incidences of tolerance and acceptance from unexpected places. We see Leo Abse and Lord Arran within the establishment being supportive of gay rights. They challenge our ingrained expectations that politicians, particularly of this era, were homophobic. Even Peter, despite his later betrayal in court, and his support to a friend, illustrates that there was support, allies and even hope, for longer than we might expect. It encourages some faith in the establishment to work in favour of queer people. Beyond that, too, Davies includes peripheral characters who supported gay men with full knowledge of the people they were around in everyday life. So, in the drama, both Norman and Thorpe experience support from people in their communities. Norman points out to the pub landlady that 'people are so nice to me wherever I go', and it seems a genuine surprise to him. That can still be the case for many queer people; the shock at being accepted, and despite the historical context, the drama makes a relevant, important point.

This point is also made through the characters, through their respective struggles with being 'out'. While there are historical, and particularly personal, reasons for it being a struggle, there is a lot in each of them that will be relatable to queer viewers. Norman's mental health struggles illustrate a stark reality for many queer people as a result of the broader discrimination or simply being raised in a heteronormative society, but also the establishment and conservative (small 'c') attitudes to sexuality within politics.

Things began to shift in 1984 when Chris Smith became the first openly gay MP. Later in 1997 he would become the Secretary of State for Culture, and later that same year Angela Eagle became the first out lesbian in parliament. While things have shifted slightly since, by 2015 the *Guardian* reported that the UK at that point had more out gay MPs than any other country.[50] In politics, then, since the 1960s, things have improved somewhat (though as with in other areas, not enough). There is a sense that in subsequent decades, there would not be another experience like Thorpe's. But Thorpe's story also serves as a warning from history; that we must move forward, prevent people from hiding themselves, and prevent the darker side of the Thorpe scandal from befalling anyone else.

Telling that story on TV is important, too, because as much as we had moved forward massively from Davies's watershed moment with *Queer as Folk* by this point, it feels as if we have not made enough progress. Davies himself, when promoting *Scandal*, reflected on the new wave of 'gay drama', citing the film *Love, Simon* (2018), which also came out that year. He said to *Digital Spy*:

> For all the success of *Love, Simon*, don't tell me that right now in some comprehensive school, some boy isn't getting his head kicked in, right this very second, because he's gay.[51]

Davies raises a good point on the broader sense – films like *Love, Simon* are the fantasy, the idealised version of what representation has done. But in tying it back to *Scandal*, we can't just have *Love, Simon* because we need to remember what has gone before, particularly for our marginalised communities. As Davies continued:

> It's that old thing that Tolstoy said: revolutions have to keep on happening. They don't just happen once. One day it might balance out and normalise, but there's tons of work to be done.[52]

That work continues through telling stories as Davies has here. There's a sense of reclaiming those stories previously told by straight-dominated media that were swept under the carpet. Something is fitting here, in that as a result of the Thorpe scandal, Davies heard the word 'homosexual' on TV for the first time, and then he was given the opportunity to retell that story on TV decades later. It's an act of both knowing your collective history and using the power of stories to keep that history alive.

Coda

Sex

The joy and pain of queer sex on screen

There's much sex in Davies's work. Sometimes it's central to the plot, like in *Queer as Folk*, and *It's a Sin*, as explored here. Sometimes it's a crucial plot point, like in *Scandal*. Sometimes it's part of the fabric of characters like in *Cucumber* and *Banana*. At other times it provides individual plot points, as in *Bob & Rose*, where it isn't a source of angst and existential crisis. Sometimes it happens as a nuclear bomb goes off or after saving the world. In short, sex is always there. As in life, really. The notable exception is with the Doctor himself, as explored in Chapter Three: 'Gay aliens?'.

Why is sex so important to queer stories? Because historically, and still in contemporary work, we don't see a level playing field. For many millennial viewers who grew up in the shadow of AIDS, this condemnation feels all too familiar – gay sex was not to be discussed. Shonda Rhimes' 2020 Netflix hit *Bridgerton* was hotly anticipated and anticipated to be 'hot'; Rhimes, known for her inclusivity in other dramas like *Grey's Anatomy* (2005–), gave people high hopes for the costume drama. However, while the drama became infamous for its sex scenes (one episode included an explicit scene, lasting nearly ten minutes, set to a Taylor Swift soundtrack), the solitary gay character was depicted sexlessly. Similar patterns occur in other big 'costume dramas' like *Downton Abbey* (2010–15), where the 'gay butler' was allowed only the most chaste of dalliances, usually with negative consequences. The impact isn't limited to the shows, but also the reaction. Case in point, *Bridgerton* aired at the same time as *It's a Sin*, a drama about gay men and AIDS, which was condemned by tabloids as 'scandalous' for its sex scenes, which were no more explicit than those in *Bridgerton*.

As part of any story, Davies uses sex like any straight drama. But more attention is paid because it's (mostly) gay men having sex. While Davies also uses the queer sensibilities of sex in his narratives, he also uses sex for storytelling or character development. We see that in *Torchwood* where, despite flashes of humour, sex between Jack and Ianto is a crucial and heart-warming character development moment. Again, keeping with Davies's trademark humour, sex in the 'office' is part of relatable character development. Likewise, there are moments across the more 'queer' dramas – *Queer as Folk, Cucumber, Banana* – where sex is a crucial emotional or character plot point. Here we look at shows such as *Queer as Folk* and *It's a Sin* in detail regarding what sex 'means' in the bigger picture.

Queer sex, politics and power, not least in *Scandal*, are all central plot strands. The drama here is more 'scandalous' with the element of a queer affair. However, like above, sex scandals in power relationships or political circles can still be scandals if straight people are involved. We see this in *It's a Sin* when Roscoe is having sex with a Conservative politician. It's a plot point as much as a political point, just as a straight person having sex with someone in power would be. Either way, a young person having sex with an older person in a position of power shows the power play, the political impact, and a sense of the abuse of power that this can create. Both the examples in Davies's writing are historic and significant in illustrating the disparity, the historic poor treatment, and the impact on queer lives even within so-called 'scandals'. It's not a huge strand in his writing but an important one on the politics and power dynamics that persist around queer sex.

The other element is that – sex happens. In *Years and Years* Daniel and Viktor have sex while the world 'ends' around them. This is where Davies substitutes straight people with gay and asks audiences to accept it. After all, it's a perfectly reasonable response, seeking out the person you care for as the world ends, and so is the animalistic human desire for connection and sex. Davies taps into a humanistic urge, one that is (almost) universal, and one that if people took a step back to think about (even the homophobes), they might see that it is irrespective of gender and sexuality. Why must Davies choose the gay couple to illustrate that in *Years and Years*? The answer is: normalisation. It's what he does with the queer characters peppered across his series; it's switching from the default 'straight' to including queer people. It's true that there are more significant reasons in *Years and Years* for Daniel and Viktor's story, but their having sex at that moment is one of those moments through which Davies is saying 'include queer stories' to show that we need to give them equal attention. We'd probably have barely discussed the storyline if the couple had been straight. Queer sex continues to be a talking point, and Davies includes much of it in his dramas.

Why is sex so critical to Davies? The answer is twofold and political. Queer sex is subversive. Not just because the right-wing press says so, but because it throws off the predominantly heterosexual nonsense of, firstly, what sex should be and, secondly, what it means. That is, if it's done right. Davies sets out to show that very queer sensibility of sex in his shows. Once again, *Cucumber* and *Banana* are adept at showing contemporary attitudes to sex and sexuality. What Davies also embraces is a sex-positive attitude where people are shown to enjoy sex and embrace it, separate from relationships, a quest for love and morality. Possibly part of the queer sex in Davies's work feels controversial because it challenges the idea of heteronormative or hetero-nonsense.

There's an element of 'explaining' queer sensibilities on sex and sexuality to staunchly heterosexual audiences, and perhaps that is why Davies has suffered the 'too much sex' and 'too explicit' criticisms or the (always amusing in context) 'ramming it down our throats' accusations. Like many other queer writers, Davies's take on sex is different for straight audiences; for many, it will be, possibly, the first time they encounter queer sex on screen. So, while, of course, Stuart's behaviour might be a slightly exaggerated version of reality, it's not *that* exaggerated in terms of the sensibilities behind it. In the 1990s, did men like Stuart have that Friday night on Canal Street? Absolutely. Or, if we look at Dean in *Banana*, do young men use apps like he does to hook up during a lunch hour or similar? Of course they do. And while this way of living isn't for everyone or not everyone in the queer community, there's a certain element of disconnect between how the straight community sees those scenes and how the queer community sees them. It goes deeper than being 'slutty', as Davies attests; there's nothing wrong with that to a point, either. It's about existing in a world with a community of people who have realised that monogamy, dating for only love, and marriage, are not the only answer. Even in 2022, this is shocking to many straight people, but it is something the queer community has long embraced.

Casanova and sex positivity

Even in the more 'heterosexual' dramas, of course, Davies is mindful of the power of sex in human nature. Casanova is, of course, driven by it. The delight of Davies's take on that story is that he emphasises Casanova's respect for women. The story also emphasises the female pleasure involved, perhaps leading to the question: is history's most infamous lover better written by a gay man? Probably. Because Casanova's understanding of sexuality has a very queer sensibility in Davies's reading: Casanova isn't a callous misogynist, using women and abandoning them. Instead, he's engaging in a sex-positive, free-love kind of attitude. Davies's *Casanova* is a critical re-writing of the long-established narrative. He casts David Tennant who has affable charm and is more 'boy next door' on the first encounter than what we traditionally think of as a 'Casanova', which works. Tennant is an unthreatening but still seductive Casanova, and the respect for women Davies works in supports this. There's queerness in the story; while Casanova remains mostly the women-loving man, we expect there to be an edge of queerness. He falls in love with what he thinks is a young man who turns out to be a woman in disguise. But he's not put off by his falling for 'him' and instead leans into it, with a 'love is love' approach. There's also some innuendo and humour around a fake penis, which keeps with the tone of the series.

That element is vital too – another trope of Davies's seen in *Casanova* is humour and sex. This is seen across his work, where sexual encounters go wrong, are awkward or just outright ridiculous. But the sheer amount of sex Casanova engages in allows him to lean into it. The retelling is written in a subtle fantasy way, with Casanova narrating his adventures to us, which helps in the retelling, the exaggeration and the ridiculousness. We see this in *Queer as Folk* through *Cucumber* and *Banana* and even *It's a Sin*. In the earlier dramas, sex is almost a funny 'anecdote' moment in the stories – we see Stuart getting up to all manner of wild adventures, or we see Dean's sexual exploits in *Banana*. They're part of a backdrop, a forming the fabric of the lives of these men. Sex is part of their lives, but also it adds an element of humour. Davies also recognises that sex can be funny, and not in a mean way, just in a messy-bodily-fluids kind of way.

This fantasy element, coupled with the attitude in *Casanova*, encapsulates part of Davies's outlook on sex – it's a ridiculous ritual that humans engage in, and the combination of body parts and bodily fluids can be hilarious. He manages to convey this in a way that isn't judgemental or mean-spirited. There's also a certain amount of respect in the way he does it, even in the more 'slutty' of his characters – they aren't doing it with an agenda or malice, they're doing it in the pursuit of gratification and the spirit of freedom from heteronormative confines of sexuality.

Queer as Folk and sex

Davies asserted the importance of queer sex from the outset in this story. *Queer as Folk* burst unapologetically onto the screen full of sex. There is a rimming scene in the first episode; it doesn't get much more unapologetic than that. The first episode sets out its stall as a no-holds-barred but also slightly tongue-in-cheek (well tongue in everywhere) look at sexual misadventures. This theme is a running thread in the show – an unapologetic, often funny, almost always as explicit as they could make it, queer rebellion of sex. It was occasionally ridiculous, raw, uncompromising, and had an emotional edge. But it was very, very queer.

Also integral to Davies's depiction of sex in *Queer as Folk* was the divorce of sex from a hunt for love. The seeking of sex in *Folk* was simply a hunt for sex. Nothing more, nothing less. Whether you see that as an accurate reflection of the queer community at that time or not, is largely irrelevant. It was a confrontational rebellion against heteronormative depictions of sex on screen. It's not about anyone seeking the one or making 'mistakes' to learn from. (Stuart, for one, does very little learning from sex, but perhaps a fair bit of teaching during the act.)

Because sex is divorced from morality in *Queer as Folk*, the show asks questions – with Nathan, and with Phil. But it doesn't offer viewers a hard-line answer; it lets them reflect. Is Stuart's sexual lifestyle sustainable or advisable? Well, that's his business; that's the personal preference the show offers up. Would we possibly want him to settle down with Vince? If we answer 'yes', is that our conditioning from a heteronormative society? Is it ok for both choices to be possible? Yes. The narrative doesn't judge Stuart, so neither should we. It lays out the problematic elements – underage sex, dangerous practices and the tragedy that befalls Phil. But it's not done in a heavy-handed or pedantic way; it presents a slice of life. That slice involves the tragic, the glorious, the fun and the ridiculous.

If sex and morality are separate in *Queer as Folk*, then by the juxtaposition of the titles alone, *It's a Sin* sits on the other end of that spectrum. That story centres on a moment when sex was the centre of the world and the centre of judgement and fear for gay men. Davies manages this with delicacy and raw honesty and that is a testament to his writing skill and holds up a mirror to the unrestrained sexuality of *Queer as Folk*.

Sex and identity:
Henry and sex and shame in *Cucumber*

Twenty years after the sexual freedom and rejection of heteronormative standards of sex, *Cucumber* ends on the devastating note that Henry has never quite been ok with being gay. For Henry, throughout the story, we see, but aren't explicitly told, that this uncertainty manifests itself in sex. Or lack of. Or lack of 'proper gay sex'. In short, Henry doesn't do or like anal sex, and this compromises his relationship with Lance and, ultimately, his perception of himself as a gay man. It fuels a sense of shame, a feeling of being an outsider, and a host of mental health issues that explain Henry's behaviour.

There are, of course, problematic elements of Henry's story. We shouldn't define 'sex' by such narrow standards or class there as being something 'wrong' with a person for not enjoying one particular sex act. Indeed, by this point in time, the sex-positive movement and a greater understanding of broader sexuality and sexual identities are increasingly spreading awareness that such definitions are outdated and heteronormative. So perhaps we should acknowledge that there is nothing 'wrong' with Henry's sexual preferences. Lance also shares blame for the harboured resentment over Henry's preferences in that reading.

However, in the context of the story, Henry's aversion to anal sex is a powerful narrative that throws light on him as a person and the broader conversations about gay identity and gay sex. For Henry, his views on anal sex have caused a mental block between him and his entire identity. Perhaps we assume there has been a sexual trauma or at least some personal mental block around the act itself. This is partly right; his mental block is tied up in shame, in a lack of acceptance of himself as a gay man. While Henry loves men – he revels in his attraction to men and their fantasies. But if he doesn't engage in anal sex, if he doesn't enjoy it, then he fears that there's some part of him that remains 'not gay'. He fears that some people might not perceive him as 'fully gay', and indeed his own ingrained prejudices make him think that of himself. As mentioned above, it's possible to be 'fully gay' without particular sex acts, but that isn't how society has conditioned Henry and other men his age to think. Indeed, women his age, too, think this way. He has been conditioned to associate particular sex acts with his identity, and a part of him keeping them separate means that he can remain a little 'not fully' gay.

Some viewers might feel anger towards Henry's story and his character. Some might agree with the characters who think that it's Henry's fault that Lance dies. Or feel anger at his denial of his identity or at his lack of engagement in sex. Particularly the latter because sex and what people do and don't do is hugely emotive, even for those who aren't directly involved in that act. Ask any asexual person whether their lack of sex confuses, and at times even enrages, vast sections of society. In the case of gay men, the very act of sex, specifically anal sex, invokes such rage from homophobes. It is what gay men are so often reduced to and it is the provocation for anger, sexual attacks and violence directed at them. In that light, is it any wonder that Henry doesn't want any part of it? But also, anal sex, when viewed as an act of sexual deviance, can be used as an act of defiance by queer men. The demonising of gay sex, and an over-focus on the logistics of it (putting aside that not all gay men do have anal sex), has made it an act of rebellion and defiance against the bigotry that is over focused on what the community does sexually. Plus, as Davies has the characters focus on this in one episode, with an in-depth explicit discussion, it's also fun for many. Davies shows, through Henry, another side to the politicisation of anal sex for gay men – the pressure to engage to be considered 'a proper gay man'. Engaging in anal sex for gay men is important beyond the physical act. It involves a heady mix of rebellion, political statement through private actions and in-community politics. Davies highlights this double-edged sword for matters of personal sexual preference and/or internalised homophobia. Because Henry's complex relationship with anal sex isn't separate from the community and wider politicised politics of anal sex, its associations, shame and a whole array of elements that have affected Henry as a gay man, manifested in the sexual act so externally politicised.

In Henry's story, Davies highlights the relationship between the queer community and sex, specifically among gay men. When Henry ventures into online dating/hook-ups for the first time, he discovers how closely sex is tied to everything. Showing him that probably seems reductive and evident to the younger members of his group. Still, for Henry, who was in a long-term relationship for over a decade before the apps took over, it's as much a revelation as it is to some straight audiences. What Henry discovers, and what Davies shows us, is how much sex and sexual preference/identity are driving factors in the dating sphere. So Tops, Bottoms, Vers, and all manner of sexual preferences lead the conversation in app hook-up culture, which are very different when Henry returns to the scene. In this, too, we get a contemporary reflection on the world of Stuart and Vince and Canal Street and their hook-up/sex culture. Not that one version entirely erased the other, but Henry's story is a marker of how sex for gay men and the way sex defines people has changed. It's also a commentary on how, for many gay men, sex has always been central in their connections, culture and identity. Suppose we combine the two dramas; together they form a unique over-arching look at the changing landscape of sex in the gay (largely male) community and this is fairly unusual in TV terms, particularly from the same writer. And the honesty of Henry's character (as well as his friends) on aging in that community is equally powerful.

Henry's story offers, in some ways, an insight into the problems sex can cause for identity in relationships. His story is, in some sense, a critical mirror of how it affects people. But in a larger sense, it's a reflection of the entirely personal impact that sex has. Henry's negative identification with sex is part of a broader homophobic culture in which he grew up and navigated his sexuality as a young man. It's a brutal illustration of what internalised homophobia does to a person, with the worst possible consequences.

Why is sex so important, then, in Davies's work?

The trouble with sex on TV between queer characters (as well as in real life), is that it often ceases to be sexy, and becomes a scandal – either within the drama itself or off-screen. But at times, queer drama is forced to overcompensate to make a point. As 'mainstream' drama wasn't allowing queer sex or even affection, then drama made for specifically queer audiences leaned into the sexual elements. So, from the original *Queer as Folk* to *The L Word* to *Looking*, sex – and often explicit sex – has been a considerable part of the narrative. Now sometimes, that's necessary. Sex is a part of human relationships and dramas, after all. For queer stories, particularly gay men in a post-AIDS world, discussion around sex, even the act of sex, has both personal and political implications. Sex is part of queer life and should be celebrated, analysed and seen in queer drama. But are there lines being crossed with over-sexualisation for the sake of over-sexualisation? Do we even see some element of fetishisation from audiences and TV makers? Quite possibly. But in line with the broader politics of Davies's stories, the sex is there to make a political or dramatic point, but also just to show queer characters having sex, just like their straight counterparts, from Stuart Jones's Canal Street escapades, through Captain Jack's fifty-first-century attitudes to sex in *Torchwood* through to scandalous sex in parliament to Henry having or not having sex. Davies's characters have sex, unapologetically, sometimes slightly politically, but also simply because it's what people do.

Chapter Seven

The future is a scary place: *Years and Years*

This chapter looks at Davies's near-future drama *Years and Years* and considers how Davies positions queer stories in an imagined future. Crucially, it isn't a show about queer people, but it does integrate queer people into the narrative.

This series, broadcast in 2019, highlights people of other nationalities, our stance on refugees and the broader prejudices. It is also worryingly prescient about the future. The clever storytelling in *Years and Years* shows that, unexpectedly, the usually 'safe' white male becomes the one to die. This is in part related to sexuality, in part related to other prejudices, and makes for a fascinating reflection on how the queer community sees itself in relation to other minority groups and how Davies challenges us to look at that.

The six-part series, set around Manchester, focuses on the multiple members of the Lyons family and people connected to them. This includes siblings Daniel, Stephen and Rosie, and their partners and children, alongside their gran, Muriel. Things begin in 2019, and move forward over the next 15 years of family life, while the world around changes rapidly as a backdrop. There's a mix of political upheavals, technological advances, economic instability and a pandemic alongside family drama. Taking place between 2019 and 2034, the six-part series follows the lives of the family members. They are witness to the ups and downs of world affairs and closer to home, the rise to power of politician Vivienne Rook, a celebrity-turned-politician whose controversial approaches divide the nation.

The show gets more 'sci-fi' as it continues; what starts as speculative drama shifts into a '*Doctor Who* for grown-ups' narrative where technology advances combine with flawed humanity to offer us a moral lesson in our present. It feels like a logical successor to *Who* in that way. Though, mindful of the period it was written in (post-Trump, post-Brexit), it lacks perhaps the eternal optimism that *Who* is infused with; the belief that humans can do good. Instead, in *Years and Years* the future is increasingly bleak. Revisiting it a few years later makes for tense, unsettling viewing, even for the elements Davies gets wrong about the future.

Predicting the future is dangerous...

There is, of course, always a slight danger with near-future sci-fi. Either it's ridiculously off base or incredibly, worryingly accurate. *Years and Years* begins in 2019 which now will mark it in ways nobody could have imagined then. Everything that follows now naturally looks a little skewed and improbable as that's what living through real-life events that feel like sci-fi will do. So, of course, when we revisit with the hindsight of a couple of years, and the impact of some world-altering events, some elements look more improbable than they did in 2018. Or perhaps elements that would have been probable without the derailing effects of 2020's global pandemic now seem less likely. Sci-fi of this nature is a tricky thing. Even if the world took a different path, the one laid out in *Years and Years* is familiar enough to be terrifying. As Sean O'Grady put it:

> The near future is an interesting place to visit. It is another country obviously and, to be sure, often enough 'dystopian', to borrow that overused expression (why does no one ever talk about 'the dystopian past'?). But it should still be plausible enough to be able to believe in it, and be a little amused, and frightened, by it.[53]

To that end, some of the stuff from the opening scenes *does* feel worryingly prescient. The younger Lyons brother, Daniel (Russell

Tovey), stands holding his sister's new-born baby and wonders aloud how anyone could entertain bringing a child into the world. His sister retorts 'thanks' (given she's just done that) and his speech that follows highlights many fears we still have beyond 2020 (and all the real-life problems that has brought). Daniel says, 'remember when we thought politics was boring' and 'I'm scared of America' – sentiments that, since 2020, have become increasingly accurate.

That the refugee camp Viktor is in (and Daniel works at) is for Ukrainian refugees after a conflict with Russia is also worryingly accurate. On the one hand, any close reading of Russian–Ukrainian politics from the past few decades could have made an educated guess that conflict might happen. But the timing is almost exact in terms of Davies's storytelling. He manages to nail the reactions of British people to Ukrainian refugees (seen early in the first episode when a colleague from Blackpool argues over the difference between refugees and asylum seekers). Of course, the Ukrainians in *Years and Years* stand for a more extensive set of issues, not least how we judge refugees based on skin colour and where they come from.

The final element that Davies got eerily correct, too, is the outbreak of Monkey Flu in the final episode. While, again, Davies is just reacting to the signs – in this case the signs in science that we were due for another pandemic – both in terms of Covid and, in 2022, Monkeypox, and its association with gay men, the parallels are frighteningly accurate.

It is more difficult to predict the technology and political elements. In technology, invariably within sci-fi, writers either are too ahead of their time or a little behind. This is because technology is more about the adoption by humans than the actual technology. It's hard to predict what will seem far-fetched. As it stands, while the integration of technology into people's lives seems normal by our contemporary standards, some of the more advanced technologies in *Years and Years*, especially 'transhumanism', seem very much still sci-fi. But, as with all Davies's sci-fi, it's the human and moral story underneath that matters the most. So really, the story is about connection and the use of technology for good, bad or indifferent purposes, and this is at the heart of all good sci-fi.

Politics is a tricky subject to navigate. As Daniel says in the first episode, after all, 'remember when politics was boring'. It is a brave writer who tried in 2017 to predict the political future, but Davies gave it a go. Thankfully one thing he got very wrong was Trump being elected for a second term. He also got the shape of British politics wrong. We didn't elect a Nigel Farage-like figure, like the one he creates in Vivienne Rook, but only really because we're tied to our archaic two-party system. But the sentiment behind her endures in British politics, and beyond. The most chilling real-world political point Davies makes is *Roe v Wade* (the US Constitutional enshrining of abortion rights) being repealed. Davies's story is a footnote in a montage of political unrest in 2027. The US got there in 2022.

The story took an idea of what many people had been feeling over the past few years and rather than creating a soap-box lecture, turned it into compelling drama. This is what Davies gets most right most of the time, even when his rage necessitates, and it's his and the growing liberal or left-leaning fear and rage he's tapping into. So, he leans into themes that validate progressive, rational and empathetic concerns. That was always the point, in much the same way as the TARDIS travels in time and space to teach us about the present. Davies perfected that in his years at *Who*, as Ben Travers at *IndieWire* said of *Years and Years*:

> The greatest trick of 'Years and Years' Russell T Davies's decades-spanning limited series examining the dangerous political and cultural trends taking over the world, is that it's not really about the future at all.[54]

We're supposed to look at it and ask, 'Hey, isn't that happening now?' The character of Daniel even sets it up before the first 'fast forward' with his lament on the state of the world today. But the near-future approach helps us (in theory at least) to see the world now with new clarity, asking ourselves, 'What if we continued this way?' Of course, it won't work; some people will watch and think Vivienne Rook has it sorted or think the government's refugee plans are a good idea. But the show does its best through drama to hold up a mirror to our current world.

The strength of that comes in using the lens of the family to tell the story; they give us focus, as Daniel D'Addario outlines in *Variety*:

> To its credit, 'Years and Years' – among the most emotionally involving, and best, series to air so far this year – keeps its aperture narrow even as the world keeps forcing its way in. This is, above all, the story of a family, one whose ordinariness makes them a powerful vehicle for telling the future.[55]

Years and Years does something different to other political or dystopian dramas, in the way it foregrounds the everyday, and at times unlikeable, characters and their low-level drama.

It is a trope often seen in novels, like the approaches taken by David Mitchell or Ali Smith. These authors are worth citing because they share a crucial trait with Davies. They are British. (So, for that matter, are Charlie Brooker, the creator of *Black Mirror,* and Jonathan Nolan, the co-creator of *Westworld*.) Britons live in the memory of what has once been; they are citizens of a power that exists now in memory and ritual but no longer as the defining force on the world stage. Little wonder that they are good at telling stories that depict shifts in historical currents, not as apocalypses demanding the rise of heroes, but as rising tides that, given their intractable power, must be endured.

Russell T Davies's writing in *Years and Years* is consistently elegant but also resonant. The critical question of our times, one so massive that it demands to be broken up into several smaller sub-questions, is about how the individual should or even could react to living through increasingly rapid change. The power of the drama, and a particular skill of Davies, is in highlighting the mundane and in finding humour in the tragic, the overpowering or the downright incompressible. It's what made his *Who* stories appeal beyond the sci-fi nerds and kids they initially were written for. In *Years and Years* we see much of this. So, for example, in terms of technology, we see fears about kids turning into technology and we see a man who has turned his household robot into a sexbot. While the latter is fairly *Torchwood* in its approach, the execution is pitch-perfect in capturing how we humans might respond to the future. Because on stumbling across her date's sexbot, Rosie does what we'd all do; phones her brothers and has a good laugh at the man's expense while they laugh at hers. It's not navel-gazing and existential worrying about whether the sexbot is a robot replacing a woman; it's (rightfully) mocking the man who thinks the best use for advanced technology is a robot to wank him off. The date in question is played by Noel Sullivan, a Welsh actor known for being 'Noel from the group Hear'Say'. He appeared in *Years and Years* after a stint on the talent show *Popstars* (he's also referenced by Nessa in *Gavin and Stacey*). Therefore, he adds an element of 'Welsh Bingo'. This kind of pop culture reference is weirdly fitting for the dystopian world of *Years and Years*. After all, in 2002 when *Popstars* aired, we wouldn't have expected to later see Noel and his sex robot on a BBC drama.

The opposite to this humour is shown in the third episode, in which their father dies. It is one of those moments where we see the day-to-day minutiae of life go on as they must. But even then, Davies aerates the heaviest, most fraught issues with wit and optimism – the serious issues then feel less a burden to us or the narrative but grist to the mental and dramatic mill. The dad had been absent from the conversation until then, and it transpires he left the family shortly after Rosie was born and lived with his new family in Leicester. He dies unexpectedly of sepsis, and the Lyons children make the trip to his funeral. Against the backdrop of the politics in this episode and the more speculative technology elements, this becomes the central plot instead – simple, family grief. We see everyone at the funeral, where advances in death care are discussed with the dad going through 'aquamation' instead of cremation (incidentally a natural and more environmentally sound alternative).

But what we also see is a very average, very human funeral. Everyone goes to the pub, sits in the corner and cries. This is the heart of what makes *Years and Years* a powerful drama and illustrates what Davies does best. Davies's trademark humour, compassion and kinetic energy infuse the six-part drama, and this makes it feel much shorter. His commitment to the everyday, the mundane and the heartbreak within sets his writing apart. He is able to put very human moments against the backdrops of great moments. It's Rose in *Doctor Who* wanting chips while encountering aliens. It's also a father dying in painfully ordinary circumstances and the response of his children.

This, too, becomes the heart of *Years and Years*; while the world burns, everyday family life carries on. There is nothing remarkable about the Lyons family, initially; there's nothing remarkable about their dad's death. But the painful ordinariness of their grief is what allows us to connect with them. Of course, the show also comes with Davies's trademark humour. The family stands giggling at the funeral, making snide remarks about their stepmother, and down a shot of their aquamated dad, all to contrast the heartbreak. When then they all break down in tears, it feels honest; it's relatable.

News media, technology and the world we live in

A 2022 Ofcom report into news consumption indicated social media as one of the top three sources for news.[56] In *Years and Years*, we see young people glued to their phones, reflecting on the world they find themselves in. Davies also uses fictional news reporting as part of the narrative. Here, in particular, this is an effective meta-narrative technique. We see in the show the world being manipulated by media, which looks a lot like our media, and therefore the effect is even stronger.

This theme is something of a staple of Davies's writing, to the point he had recurring newsreader characters in *Doctor Who*. This use of fictional news broadcasts helps ground the work in the present day, a standard of historical and futuristic drama, and something Davies utilises extensively in *Doctor Who* to similar effect.

Transhumanism and metaphors for otherness

The first way in which queer experience or references are worked into an otherwise not queer-centric script is something of a 'bait and switch' and back again. In the first episode, we see a teenager googling 'what is trans' and her parents sitting down to chat with her offering understanding and acceptance. We assume, particularly given Davies's track record, that the episode will be about trans issues. What it's actually about is technology. Bethany is taking the perceived 'Gen-Z' dependence on technology to the next level. She wants to transcend her physical boundaries and become code. Her parents are shown as accepting, embracing even, the possibility of a transgender child; they are less so with the idea of a transhuman child.

Bethany's story *concerns* technology and how far we'll go with it. It's about dependence and the notion that more is always better. It's about government control and all those scary tech elements that are less sci-fi than near enough reality, with just enough of a dramatic twist. It's an imperfect metaphor at times, as many about technology are. After all, we can rarely predict what will be beneficial and what will turn out to be dangerous. But for the sake of drama, Bethany's story takes this to the extreme.

But despite the 'bait and switch' element which makes us assume that Bethany's story was about queerness when it becomes about something else, it could be argued that the story is possibly about both. Throughout her life, Bethany's parents have declared her wishes at best 'strange' or at worst 'dangerous'. Bethany's engagement with her transhuman identity ends up being dangerous as she, along with her friend, connects with 'backstreet' surgeons, and she lacks an understanding of the technology. This can be viewed as analogous for what trans people go through. That, coupled with her feeling that nobody understands her, means her interest is dismissed as a 'fad' by everyone except for a small subset of fellow transhumanity advocates. The way Bethany describes feeling at odds with her body, saying that she doesn't feel connected to it, and is almost repulsed by it, is an imperfect metaphor, too, but one that stands up. There's a caveat to her story: Rosie's younger child is trans. We see their story unfold in the backdrop of the narrative, with the family fully accepting her, without it being a central part of the story. This is a lovely piece of incidental queer inclusion and a statement that strengthens the metaphor of Bethany's transhuman narrative.

It can, of course, be both. Davies can be commenting on technology – its insidious, potentially dangerous nature – and using an analogy for the trans experience. In particular, Bethany's feeling at odds with her body, and the lack of understanding from those who aren't transhuman, is a powerful analogy for the trans experience. Her journey also speaks to the broader 'queer' experience that Davies comments on in *Years and Years*: the way the outsiders, for sexuality, gender, or even disability (as Rosie shows), are the groups so easily made vulnerable when politics is raging around. They are also made to feel the real personal impact, even when larger society thinks 'it doesn't happen to people like us'.

Queer stories, sex and the fear

In *Years and Years*, the queer characters start as something Davies has, by this point, mastered – they're just queer. As the Lyons family is brilliantly diverse anyway, it seems completely normal that Daniel is gay (because it is). At first, he and his partner are simply rounding up a diverse contemporary family, even when Daniel simultaneously has his head turned by an attractive Ukrainian, Viktor. He starts to realise his husband is, well, a bit of an idiot, and it seems that this is the sort of human sub-plot against political sci-fi that Davies is so good at. The point of *Years and Years* is that we care about the crumbling world, seeing it through the lens of the Lyons family. It also makes sense that they will continue to have personal dramas against that backdrop. Even when Daniel goes to Viktor and quite literally has sex as the world ends, it seems a human way into a much bigger conversation.

But the story is more complex, more brilliant than that. Firstly, making Daniel the 'big gay brother' (as Rosie calls him at one point) looks like a charming way to integrate representation into the story. Adding to that, there is Russell Tovey's commitment to playing gay characters because it serves him as a performer, as he said in 2019 to *Gay Times*:

> It's like me saying I could never play a straight character because I will not know a straight person's thoughts. I've always been out and happy with the range of characters I've been offered.[57]

Tovey has been, like Davies, outspoken on the desire to play gay roles, and this is another of them. He has played a handful of straight roles in his career, but as he's been able to be more discerning, he's focused what he says yes to. Given, too, that he's worked with Davies before, the likelihood is that Daniel was written with Tovey in mind, or at least with him as one of the favoured options. This is an essential sidetone as it feeds into the more extensive conversation that Davies is creating around allowing queer actors to be given roles that, as Tovey says in the quote above, serve their life experiences. It's something neither straight actors nor straight audiences likely think of, but as picked up in the chapter on queer characters, *Years and Years* was part of furthering this conversation.

The simple act of representation, too, is vital in the first three episodes of *Years and Years*. While there are 'queer' plot points with Daniel, mostly, he's just there, being gay, part of the story. That fuels the element of the everyday backdrop to life – the Lyons family is witnessing history, and Daniel, as a gay man, is part of that. It strikes a good balance having him just being there, being gay, and moving towards a plot where his queerness is central to the commentary in the broader world.

Sex and queerness

The first episode of *Years and Years* ends with Russell Tovey fucking a man as the world ends. That seems a flippant summary, but for gay men, sex has always been, and still is, a political act. This is seemingly apt from the writer who brought the world *Queer as Folk* and caused much clutching of pearls when gay characters appeared in his *Doctor Who*. The story of gay characters Daniel and Viktor in *Years and Years* is as much a political act as any of the broader politics of the story. A gay man fucking an illegal immigrant as the world edges towards nuclear disaster is the opening gambit of one of the most important gay stories on TV in recent years. Being gay is, after all, still a political act. Simply existing in the world becomes a political act.

'People like us' is the critical line from Tovey's character Daniel in the fourth episode. Daniel is a middle-class man, comfortably employed within the establishment (he's a civil servant, the height of generic middle-class acceptance, or at least, the height of being seen as part of the establishment). He couldn't be more 'normal' and 'safe'. Worrying about his sexuality has been a relatively minor part of his life. Later in the episode, his brother Stephen reminisces about being born in the 1980s and how good life was for a while for their generation. For gay men like Daniel, it should have proven a 'golden age' to be gay – an age where marriage became legal, tolerance increased, and gay people gained rights and were socially accepted. For the most part, Davies paints that picture of the future – a time where gay marriage is normalised, and prejudice seems limited, at least in the middle-class bubble of the Lyons family. They're painted as liberals, accepting of one niece, potentially, having a girlfriend, being trans and a nephew wearing a dress.

It seems then that the future for gay people is one aspect of Russell T Davies's dystopian vision that isn't as bad. In one way, it's almost victorious. Davies has for years worked on 'normalising' gay people on TV. In an interview with *New Statesman* in 2018,[58] he commented on this, saying, 'Whatever I worked on, I put a gay character in. I put a lesbian vicar into a show. I put gay teenagers into *Children's Ward*.' And, of course, *Doctor Who*, under Davies's tenure, had gay characters peppered across time and space, which allowed Davies to imagine various futures and civilisations where gay and trans people were accepted. *Years and Years* might seem like a 'real world' version of this same philosophy.

The only time any character in the series went out of their way to comment on either sexuality or gender was when Grandmother Muriel said, 'I'm not prejudiced…I don't like people who wear sunglasses indoors.' This is a line that Davies later admitted on Instagram was stolen from an episode of *Coronation Street* from the 1970s. On 21 May 2019, he posted a picture of the scene with the caption: 'CONFESS. I stole that line off 1970s Coronation Street. Len Fairclough employed a young black lad, who was surprised Len wasn't prejudiced. "Oh I'm prejudiced," said Len…Great lines never die! Wish I know who wrote it.'[59]

There is perhaps, too, a double meaning here with that borrowed line from decades earlier, of the racism towards Viktor and homophobia being commented on. The near future seems to be enlightened regarding sexuality, if nothing else. But being gay in Davies's world remains a political act, both within the world and as a televisual statement.

Within the show, there's a slow burn of just how dangerous it still is to be gay. It's in keeping with the domestic window on the broader world that the show masters. In the fourth episode, Daniel talks of the reality of Viktor being executed and says, 'I can't believe I'm saying that sat in the garden.' This exemplifies what *Years and Years* was saying overall; the changes in the world aren't played out in political debates but in the homes and gardens of those it affects. At the end of the episode, the Lyons family's impact of all this politics is felt over a simple phone call in the living room when they learn Daniel is dead.

Bury your gays...

The introduction of Viktor is a way for Daniel's view of the world to be disrupted, ultimately in a tragic way. He's not blind to it anyway; he's a liberal thirty-something who works in local housing. As he later comments, he's seen things; he's aware of what happens to people from less liberal countries. But there's being aware and being in it. Through Viktor, he learns first-hand the impact; his parents gave up Viktor to the authorities, who tortured him. The whole story of his not returning to Ukraine rests on him being gay; if he goes home, he'll be arrested, possibly worse. As the political dominos fall across Europe, the rights and safety of Viktor, not just as a refugee and asylum seeker but as a gay man, are the narrative Davies brings home.

Within the narrative and for viewers, this is a stark reminder of the closeness of persecution for being gay and the intolerance that contrasts with the comfortable world of the Lyons family. This is not some dystopian future, as with much of Davies's story; it's happening now, except many people choose not to see it. When a lesbian couple is attacked in England, we are reminded that persecution of queer people does not just happen abroad. Yet, we deport people to countries where, because of their sexuality, they are imprisoned, even sentenced to death.

Davies weaves a slow burn on this. Initially, it looks like Viktor will be helped by the friendly middle-class British family. After all, with gay marriage long ago legalised and him being an asylum seeker and already in the UK, it seems like a hopeful, liberal inclusivity subplot. However, slowly over the first three episodes, all that changes.

This works on two fronts – the dramatic and the political – from a dramatic point of view, the story builds slowly with a series of small twists and turns.

At first, it seems *Years and Years* may escape the trope of a tragic gay story. Viktor is deported but escapes to a tolerant Spain, as a kind of 'up yours' to a Britain falling apart. As Daniel and Viktor struggle to get home to the UK through increasingly desperate measures, they become refugees, the kind of people Daniel has watched on the news, crammed into tiny boats crossing the channel. As with many of those stories, it ends in tragedy. 'It doesn't happen to people like us,' thinks Daniel, sure in his comfortable status. And yet it is his lifeless body that washes up on a beach.

This is a difficult moment on many levels. Again, there are echoes of the 'bury your gays' TV trope. However, the story itself is compelling and fitting with the narrative, if still shocking, as such deaths should be.

There is a little inverting of this here, too; we would have expected Viktor to be killed, not Daniel. He's the 'new' character; the one Daniel cheats on his husband with. He's framed as 'in danger' for much of the series. It's a clever twist when Daniel dies, the guy we expect to be 'safe'. After all, he's part of our central family, he's played by a more famous actor, he's good looking – the list goes on. Of course, this is a well-known page out of the Russell T Davies playbook; kill someone off when the audience least expects it. From Phil in *Queer as Folk* to Ianto in *Torchwood*, this is part of his longstanding way of showing real life in drama – in real life, people die unexpectedly, and it hurts. That's, in part, what happens to Daniel.

Broader, and dare we say it, bolder than that, there is a message to all gay men like Daniel – not to put too much trust in the idea that you're 'safe' somehow, that you aren't 'Viktor'. Indeed, Daniel thinks he can save Viktor. He goes to his death, firmly believing that he can save him. He is, after all, a white, middle-class, British gay man. He's 'safe', nobody is coming for him, and he can help others like him or at least help the man he loves. The chilling reminder Davies gives us is that we're only as safe as one political vote, one homophobe and one bad piece of luck.

The story of Viktor starts as a narrative of people from 'other countries' and the dangers they face. Slowly Davies forces the audience to face up to the knowledge that this is a particular gay issue, to remind them that being gay is still dangerous for many people. The fact that he uses a Ukrainian is vital too – he's white, he's 'the right sort' of refugee. But Davies challenges the audience further. When Viktor tries to find help, he tries countries we consider 'safe' – Spain, France – neither are willing to help. Both are one political strike away from being a terrifying place for gay people. We don't see the UK becoming that; he doesn't say it, but he doesn't have to.

This storyline also reminds us that campaigning for the right to exist as gay people is not a thing of the past. While *Years and Years* is futuristic, the point is that it comments on what is happening right now. We are still one bad election and one political coup away from another country being a dangerous place to be gay – adding, of course, to the number of places where it is already hazardous to be gay. But the twist is the way that Daniel gets caught up in it. Ultimately, it's not a story about how it's dangerous for people in 'foreign countries' to be gay; it's a lesson in how easily it can be for people like Daniel to get caught up in danger.

While it's a 'bury your gays' moment, it's for a purpose. The feeling of 'there but for the grace of god' (or sheer luck of birth and circumstance) is vital for queer people born into relative privilege. As Daniel's brother Stephen says earlier in the episode, they had it pretty good, people his and Daniel's age; they were born in a 'pause', as he puts it. Without significant political turmoil, they reaped all the benefits from previous generations of turmoil. That's particularly true for queer people Daniel's age; he came of age post-Stonewall, post-decriminalisation, post-AIDS and with gay marriage on the horizon. Things weren't perfect – he would be the generation who grew up under Section 28 – but he grew up under a fair amount of privilege. It's easy to assume – especially for rights that were hard-won by generations before – that those rights aren't glorified. Davies is reminding us all that they aren't.

He continues this theme with what happens to Viktor next. After Daniel's death, Viktor is detained as a refugee, but we assume everything will be ok now, that the Lyons family will look after him. They do, to a point; Edith keeps helping him, the activist that she is. But in a chilling scene, we see Stephen visit at Christmas and tell Viktor, 'it's your fault he's dead'. This is a man talking out of grief, maybe. But later, we see Stephen use his job to send Viktor to a concentration camp. The UK has got to that point by now. A gay refugee is, of course, the perfect candidate to 'disappear' to a camp. We stop and ask, would Stephen have done that if Daniel had a wife? The honest answer has to be, no. The more chilling question is, what would the outcry be if a TV show had him do that to a wife? It's an interesting, uncomfortable question for queer and straight audiences alike. This theme is not just about queerness, there's also a strong pro-immigration, anti-Brexit rhetoric in *Years and Years*. When we see Viktor interred in a camp that the government is flooding with people who have Monkey Flu, and he's left, among other 'unwanted' or 'undesirable' groups to die, we are reminded of pandemics past and present. (That there is also, in the real world, homophobic rhetoric around Monkeypox and the gay community is a chilling footnote.)

It's hard to explain, perhaps to someone not from the LGBTQ+ community, just what a chilling streak of recognition the fourth episode of *Years and Years* brought out: the sense of fear, tightness in the chest watching the chase across Europe, that all-too-familiar feeling of 'will we be noticed'. Their attempt to escape across Europe is also a neat metaphor – they're hiding, seconds away from being 'discovered' and encountering the terrifying consequences. It's a gay tale as old as time – the sight of Daniel's lifeless body on the beach. Hearing Viktor recount the loss of his lover to a family that is not his, the fear of now being rejected by them as well hangs in the air.

Having sex in the face of an apocalypse might be a political statement. But so, for gay people, it is in love. Davies reminds us of that in true tragic form. It's a rallying cry both to politics and to love.

A near and present future

This story, among the many complex ones in *Years and Years*, brings home what Davies is trying to say. Although there are two more episodes that follow, and many other strands to tie up, Daniel's death distils the message of the show – the future is nearer and more dangerous than you think. For all the political and technological speculation, that, too, is where the point of the show lies – the humanity and the human damage at the heart of it. The Lyons family may take part in political action across their story in various ways, but the story that will stick with them, and with us as viewers, is Daniel's death. It becomes about the human impact of world events.

While *Years and Years* ultimately becomes about witnessing history, as Edith says in the final episode, 'we just lived through it', the combination of the queer story and the immigration story of Viktor remains with viewers.

Coda

Queer characters

We have seen in Chapters 1–3 that Davies was incorporating queer characters, in the words of the tabloid press, before it was 'trendy'. He did this in part as a political act and in part as a writer just writing their experience (of course, when your experience is political, that's also unavoidable). Cultural history for queer stories is part of a series of 'hidden histories', the narratives that were kept tucked away or hidden in plain sight, from the writers and artists who weren't able to be themselves or tell their stories, who still belong to that story, or to those who began to take those tentative steps but could not fully be themselves or tell their stories.

Queer cultural history is a complex one. There are the 'hidden histories' of literature from the likes of E. M. Forster or the stage works of Tennessee Williams. These men being specific examples of a larger group who didn't write about their 'real life' in fiction, who dared not reveal it to the world. Others were punished for being more open, such as Gore Vidal, whose work was blacklisted by the *New York Times* for its gay themes. There were, of course, those who broke through – Christopher Isherwood was open about his sexuality for all of his career and included queer characters in his work – most notably in *Good-bye to Berlin* (1939). Open about his sexuality while writing about his community, too, was Armistead Maupin with *Tales of the City*, serialised in 1978 and published that same year. It was later adapted for TV, and it managed to depict an out, proud, and largely happy, queer community. These are probably two of the most famous examples, and many other authors paved the way, such as Edmund White,

Andrew Holleran and Manuel Puig, who all told stories of gay men in literature during the years when it was still a risk. These writers were forerunners in carving out a culture of queer people at a time when TV and film certainly weren't giving LGBTQ+ characters a look-in, aside from when coded as villains or as figures of fun.

Variety of queer characters

Davies achieves significance in the variety of queer characters he incorporates in his writing. This is important, particularly in his early work when queer characters were very much of the 'token gay friend' variety on TV, and little more. Indeed, Peter Goodwin writes that 'independent production allowed new and alternative voices into television',[60] which Davies certainly did in *Queer as Folk*. Not only were there different types of 'gay men', but they were also just an array of characters. In particular, a class spectrum that showed working-class people could be gay too (something that was a hangover from Davies's love of soaps and something of a precursor to Antony Cotton's eventual triumphant *Coronation Street* role as a gay working-class character). In *Bob & Rose*, Davies shows the quiet, football-loving, 'away from the height of the "scene"', Bob as a central character. When we move to *It's a Sin*, the group of friends in that perhaps best illustrates Davies's commitment to showing many types of gay men; from the contradictory young-Tory-gay-man Ritchie to the southeast Asian teaching assistant in Ash, through to quiet, nerdy Colin and camp-as-Christmas Black man Roscoe. They illustrate many faces of queerness, and of course, the tragic face of the impact of AIDS.

Equally, Davies shows many ways to be queer. From Bob in *Bob & Rose* not having a label for his sexuality and to *Torchwood* and its fluid approach to gender and sexuality; almost from its opening moments, for example, the lead character, Captain Jack Harkness, nonchalantly mentions he was once pregnant. While gender fluidity isn't a central aspect of Jack's character, it's another reference to fifty-first-century concepts of gender and sexuality where he's from, being more evolved than twenty-first-century ones. Later, the other lead characters discuss Jack's sexuality. The culture website AfterElton opined that *Torchwood*'s most significant breakthrough might have been 'queer representation', by showing Captain Jack as a character whose bisexuality is explored but isn't his only character trait.[61] Equally, with the 'incidentally queer' characters in *Who*, from Midshipman Frame to, of course, Captain Jack, through to Luke Smith in *The Sarah Jane Adventures*, Davies laid down the possibilities to reflect the everyday queerness of the real world across time and space. As he said in a 2019 interview with *The Times*:

> It's been 20 years since *Queer as Folk*. Things are so much better than they were 20 years ago, but I do wonder, if you took soap operas out of the equation, how many gay characters would there be on television? I'm not sure the figure would be very encouraging. When I left *Doctor Who*, I pledged that I would write gay drama from now on. People laughed at me for making such a bold statement, but it's exactly what I've done, and I'm proud of living up to my promise.[62]

Davies has consistently been making queer drama and only queer drama since *Who*, using his powers to politically fight for the voices of queer writers and characters across TV. Why is that important, particularly in the second decade of the twenty-first century? As Davies said in the same interview:

> Simply being gay in the twenty-first century is a political act. There is not one day when we're not dragged into the headlines and either accused of something or used as an example, even without us doing anything. In America, it's even worse. You can guarantee that gay rights will be front and centre of the debate in an election. That politicises you.[63]

So, how has he led the conversation on TV around queer characters? Are his queer characters leading the way?

Political versus incidental queerness

There's a sense in writing queer TV that including a queer character becomes inherently political, or 'woke', to use a word beloved of the tabloid press. Indeed, it is; including queer characters remains, even today, inherently political. Davies saw this, again, when he cast Yasmin Finney (a transwoman) in *Doctor Who*. The reality is that existing as queer in stories on TV or performing in them as a queer actor remains a political act and will remain so until the playing field is levelled, when accurate and broad and equal representation is achieved. Even then, much of Davies's TV – from *Scandal* to *Sin* – has focused on rewriting and reclaiming history to include the stories not told.

So, yes, Davies's queer characters are political. Their inclusion is political, and their stories are political. Even though they don't all have a political story themselves, their impact is equally important. For example, Thorpe is influential in reclaiming that narrative for queer people telling their history. The *Sin* characters are essential for giving voice to that era of history. But the incidentally queer characters, too, are vital.

Midshipman Frame, who smiles across the bar at Captain Jack at 'The End of Time', is just as significant as a queer character as Stuart and Vince are. Or, despite their story not being *about* being queer, so are Viktor and Daniel in *Years and Years* because their inclusion means that stories about queer people, not just queer stories, are being told. That is something Davies has also become adept at. The way he incidentally made queer characters part of the fabric of *Who* was a testament to the fact that they exist as part of the fabric of the world (or worlds, in this case). That incidental queerness is essential, and far from incidental.

However, you can't do all of the things. Even when you do the best with good intentions, this is how it lands. In 2003, in the *Guardian*, Davies recalled hearing the impact of his work and the threefold impact it had:

> And I still don't know the answer. Come back in twenty years. But one story, in particular, haunts me and shows the difficulty of applying a simple 'good' or 'bad'. A gay teacher told me Nathan inspired a 15-year-old boy at his school to

come out. (Good.) In the yard, he was beaten up so severely that he had his cheekbones crushed. (Bad.) The teacher was so shocked that he and other staff members came out. (Good.) They formed a policy against homophobic bully-ing to the extent that the word 'gay' is no longer used as an insult in that school. (Good.) But weigh it up. Do three Goods cancel one Bad? Is that policy worth that kid's face? Am I responsible? For the face or the policy? When I say that I don't know, I mean it. I will never know.[64]

You can't represent all of time and space

This feeds into the element, too, of the idea that as much as Davies's queer characters are essential, incidental and political alike, some criticise him that he 'doesn't go far enough' or 'doesn't represent [insert type of queer person here]'. The honest answer is, no, he doesn't. Chapter Two: 'Can you show that on TV?' outlined how *Queer as Folk* tried to depict archetypes rather than 'realistic' or 'nuanced' characters. There was more criticism, too, when *Sin* aired, that the diversity of queer characters and queer women wasn't seen there either. The argument is that it was a very particular slice of life and moment in history and the characters perhaps served that. The irony, too, is that probably the most diverse depiction of the community comes in *Cucumber* and *Banana*, arguably the most overlooked of Davies's work. To link to the point above, the characters in those shows feel most diverse because they are the most contemporary in terms of the time of writing and when they are set.

All this illustrates why Davies's work is needed in queer stories; we don't have enough of them. One man's stories on the one side get derided by the right-wing press for being 'too queer' and on the other side by the community or queer press for being 'not queer enough'. Or he is putting 'too many gay characters in' or 'not enough'. The prob-lem isn't actually (usually) Davies's writing; it's that we're expecting a handful of writers, Davies included, to serve all of the queer identities and stories out there with a handful of programmes.

In short, we're expecting Russell T Davies to be the queer Doctor and solve all the problems of queer time and space armed with, in his case, not a TARDIS but a single script. As much as Davies's mind might be as infinite as the Doctor's, he can't be all things to all people.

Davies and all other writers should be held to account for their missteps – respectfully and without a Twitter mob, hopefully – but criticism should be constructive. So, in Davies's case, the critique of *Torchwood* and Ianto's story is valid, rooted in queer trauma of the past, and grounded, too, in a dramatic critique of the work. Similarly, so is the critique of Nathan's story in *Queer as Folk*, both in context and acknowledging that the seduction of a minor was never, and should never have been regarded, as 'ok'. Again, a critique of the work in context is valid. What isn't valid is the idea that Davies isn't showing the 'right kind of' gays or 'enough of…' or 'too much of…' because he can't be solely responsible for depicting all of queer time and space, even with a TARDIS.

Queer actors for queer roles

> 'Gay men always say that a handsome man on television is gay. So in the 1980s, we always used to say Phillip Schofield was gay,' Davies laughs. 'The lawyer [for *It's a Sin*] said, "No, you don't need to clear this with Schofield because he's straight. He's married with children; we don't need to check that." Only now he's come out! Isn't that weird?'[65]

As the title of Davies's iconic show says, 'there's nowt as queer as folk' and no predicting what might happen. Schofield's inclusion in that category now resembles a loving nod to the previously closeted TV presenter. When *It's a Sin* aired, it seemed a happy coincidence that he'd since come out. Of course, real life is seldom so smooth, and since the program aired – and indeed since the original draft of this book – Schofield has undertaken a very public fall from grace, which perhaps moves the joke back into slightly awkward territory, the blurring of lines between his coming out and other allegations against him making the situation less of a celebration than it once was.

The ongoing debate around 'queer actors for queer roles' is linked to this. Davies has been vocal and somewhat at the heart of the debate –

which rages far beyond him – of whether casting queer actors in queer roles should be standard practice. It has rumbled on across stage and screen for many years, and there's no clear-cut answer for many. For Davies, he has come down hard on the side of 'queer actors for queer roles', something that came up a lot while doing press for *It's a Sin*. Of that process, in *The Hollywood Reporter* in 2022, he said:

> Now, I don't just cast gay actors – I cast *out* gay actors. There's a great bed of actors now who are out of the closet, which is a brave new world to me. *It's a Sin* genuinely had a great big queer energy that rattled off the screen. I love the fact that it pisses people off.[66]

It's also tremendously queer energy to deliberately rile up the (straight) folks like that, or more accurately, the straight folks with a subscription to the *Daily Mail*. This wasn't an option when Davies made his first iconic queer drama. Firstly, going to press with that argument would likely have been detrimental to the show, but there weren't actors to choose from in the same way. As Davies remembered: 'It didn't exist as an argument because back then I kind of assumed that we couldn't cast gay actors. There just weren't enough out gay actors.'[67] Davies has worked in TV long enough to have seen this evolution, from fearful closeted silence to tentative first steps to those embracing queer roles. That is not to say that Davies has anything but respect for the men who helped make his iconic series. He recalls, again in *The Hollywood Reporter*, the *Queer as Folk* cast:

> The marvellous straight actors who we cast [including Aidan Gillen and Charlie Hunnam] were the foot soldiers and generals that led me to the luxury of being in this position. In 1998 if you would ask agents for a gay actor, there was no such thing.[68]

Davies isn't saying in his calls for casting – not even calls, just his commitment to our actors – that we were wrong to do otherwise. It's more a sense that: as times have changed, as attitudes have changed, then when we can, perhaps we should. It's ok, too, for things to evolve. There has been a natural evolution in how we write queer characters for screen (and beyond) as society has evolved, and the conversations about casting queer characters, too, has evolved. It was, after all, a different time. In the present day, too, we have to sit with the uncomfortable truth that we had to let straight actors pave the way for queer ones. As he continues about *Queer as Folk*'s cast:

> Lots of people we knew were gay, but a lot of actors ran away from it because they couldn't have faced the press launch where they would've been interrogated about it. There were some gay actors in it – Antony Cotton (Alexander) has been on *Coronation Street* ever since, and he's possibly the most famous gay man in Britain now.[69]

Times do change, thankfully, and by the time *It's a Sin* came around, there were an array of young queer actors Davies could cast in his drama. Perhaps more significant was the older actor guest starring in the first episode, in the form of Neil Patrick Harris, a gay man, happily 'out' and married to a man (David Burtka) who has been 'out' for much of a career spanning being a child star (*Doogie Howser MD*) through Broadway (*Rent, Hedwig and the Angry Inch*), TV sitcom (*How I Met Your Mother*), and more. Harris, however, has rarely played 'out' gay roles. His role as Henry in *It's a Sin* was a departure from his screen roles (Hedwig is an iconic queer role, as is the Emcee in *Cabaret*, which he has also been in, and which Callum Howells, who played his protégé Colin, has also recently played). In TV, he's best known for the womanising Barney Stinson in *How I Met Your Mother*, so playing Henry was a departure from that style of acting and type of role. Though he only appears in one episode, Henry might be Harris's finest performance to date. It's nuanced and sensitive and draws on his experience of a life that parallels his character's. Harris is old enough – like Davies – to remember the impact of AIDS on the community when he was a young man, to have suffered the loss of that and the impact on his own life. It's here, perhaps, more so than with the younger cast members, that we feel the weight of that. The queer energy of the young cast is important, but so is offering opportunities like this, to play men who share their experience, to actors like Harris. He went on after *It's a Sin* to star in Darren Star's comedy *Uncoupled* as a gay man, becoming a leading man in a show once more. Still, as a gay man, that feels a little like the confidence of Davies casting him, giving him a push towards a show where he could perhaps embrace a bit more of his whole self than in previous roles. Perhaps, in addition, Davies's stance on such things is essential.

It's crucial, too, because over the years that Davies has been writing for TV, times have naturally changed, but, also, younger generations of actors have come up through the ranks. Many of those younger actors, because of the positive shifts in society, are much more comfortable being 'out' if they are queer. Many, too, actively seek out queer roles (when they have the luxury of doing so) because they want to contribute to the telling of the kinds of queer stories they have benefited from, or simply because they enjoy playing roles aligned with personal experience. In short there are more 'out' queer actors now, enthusiastic about queer roles and about talking about those roles if cast in them.

The younger generation, again – Callum Howells, Olly Alexander, Nathaniel Curtis and Omari Douglas, to cite the *It's a Sin* cast – are entering the world of acting, *wanting* to be who they are and owning it. Those who have decided to be 'out', or at least not hide their sexuality, want to explore roles that reflect that. Is Davies saying they can't play straight? No, of course not, though, some like Tovey, by and large, choose not to play straight (of course, once given the luxury of being able to choose parts). But what Davies and these actors are advocating for is a chance to use their experience and acting skills, but also to feel comfortable on set. There is, after all, a shared language of queer people. This shared experience allows for a deeper delve into the material, accessing some spaces and emotions with the safety and support of a queer team. For some pieces like *It's a Sin*, that feels important, too. Davies isn't asking for a blanket ruling from Equity or similar, but as a queer man writing queer drama, it's his prerogative to cast as he sees fit. It's also undeniable that there is a particular lived experience that can be brought to the work by queer actors.

Of course, Davies isn't above being political, even a bit mischievous, to make the point. At which point, with queer actors still struggling against the wider homophobic machine, you have to say, good for him, really:

> All those straight people who sit there go, 'Oh, I'm perfectly happy with homosexuality, but don't you dare not cast me.' I know I've upset some people I've cast in the past who do not appreciate the decision.[70]

Is this a bit of pearl-clutching, after all the headlines and homophobia that Davies has encountered for breaking down the doors with queer characters? Well, it feels like a little bit of vindication that he can still upset them, just a little bit, with controversy.

Chapter Eight

Know your history:
It's a Sin

Davies's great labour of love, one which bookends neatly with *Queer as Folk*, was his plan to write a series depicting gay life during the 1980s and the UK AIDS crisis based on his and his friends' experiences, commemorating the generation who lost their lives to the illness. Davies told Ben Dowell of *Radio Times* about these plans, saying that it was 'the most research-based piece I will ever do'.[71] Davies has also talked of the script being a tough pitch due to the subject matter. He described being asked to start the story in an AIDS ward in the 1990s, then flashing back to the 1980s – a concept he dismissed as 'unbelievably crass'.[72] In fact he continued to refuse and instead waited it out until a new head of department was in place as he stated in *PinkNews*: 'In my experiences, all the bosses will leave their jobs every two or three years. So just sit still and the right person will enter the scat again.'[73] Then, under the right person, *It's a Sin* was commissioned five years after that initial conversation. That series was produced by Red Productions for Channel 4 and broadcast in 2021.

Pandemic parallels

It's a Sin began filming on 7 October 2019 – under the working title of *Boys* – and completed filming on 31 January 2020. The fact that it finished filming just before another pandemic happened, and would air during its ongoing impact, was something that couldn't have been foreseen – or maybe it could, given the way Davies, by paying attention, predicted as much in *Years and Years*. However, an AIDS drama airing during Covid added an extra echo of resonance and one we cannot, and should not, try to ignore.

Pandemics aren't interchangeable, but the reality of watching a TV drama about one pandemic while living through another must be taken into consideration. It was less than ideal, too, given that the comparison to Covid, while unavoidable, is also problematic. While comparisons with other pandemics do make a certain amount of sense on a surface level, AIDS and Covid are markedly different. Covid is airborne for starters, making transmission entirely different. The morality attributed to AIDS was different because it affected queer people (along with other groups deemed 'unacceptable' to society like drug users and sex workers, as well as racist connotations with the pandemic having started in Africa). Meanwhile, Covid was a worldwide phenomenon, and while some groups were disproportionately affected, it did not carry the same stigma as AIDS did (and still does).

And so, after so long getting *It's a Sin* made, Davies's hard-won work on AIDS ended inevitably being compared to what the wider world had just lived through in 2020–1. In one respect, it might have drawn on empathy, or at least shared experience of the fear, of an unknown virus that any viewer could now comprehend. This was picked up in reviews; The series was praised by Lucy Mangan of the *Guardian*, who called it a 'poignant masterpiece'.[74] Mangan drew comparisons to the Covid pandemic, expanding that in its wake she felt that people could 'empathise that bit more with the fear, uncertainty, and responses rational and irrational to the emergence of a new disease'.[75] That creation of empathy is a good thing. But there is a fine line between feeling empathy and equating the two viruses.

With Covid, there was less (not none, but less) of a way to put a moral value on who got it and who didn't. With AIDS, there was a very easy way to make scapegoats of those who got it; it was, after all, their 'fault' for being queer. So while we can make analogies between pandemics, how humans respond to disease and collective fear, the key component missing from Covid was homophobia. With AIDS, the underlying message was that these men deserved to die because of who they were.

Davies responds to both the setting of his drama and the context of its broadcast with a sentiment that seems ripped directly from the era of AIDS. He said to *The Times* in January 2021: 'Out of crisis comes great art – and out of that I think great things will come.'[76] That sentiment sounds very much like David Roman, writing on early AIDS drama, who said: 'Great art was forgone in favour of great ritual.'[77] However, maybe, with time and distance, what Davies can achieve is, indeed, great art out of the crisis.

What stories to tell?

How do you start an AIDS narrative? As explored later in this chapter, it's been done many times, and as Davies said:

> But you're scared of doing it justice. [He'd watched the great seminal Aids dramas – *The Normal Heart*, *Angels in America*.] And how can you live up to that? So it took me a long time to think of the things that hadn't already been said. There's a great temptation with Aids to fall into that argument of saying, 'All those lives lost – these might have been people who discovered the cure for cancer, they could have been doctors and professors, they could have enhanced society.'[78]

Interestingly, given that Davies namechecked *Angels in America* there, within the cast of *It's a Sin*, was Susan Brown, who had recently performed in the National Theatre's revival of *Angels* (2017/2018). There is a long-standing tradition of actors moving between AIDS narratives on stage and screen. While, particularly considering AIDS, the reluctance of some actors to take on 'gay' roles and associated prejudices was compounded, others leaned into it as a form of activism – making themselves as actors visible in gay roles, and AIDS dramas. Stephen Spinella and Joel Grey are two such actors who have taken parts in multiple AIDS and gay dramas across their careers.

Although a straight female actor, Brown's, appearance in two AIDS dramas in quick succession feels like a little nod to this.

It's a Sin was seminal in that it was one of the only versions of the story from a British perspective and one that, thanks to the distance of time that many other writers didn't have, was for many younger viewers their first insight into the AIDS story. For older viewers it was a painful, but cathartic, revisiting of that time.

Davies feels like a logical choice in British TV writers to tell this story, given his history with queer drama. The fact that it was also a hard-won show in terms of getting made is also indicative that perhaps things haven't moved on as much as we would like since *Queer as Folk*. With that, too, the work Davies has done in queer TV over the past two decades led to telling this story.

The drama, formed of five episodes, follows a group of friends who meet in 1981 over the next decade. Their lives in London are soon impacted by AIDS, and through various losses, they're shown living out their lives in the face of AIDS. The story ends in 1991 with their group altered greatly by the intervening decade. We're introduced to the group in the first episode, when, in September 1981, their lives converge. We meet Roscoe running away from home before his homophobic father can send him back to Nigeria. Ritchie moves to London from the Isle of Wight for university and looks forward to escaping from his strict parents. Ritchie meets Jill at university. Meanwhile, Colin arrives in London from Wales and begins an apprenticeship at a tailor's.

They all live in a run-down London flat called 'The Pink Palace'. The first death of the series is the friend Colin made at work – Henry – who dies of a mysterious 'rare cancer'. The next episodes see the impact of AIDS seep into their lives while they are also trying to carve out love and life in their twenties in London. At the close of the penultimate episode, Ritchie joins his friends in a protest against pharmaceutical firms profiting from AIDS. At the end of the protest, while getting arrested with his friends, Ritchie declares he will live. In the final episode, it is November 1991, and Ritchie's condition has worsened. He and Ash confess their feelings for one another while Jill helps care for Ritche. But when his parents discover, he's ill, and the truth of his illness, they take him home to the Isle of Wight. Ritchie's agent gives Jill and Roscoe his latest royalty cheque and tells them to use it to visit him. They do, but Ritchie's mum keeps them away. Despite trying, Jill meets with her one morning and learns Ritchie died alone the day before. Jill and Roscoe return to London. While Roscoe visits his parents, Jill continues supporting gay men with AIDS. We see Ritchie, Colin and everyone else one more time in a joyous flashback from years earlier.

Know your history

It's a Sin doesn't exist in isolation. It stands on the shoulders of over thirty years of HIV and AIDS stories. From the very beginning, the community used performance and storytelling to memorialise and as a means of activism. This was partly because the links between the queer and artistic communities were strong. Both saw art and stories as a way to respond. It was also a means to record a pandemic, being ignored by larger areas of society. Plays, novels, and later TV and film about AIDS have always existed for two key reasons: as a memorial to those lost and as an activist tool. *It's a Sin* carries on both traditions and builds on them.

David Roman was referenced earlier in this chapter, commenting that 'great art was forgone in favour of great ritual', which was the purpose of many early AIDS dramas. The gay community had connections both with AIDS and with theatrical communities, which meant that in urban centres with a high number of gay men, performance was an obvious tool to use to respond to the AIDS crisis. In the UK and the US, this meant that performance to raise money or awareness was a natural progression from using performance as a response to AIDS. These included Paul Rudnick's *Jeffery* (1996), Steven Dietz's *Lonely Planet* (1994) and Terrence McNally's *Love! Valour! Compassion!* (1995). *The Normal Heart* (1985) by Larry Kramer is a seminal text in AIDS theatre. Kramer's work combines an activist message with an emotional connection, which is something Davies is also familiar with. *It's a Sin* builds on these plays' long legacy. Still, in particular, Kramer is conscious in his angry, emotional activist voice in his writing of standing on the shoulders of other queer men and paving the way for the future, much like Davies is in *Sin* and across his work. It's reminiscent of the speech in Larry Kramer's seminal *The Normal Heart* that begins 'I belong to a culture' in which protagonist Ned Weeks recalls the gay men of history who have been lost: Walt Whitman, Herman Melville, Tennessee Williams, Byron, E. M. Forster, Lorca, Auden, and so on. Here, a through-line of queer culture in its hidden histories and struggles is interconnected. In telling AIDS stories, this is vital. This legacy is important, as it is what Davies draws on and what he gives an alternative narrative to.

There's also a shortage of original British works. In terms of theatrical output on AIDS, these are limited to Kevin Elyot's *My Night with Reg* (1994) and Andy Kirby's *Compromised Immunity* (1986), both created by Gay Sweatshop Company. Elyot's work was moderately successful; it spawned a film version and transferred to New York, albeit in a small off-Broadway theatre. In other British writing, the closest any other text comes to being an 'AIDS Play' is Mark Ravenhill's much later text, *Some Explicit Polaroids* (1999). In Ravenhill, AIDS is part of the tapestry of the character's world. Like Elyot, the focus was effect and impact rather than a political or medical analysis of the condition. This small output of British AIDS plays indicates that depictions of AIDS in original British productions were limited. The lack of British-originated AIDS plays can be linked to various socio-cultural factors, as well as to the theatrical landscape of the UK. In the UK, the provision of healthcare, combined with the later impact of the epidemic, meant that the UK's cultural and political response differed from that of the US. Davies's writing becomes even more important in light of this, highlighting the activist history of AIDS in the UK, as well as the stories of those affected.

The different responses in activism and protest cited above are reflected in these theatrical responses; in the UK, dramas such as Elyot's and Ravenhill's, looked at AIDS through its emotional impact on people and relationships as part of a wider set of issues in their lives. In the UK, where healthcare was a given, and the government treated AIDS seriously from the outset, the theatrical discussion shifted to the personal impact. British writers also wrote later than their American counterparts, not so much following a lead, but offering a different perspective and account. It stands to reason, therefore, that the most prominent theatrical texts on AIDS in the UK were two which combined the domestic, emotional response to AIDS with the political facets. This is something that Davies has done throughout his career, and we see this in *It's a Sin*.

Here, you can feel Davies standing on the shoulders of what went before, the good and bad. You can feel the honesty missing from *Philadelphia* (1993) or even films like *Holding the Man* (2015), where everything is a bit clean and nice. Instead, you can feel the same visceral urgency of action that was present in stage dramas. You can feel the political anger of Kushner in *Angels in America* and the raw grief Kramer shows in *The Normal Heart*. But you can also feel Davies opening these dramas, filling in the gaps of stories they didn't tell.

Crucially, Davies also tells the British story of that era that didn't get told. On stage, British theatre had a handful of 'gay plays' that companies like Gay Sweatshop and smaller fringe theatres performed. The UK didn't have an *Angels* or *The Normal Heart*. The only real 'AIDS play' to have prominent productions was Kevin Elyot's *My Night with Reg*, which worked as a British response. It was funny, self-deprecating, and skirted the issue in typically British fashion. TV continued to skirt the issue, except in medical dramas and with muted soap mentions. By the time Davies himself was writing his seminal *Queer as Folk* in the 1990s, it felt like the moment had passed for that story. And instead, *Queer as Folk* focuses on the post AIDS world for gay men.

It's A Sin fills a historical gap in those stories. The plays, the literature, and even the passing references on TV, were responding 'in real time' or thereabouts. They were a combination of written-in-the-moment grief and rage or a 'what can we get past the censors?' approach to sharing the stories. With time and distance, Davies can side-step those elements and deliver a sense of perspective not seen in other dramas. Davies now has the luxury of perspective and time to be selective about which stories to tell and how they are told.

How does Davies tell that story?

The way to tell AIDS stories has always been to humanise them. When the world was ostracising, demonising those with AIDS, the early AIDS dramas sought to make the virus human, to enforce compassion. Thirty years later, Davies's approach is the same, but for a different end – to humanise history. To make the story effective, the characters depicted must come out of history and into the present. Davies, whose skill has always been his believable characters and his empathy, does this in a typically emotive style.

He shows friendship, too; we, as viewers, are pulled into the friendship circle. The first episode sets up an inter-generational circle of queer characters, from the university students Ritchie, Jill and Ash to young Colin, the tailor's apprentice. Meanwhile, they have older mentor characters in 'Gloria', the older man in Ritchie and Ash's circle, or Henry, the older tailor who mentors Colin in queerness as much as tailoring. The circle of friends becomes ever more important as it inevitably starts to shrink.

We first see the older characters go. This is extremely central because while it replicates what was happening at the time – people being lost – Davies also references the lost generation of queer elders. What we see with Gloria and Henry used to be the norm; older queer people, in this case, men, informally 'mentoring' younger ones, particularly in the workplace or in the straight society, like Henry with Colin. But also more broadly, being perhaps a father or uncle-like figure who has lived through what the younger generation is going through and been an outsider to their own family – as we see with Roscoe in the series. Many queer young people needed that. AIDS wiped out a generation of elders. The people of Ritchie and his contemporaries' generation, and the ones after that, grew up without those elders. Many of them watched them die. The older narratives on AIDS perhaps didn't address this as they were still in the midst of it. But with some distance, Davies can include this, highlighting the ongoing influence of this loss.

Of course, the loss of the contemporaries of the younger generation of gay men accompanies this. The power of losing someone your age when you are both still young is dramatic, and the losses are profound as they start to add up in *It's a Sin*. Davies employs his classic approach of 'killing off the unexpected one' with sweet, quiet Colin. We sort of know when we start watching the series that we're going to watch Ritchie die – given the premise, it seems obvious – and we expect some other deaths along the way. But Colin isn't who we expect to see die. This both plays into audience assumptions, as well as dramatically offering a sucker punch. It plays into expectations because we naively assume that Colin won't get sick, because he's a 'good' boy. Because we don't see him having sex like the other boys in the story, we assume he's safe. That's exactly the subtle political point Davies is making – there are 'good' and 'bad' narratives of AIDS we have all absorbed over the years. Colin's death should be no more shocking than anyone else's, but it is. That highlights the audience's prejudices and assumptions; it sits uncomfortably with the emotion of losing Colin.

However, all the deaths are devastating, and Davies is unflinching in the reality of AIDS at that time. It's a hard watch, and rightly so. We find Henry dying alone in a hospital ward that nobody will enter; his partner has gone home, leaving him having no visitors, until Colin appears, lying about being his nephew. We see his body unceremoniously wrapped and taken to the morgue by hospital employees afraid to touch him. We see Gloria taken home by his parents, revolted by him; they burn all his belongings after his death. Later we see the reality of the physical impact of AIDS on Colin and Ritchie. Colin gets dementia; he's sexually inappropriate, masturbating in front of his friends and loses the capacity to edit his thoughts. Then he slips into a waking coma and is all but gone but still alive while his friends and mother look on. We see Ritchie, too, move through all manner of medication, going to bed at 7pm and being cared for by Jill. It's a slow burn and an unflinching look at the physical impact. Davies doesn't play it hard in showing the medical, but the glimpses are enough. We see Ritchie's room at home getting populated by medical equipment, and we're slowly aware of the physical impact and decline on these characters. We're forced also to confront the kind of medical reality it's often too easy to look away from.

That's key to the difficult parts of *It's a Sin*; Davies forces us to look at the uncomfortable. But in so doing, he pulls us in with the heart and love within the story. So many AIDS dramas rest on the notion of community, of chosen family; from *The Normal Heart* to *Rent*, the idea of a community coming together to care for those sick and dying is at the heart of those stories, and *It's a Sin* is no different. What Davies gives us is an insight into how communities rallied, and those who fell through the cracks. For every Colin, there's a Gloria, destined to be with a family who didn't love them at their worst as they should. For every Ritchie with friends desperate to care for him, there was a Henry all but forgotten. Davies shows us both sides. But ultimately, that story of community, learning, changing and rallying comes out. The fact that the community extends to parents – like Colin's lovely mam, through to women like Jill – is a reminder that against the difficulty there was hope and community.

The story starts with friendship and ends with friendship. We see the group finding each other – a classic story of queer chosen family – we see the happy, carefree times that mirror times depicted in *Queer as Folk*, *Cucumber*, *Banana*, even *Bob & Rose*, but we also know they're doomed to heartbreak. The use of the joy of humour before that is what makes it effective. Even in the face of the worst of times, there's humour, triumph and love – romantic, sexual and platonic. The story is powerful for those universal themes. It's also what made it accessible to straight audiences seeing the reality of AIDS for the first time. It's what made it so powerful. Both queer and straight audiences, old and young, were pulled into the story.

Importance and impact

It was, of course, an anticipated drama. In January 2021, *The Times* called it 'the most talked-about show of the moment'.[79] It was likely to get attention with the pedigree of Davies and the potentially controversial subject matter – or at least homophobe-inducing subject matter. The first episode, when aired on Channel 4, was watched by 1.6 million people, a benchmark provided by the launch of *Deadwater Fell*, a year previously. It was Channel 4's best-performing drama among young viewers (in the sixteen to thirty-four age bracket). Catch-up views hit 2.5 million within three days. Channel 4 revealed on 4 February 2021 that the series had to that point gained 6.5 million views on All 4.[80] This gave the streaming service its highest monthly figures for January, nearly doubling the previous highest figure. The series was the biggest hit to date on the channel's streaming service, becoming the 'most binged new series' on there. By 1 March, this number had gone up to 18.9 million. The same press release from Channel 4 also reported on the drive in HIV testing catalogued following the drama during HIV Testing Week 2021.

The critical consensus too was positive; it went on to have multiple award nominations, on top of record-breaking viewing figures. However, in terms of awards, it wasn't the board-sweeping success the public response indicated.

Difficult queer TV

Despite being nominated for many awards at the BAFTAs, Russell T Davies's seminal series on the AIDS pandemic didn't take any home. Was this because we still can't say AIDS on TV? Was it because we don't want to acknowledge queer TV as doing the best work on TV? Yes, almost certainly, to both questions. But also, it could be because *It's a Sin* is *difficult* queer TV.

It's a Sin was important TV; the response on social media said it all in many ways: shock and sadness. Many people were hearing this story for the first time, or at least in a way that made them listen.

Or, on the flip side, for those familiar with the story, it was an emotional reckoning like no other. The idea that you know what's coming and can do nothing to stop it is, well, let's face it, the biggest allegory for AIDS you could ask for. I struggled, too, hearing friends, acquaintances and strangers who had lived the story talking about reliving it. *It's a Sin* was complex for those who knew the story, who lived it, or who already had educated themselves, knew their history.

There have been valid critiques of how the story was told. But in the short version, we can't expect one show about AIDS to tell *all* the AIDS stories. It proves the point we need more stories. We have dozens, if not hundreds, of TV stories about cancer. We never expect one to represent all people with cancer – because we have a choice of so many, it doesn't matter.

In the same way, we don't expect every romantic drama about straight people to be everyone's experience, but we often do for queer ones. Because for straight ones, flip the channel, and there's another. For gay ones, wait until next year.

On the one hand, it didn't matter. Because *It's a Sin did* get the attention of people outside the community, outside the people who already knew the story. That was amazing; that was the thing it perhaps did best, telling that story. But its undoing made it so powerful: it was honest, raw and real.

The scene that springs to mind is not any of the hospital scenes and the brutal realities of what happened to these men (in this instance, given men were the focus), it's the scene early on, an awkward bedroom encounter where Ash tells Ritchie that he 'needs a wash'. In all, its awkwardness captures the realities of sexual encounters between men and at once all the things you've never been told until you have. Why this moment? Because I've so rarely seen conversations like that on TV. It's about sex and not about sex. Other shows that did it well were *The L Word* and HBO's *Looking*, and yes, even the original *Queer as Folk*. It's as much a boring detail as it is a revolutionary one because we aren't allowed to talk logistics of gay sex, but it's a large part of life. Again, on the contrary, we get a *lot* of straight sex in our lives.

It's not about the sex in that it's the kind of detail that resonates if you're connected to the community. It's the kind of authenticity, dare I say, to the story that made it powerful. But it's also a story that sits in the less glossy moments, which is both its power and undoing. Because talking about needing to wash your bum before sex is funny, but it's also uncomfortable. It's all the things we're told we're not to talk about in polite company. It's all the things about gay men that form part of the mockery (and I won't speak of that in detail as it's not my place). It's discomfort for an audience.

And that's what *It's a Sin* did so well; it sat in the discomfort of the story and the discomfort of straight audiences. The story doesn't gloss over the horrors of AIDS, of course. But it also didn't present a group of straight-conforming and 'adorable' gay men or gay men's experiences. It presented messy, flawed gay men doing things that made each other uncomfortable, doing morally questionable things, making poor life choices, and making life choices wider society frowned upon. None of it was sanitised, and that's the difference.

That's the uncomfortable element. In recent years, straight audiences, in particular, have embraced 'queer shows' but only on their terms, only the 'safe' ones. The shows with huge fan followings – *Schitt's Creek*, *Love, Victor* and *Heartstopper* – are three of the most successful ones that show *safe* portrayals of gay men. They're heteronormative, sweet and romantic.

This is in no way an attack on these shows. *Heartstopper* is a phenomenal thing we all needed and never before had the likes of. I believe *Love, Victor* is charming and wonderful. They have a place for young and older audiences. So do the charming, inoffensive, but enormously important shows like *Schitt's Creek*. We need these 'safe spaces' of queer TV where all is well. But we need difficult TV, too. These shows are all shows that straight audiences feel 'safe' with because they replicate versions of the world they feel safe in, one in which gay men follow heteronormative patterns, focusing on love and romance (and, again, hurrah for that). They are an easy stepping stone into the queer experience and should be applauded.

It's a Sin wasn't a stepping stone; it was a full-on baptism of fire. That's perhaps why it struggled to win awards and why it was difficult to sustain the interest beyond that initial shock moment – because it was a shock. That's also perhaps why it'll take a while for the show to truly be appreciated for what it was.

What was it? A rallying cry for paying attention to history while also making sure history was told.

In the end, too, the awards won't matter. *It's a Sin* will have a long life, being viewed by people who need it. Just as the 'important' gay works have done before, it's critical to note that it comes from its legacy of AIDS drama, originating on the stage, too, and owes its debt to history. From Larry Kramer's *The Normal Heart* to Tony Kushner's *Angels in America* and also *Rent*. Perhaps the best we can ask is for those who saw *It's a Sin* to seek out those stories, too, to see what went before, and to demand more, demand history be told.

Also, as a footnote, I know the show is named after the Pet Shop Boys' song, but I can't help but hear Harper in *Angels* every time: 'It's a sin, and it's killing us.' Maybe there's something in that…

Part of a legacy and opening a door

Not every story is in *It's a Sin*. A key element of criticism of the series is that it doesn't represent all the affected people. Are the women in the show a good representation of women? Can we do better with Black characters in LGBTQ+ stories? These are valid questions, but the question of 'Why doesn't *It's a Sin* represent everyone?' should be reframed as 'Why are we expecting this one TV series to do it all?' We should be grateful this story now exists while being mindful that it is only part of a larger narrative.

It must exist now because, for many, tragically, it's the first time they are hearing this story. For others, tragically, it's the first time they are seeing their story told. For those reasons, shocking and compassionate moments are important in equal measure. In the UK, a whole generation had a history of LGBTQ+ culture erased from their education and mostly from their lives, by the impact of Section 28. When gay lives couldn't be discussed in schools or in any 'official' capacity, a whole chunk of history disappeared.

It is perfectly reasonable to interrogate the representation seen in Davies's series as we would any series. But we cannot hold him responsible for a deficit in thirty years of TV stories because we still don't have the LGBTQ+ stories on TV that we need, and we haven't told the AIDS stories we need to.

It's A Sin fills a gap and continues this long legacy of vital stories. Davies does what he does best in putting his stamp on this; he devastates us but ends the story with joy and, more importantly, with hope. Anyone who has watched anything he's written knows that dealing with loss, with character death, head-on, is something he's never shied away from. Here it's done with typical honesty, unflinchingly, and just like in real life, often when we least expect it. Davies's other hallmark is humour, and that's here, too, where you least expect it because that's what life is, light and shade. Just because a person becomes ill doesn't mean the world stops around them; life goes on. There's an unspoken additional chapter to Davies's story, maybe one he'll explore later, that the community went on without those who were lost. They went on and lived and lost more, and also laughed more. That's the unspoken tragic note in the series; Davies and others are left to tell those stories.

While people of all generations are talking about being devastated by the stories about AIDS that they're hearing for the first time in *It's a Sin* or by the memories that it brings back, it feels like Davies's message of hope will be the one that endures, that this is the 'new' message for this generation of telling AIDS stories.

We can still revisit the anger and the grief that is a call to action and activism. We can sit with the sadness that is a memorial to those lost, but we can also find the hope that Davies shows us – the chosen families, the caring relationships, the family that rallied around and that started taking activist action and political engagement – and use those lessons for this next stage in telling these stories.

Coda

AIDS

It might seem that Davies didn't write about AIDS before *It's a Sin*, but that's not strictly true. The threads are there in *Queer as Folk*, and, as we have seen, in *Torchwood*. But it's also there, indirectly, in his activist writing. AIDS changed how queer writers wrote, and Davies is part of that conversation. In *Years and Years*, Davies invokes the words and spirit of past generations. In 1983 Larry Kramer stated in *The Native*: 'If this article doesn't scare the shit out of you, we're in real trouble. If what you're hearing doesn't rouse you to anger, fury, rage, and action, gay men will have no future here on earth.'[81] Kramer continued to use his writing as a force for activism. Through his play *The Normal Heart* (1985), he achieved more in the way of activism than arguably anything else he did. Kramer and others like Tony Kushner and Kevin Elyot wrote their activism through entertainment. For them, the vehicle was the theatre; for Davies, it has always been TV. Instead of the podium and a march, Davies uses the power of a TV screen. Reaching into living rooms, where comfortable life might have blinded many to the fight that still goes on, again, he is confronting people with these scenes, echoing Kramer. He's asking, as Kramer did in his AIDS play *The Normal Heart*, 'How long does it take before you get angry and fight back?' He would do this again with *It's a Sin*, and these two dramas illustrate that Davies is more than the guy who writes gay drama or puts gay characters in a show about aliens. He is a true activist in his writing.

One of the first ways Davies was able to integrate queer representation and queer issues into his work was through *Children's Ward*, which included a reference to AIDS. This was 1993, and the impact of the AIDS pandemic was being felt. There had been public information films and thousands of deaths, yet due to the homophobic, right-wing government and the impact of Section 28, the conversations about AIDS with young people weren't happening. Or if they were happening, it was through the lens of homophobia. In writing for *Children's Ward*, Davies drew attention to this, in an episode about a teenage boy contracting HIV.

The overall storyline was designed to show that it isn't only gay people who get HIV – the boy gets it from a blood transfusion. Davies's writing also opens the broader conversation about homophobia. TV storylines at that time were largely negative, and homophobia presented a challenge to any discussion on HIV/AIDS, and Davies had just a small corner of children's TV. For many, too, this might have been the first accurate depiction of HIV they saw, and it challenged other perceptions, which was important.

AIDS and *Queer as Folk*

The gay press criticised *Queer as Folk* for not addressing the issue of the AIDS epidemic. However, Davies has since commented that this was a deliberate choice; in his eyes, the community had seen enough heartbreak over AIDS, and he wanted to separate this watershed moment in drama from it. Davies did what many writers for the stage did post-AIDS: he found things to celebrate and get lost in rather than dwell on the pain of AIDS.

AIDS does exist in the *Queer as Folk* universe – we see Stuart pinning on an AIDS ribbon before a meeting. In true Stuart style, he does it to signify to another man he's gay (and in Stuart style, to lead him to have sex in the work toilets). In the same episode (Series 1, Episode 2), Romey (the mother of Stuart's baby via sperm donation) asks him to sign various documents relating to the baby. In one of these, she says '...if you get ill'. They talk around it and never mention 'AIDS', but it is implied. While Davies early on chooses to gloss over the issue, he acknowledges the reality of AIDS in the world.

In one respect, this is a glossing over of AIDS; at this point, AIDS was a chapter far from over. Does Davies's writing make light of it? There's a moment where Stuart shouts to another man asking how his boyfriend is, and the man replies, 'Still dead.' Was this, too, a reference to AIDS? Possibly, given that the man is Stuart's age. Also, as mentioned above, Stuart uses an AIDS ribbon to mark himself out as gay, which is a nod to other methods in decades past, like handkerchief codes. Is this an uncomfortable moment? Possibly. Some could have felt it was inappropriate. But we also see from Stuart's response to Romey that his attitude towards AIDS is one of 'turning a blind eye'. His promiscuity and a lack of conversation around safe sex in the show might suggest that Stuart engages in 'risky sex'. But the point is, he is a character, a flawed one on many levels, and this might be one of his flaws. Davies isn't positing Stuart as a role model; he's presenting a character and, to go back to the archetypes discussion, a certain 'kind' of gay man through using an AIDS ribbon to indicate his sexuality and procure sex, his dismissal of Romey's concerns and his sexual behaviour.

Stuart's attitude to AIDS is essential, too, as it represents, as all the characters in *Queer as Folk* are supposed to, a facet of gay society at that point in time. Stuart, at almost thirty, is old enough to remember AIDS but not old enough to have fully lived through the worst of it. Therefore, he represents a younger generation who is slightly 'over it' or doesn't appreciate the impact. Again, not all younger men were like this, but some were: feeling like the worst had passed, or just not wanting to have their lives dictated by it, as they'd seen in the generation before. Or perhaps, too, it was a case of sheer ignorance, as they had done most of their schooling under Section 28. They were denied any actual acknowledgement of queer people beyond the narrative of 'Don't Die of Ignorance' (the AIDS awareness campaign rooted in Thatcherite homophobia). So, while Davies is commenting by not fully engaging with AIDS through Stuart, he is also commenting on some gay men's response to the crisis in this era.

Is Stuart himself a symbol of something more towards AIDS, the men who came of age in the era of AIDS and chose to believe it wouldn't happen to them? Stuart believes he's invincible on many levels, why not against AIDS, too? He's also a Peter Pan character, immune to growing up and being responsible. So, again, why not be

AIDS

invincible in the face of AIDS? Is this the narrative many previous
(and future) AIDS dramas would want? No, there was in those an
overriding sense of 'responsibility', but as discussed in the previous
chapter Stuart Jones is not a role model. We see it elsewhere in his
attitude to drugs (he takes dog worming pills without much thought)
and even his reckless driving 'skills'. Stuart Jones believes nothing can
kill him, least of all AIDS. But beyond that, he's a certain kind of man,
the kind of man who thinks, 'if I'm likely to die of AIDS then I might
as well live'. Stuart, like Henry in *Cucumber*, is a product of the trauma
of the AIDS years on gay men, even if perhaps he isn't aware of it, and
writing him, too, is a way for Davies to show the broader impacts.

As much as it is a 'glossing over' of the impact of AIDS, *Queer as
Folk* also serves an essential purpose on TV – a statement that gay
men were more than AIDS. By the time it aired, AIDS had been the
central narrative of gay men in real life and media/culture and news
for a decade. Rightly so, as it was an emergency, there was also a
sense of fatigue with only bad news stories, reducing gay men only to
stories about AIDS. What Davies did in choosing not to incorporate
AIDS heavily, was to make a statement that there is more to the gay
community than just the virus. The focus of *Queer as Folk* was on the
relationship between the group of men (and the women, peripherally)
rather than letting AIDS take the forefront, reminding viewers that
gay men are more than just the headlines.

In Phil's death, we see the shadow of AIDS, indirectly, proving that
perhaps you don't have to talk about AIDS for it to be present in the
narrative. Phil dies tragically and far too young. At his funeral, we get
a sense of world-weariness about it and a sense of the hangover of
AIDS. Firstly, Phil had planned his funeral, at only thirty-ish. Straight
people, by and large, haven't had to do that. Despite Stuart declaring it
weird, Vince also confirms he's planned his. It's subtle, but the impact
of AIDS influenced this. Having watched what happened to others,
there is a consciousness that dying young might be a reality for many
of them. Has Stuart secretly planned his? Maybe. Or maybe he assumes
Vince would do it for him.

The show also gives a sense of the funeral as a social occasion. As morbid as it is, the idea of all the men coming together (and when we see Phil's funeral, it's all young men aside from his family) reflects on the funerals of those who have died of AIDS. There's also the campish frivolous side to such a funeral – from Phil's requesting 'D.I.S.C.O.' read aloud by Vince to the after-party being something of a combined catch-up and cruise for the guests. Dark? Yes. Indicative of the reality for many, also, yes. Also indicative of Davies referencing the impact of AIDS and how it has shifted and changed the community without directly saying it. We see this in a couple of darker and more serious moments, too.

There's also a sense of *Queer as Folk* being a transition piece between the AIDS-dominated narrative work of the previous years, towards a future that would acknowledge the pandemic and incorporate other facets of gay life. The carefree nature of Stuart, Vince and others gave both a nod to an earlier carefree time and a nod to a hopeful future. They have problems, sure – they often create problems for themselves – but their problems aren't just related to AIDS. That felt, too, like a statement affecting gay men, not the one issue that had been the focus. It also looks forward to a world where gay men live with the impact of AIDS and the reality of HIV in their everyday lives, but their stories and lives aren't dominated by it.

As many other shows would pick up in the coming decade, gay men needed good news stories. After a decade of stories about death and the loss that AIDS brought, there was also a need for light relief. It's not hyperbole to say that after being defined by tragedy, perhaps the community needed the antics of Stuart and Vince as much as maybe Davies needed to write about them. There is, too, the capacity for simultaneously being a conscious, political gay man (or other queer denomination) and enjoying the fun of Vince and Stuart. After all, the straight community had *Sex and the City* at this time, which wasn't claiming to be either documentary or political commentary. So *Queer as Folk* offered a similar, exaggerated version of what perhaps life 'could' be like.

Jack, infected blood and 'Children of Earth'

In the final TV instalment of *Torchwood*, there was a storyline involving infected blood that bears more than a passing correlation to AIDS narratives. Ultimately though, and unfortunately, it wasn't one that was particularly effective, and it was at times outright questionable in its approach.

There is a strange, slightly uncomfortable element of that story in light of Jack Harkness as a queer man; the use of his blood is central to the plot. To summarise the plot of *Torchwood: Miracle Day* (the title of the fourth series of *Torchwood*), on the same day across the Earth, the concept of death is suddenly erased when it is found that people who have suffered mortal wounds or fatal diseases are unable to die. This is initially seen as a religious miracle, but the absence of deaths begins to strain medical resources and spread diseases around the globe; the world's governments estimate that unless something is done, within four months the world will be unable to sustain the population growth. Meanwhile, Jack's immortality disappears. Against the backdrop of the world, governments institute a plan to bring those people that would typically have died from illnesses or injury into camps without exception. Torchwood infiltrates a camp and discovers the patients incinerated in the camps. Team Torchwood reveals this to the world, hoping governments will be forced to stop, but they are seen as justified.

Meanwhile, there's a link to leading Catholic families via Jack and a strange bloodletting ceremony he'd been part of. Eventually, Jack traces things back to his blood, getting into 'the Blessing' (a link that powered the 'Miracle Day'). The only way to stop the 'Miracle Day' and let everyone affected die is to put Jack's 'mortal' blood back into 'the Blessing'. They do, and Jack's immortality is restored, and death is returned to the world.

This plot is tricky to wrap your head around in more ways than one. In one respect making the queer character's infected blood, the 'saviour' element for the planet is a good thing. As discussed in the section on his character, Captain Jack is hugely important for this. Yet something about this doesn't sit quite right; infected blood and queer male characters simply never will. Coupled with it being *Jack* specifically – the self-styled 'slutty bisexual' who we know has had sex with all of time and space by this point – the two make for slightly uncomfortable viewing.

Davies had to be aware of the implications of this – the man who spent nearly a decade trying to get his own AIDS drama made. Any gay man who lived through the 1980s and 1990s could not fail to see the implications of using blood in any narrative in this way – metaphorically or literally (Davies does both here). The power, the danger of blood is so ingrained in people who lived through AIDS in that era. Davies must have written this deliberately, with good intentions, but it somehow feels uncomfortable. It's probably meant to feel redemptive; we learn that the queer man's blood can fix things, but only after he is blamed, after the damage is done, and when his blood is used, people will still die. It's a clumsy metaphor or analogy for AIDS and one that falls just short of working.

Other allusions to AIDS

AIDS is not absent from Davies's other work, whether in the periphery of life or other allusions. As discussed in the chapter on *Years and Years* (Chapter Seven: 'The future is a scary place'), there are subtle allusions to AIDS in the Monkey Flu epidemic. It feels more pointed given the 2022 rise in Monkeypox. The rhetoric mirrored AIDS more clearly, but even when Davies was writing, the allusions were clear. There are also obviously mirrors in how Covid was framed and the treatment of different groups. But in the broader spectrum of Davies's work, we can confidently read the allusions to AIDS, mainly as we know he was thinking about writing *It's a Sin* at this point in his career.

In *Years and Years*, then, when Monkey Flu takes hold, we see the government (under right-wing Vivienne Rook) put people into camps. They're essentially left to die/be extradited from society. While there is a bigger analogy at work – right-wing governments removing 'undesirable' people from society (immigrants, people of colour, poor people) – the fact that Viktor, a gay man, is one of these groups, too, is a clear analogy to AIDS. The idea of isolating gay men during AIDS is, after all, not new. AIDS wards kept men isolated (as Davies shows in *It's a Sin*) initially through fear of the illness, but also with underlying homophobia. It is not a stretch for camps and permanent removal from society to be part of such a plan. In *Years and Years*, Davies shows us the future through an alternate version of the past – what if the extreme right-wing views had won in AIDS, would we have seen AIDS camps? Quite possibly.

The element that stopped that, and what Davies also shows in *Years and Years*, is community mobilisation; in AIDS, community action was meant to care for those with AIDS and fight again. In *Years and Years*, Davies shows the community fighting back – led, of course, in this instance by Edith. In a neat mirror to the 'Jills' of the world, as shown in *It's a Sin*, Edith is the person who has a personal connection in Viktor, which is the start of her reason to help, yet she is conscious of the bigger picture. In showing a woman riding in and taking direct action, we can see Davies referencing the women who fought the battles of AIDS activism. While Edith and the Monkey Flu storyline in *Years and Years* together form a commentary on bigger issues, they, too, have strong links to AIDS history and activism, here subtly referenced by Davies before he wrote his full AIDS drama in *It's a Sin*.

Cucumber and *Banana* and the longer reach of AIDS

The most overt/direct references to AIDS come in *Cucumber* and *Banana*, where the long-term impact of it is shown. Generally, attitudes towards safe sex from the younger and older generations are also seen (more directly addressed here than in *Queer as Folk*). But, they are also shown in Henry's conversation with his date about it. It was a robust conversation, and it was the first time that Davies addressed those times.

As Henry sits in a diner with a gay man he's just met, they have an honest conversation about the fears of those times. It seems, perhaps, to straight audiences an odd conversation to have with a stranger. Here, Davies is showing the trauma bond that gay men who lived through that era have. For Henry, too, it's an interesting conversation, representing a contrast to the likely conversations of the generation shown in *It's a Sin* later. Henry's generation both knew the worst of

AIDS, and at the same time, no different, they weren't old enough to either remember or experience the carefree pre-AIDS era. They also weren't the 'first generation' affected, they were the 'second wave'. Henry's generation feels both a sense of never knowing different and longing for something they almost had.

The honesty with which Henry talks about his generation's fear of AIDS and its impact on his life, and sex life, is refreshingly candid and unheard of on TV. In AIDS stories, we often see the *It's a Sin* or even what we might call the *Casualty* model – the medical moments, the moments where people are impacted because they have it (and most likely on TV, dying of it). What we get with Henry is a reflection on living with AIDS in the broader sense – living in a world where it still affects life. Again, this might be something of a revelation for straight audiences for whom AIDS has likely faded into 'something of the past', but for Henry, it is still authentic for both the impact on life/ sex and the long-term emotional impact.

The emotional trauma he refers to in the conversation is something rarely addressed and is confronted honestly here, too. While Henry does not have HIV himself, living through the worst years of the pandemic has left emotional scars on him and many gay men. He recalls the fear of wondering if he had HIV, of checking his body, and the compulsive fear around every new mark/illness. While that fear might be a thing of the past for those who lived through it as Henry's generation did as twenty-somethings, that age of fear is hard to shake. *Cucumber* is very powerful in a brief scene acknowledging what little queer TV has done; how scarred a generation of gay men is from that fear, and the long-ranging impact of living through AIDS on them.

It's a Sin and the morality of sex

It is, of course, in *It's a Sin* that Davies addresses AIDS head-on, and the full impact of that is discussed in Chapter Eight: 'Know your history'. However, the subject is worth considering separately as a bookend to *Queer as Folk*.

Davies weaves a fine line in *It's a Sin*, between showing sexual free-dom and the unintentional but unfortunate and deadly consequences of that. He asks challenging questions on the morality of sex under the siege of AIDS and acknowledges that not everyone responded 'well' to it. On the one hand, he has Jill telling Ritchie it's pointless to attribute blame to who might have given him AIDS or whom he might have infected. On the other hand, the group talks about Colin and the fact that he didn't sleep around and still died of AIDS. We see the extremes of sexual approaches in Colin, who only had sex with one boy, and Ritchie, who revels in the hundreds he has. Between them are Roscoe and Ash, who seem to tread a middle ground – they are still sexually free but perhaps not quite as much as Ritchie.

Firstly, Davies gives us an honest look at gay men disregarding the guidance on safe sex. When Donald and Ritchie are having sex, they have a conversation about condoms, and even try to use one. They both agree they prefer sex without and decide to disregard the advice to use them. Ritchie says, 'I'm clean' even though he hasn't been tested at that point. Davies here reflects the mentality of some gay men at the time. The idea of 'it won't happen to me' is a human defence mechanism and a natural response to being told 'stop having sex'. For the gay community, too, sex was integral (for some, not all) and part of the rebellion, the political statement and nonconformism. After all, if gay men were attacked, stigmatised and ostracised for having sex in the first place, continuing in the face of danger became another form of rebellion. But we also see the more complicated angle of what happened to Ritchie, too: shame and sex. When in the hospital, he confesses to Jill and Ash that he carried on having sex even when he knew.

Here Davies builds on Larry Kramer's work and reflects on divisions in the gay community, something that Kramer was part of. In multiple articles for the gay newspaper *The Native*, Kramer called on gay men to stop having sex. It was his only sensible answer, but much of the gay community rebelled. We see this play out in *It's a Sin* when Jill asks why they don't just stop. Kramer asked the same thing, and just as Ritchie (and the others more subtly) said they wouldn't be stopped, so did many men. Davies does a fine job of illustrating different men's approaches through the central characters. Ritchie defiantly leans into sex, Roscoe seems to lean into how he can *use* sex with his wealthy MP, and the safety of money and security in the face of danger becomes a real saviour for him.

On the other hand, Ash seems to lean into, if not celibacy, but a more moderated sex life (coupled with the fact that he now works in a school and is more outwardly conservative). Kramer in *The Normal Heart* asked (more accurately, screamed) shouldn't men stop having sex if it was killing them? Davies enters this debate again with *It's a Sin*. Kramer did it from the white-hot furnace of the moment when nobody knew enough, so doing what little there was – not having sex – might seem logical. Davies can step back and look at why people like Ritchie might not. He can also see the power of sex at that moment.

Ritchie continues, sure that he will be 'fine', through youthful rebellion, defiance of society and sheer wilfulness. We might even read it as selfishness. After all, we find out Ritchie is a Tory; he defends Thatcher's Section 28 stance. We might judge any of his takes on sexuality. However, Jill distils it perfectly after he dies; he is ashamed. Much of what Ritchie did, came from shame: from his parents and society. First, he channelled it into promiscuity, but later, because he was ashamed of who he was, he wilfully infected others. It's a powerful speech and, from the point of view of Davies as a gay man, a powerful thing to admit; the dark things gay men have done and continue to do because of shame. Ritchie's is one response; many others damaged the mental and physical health of gay men and continue to do so. It was just unfortunate for the generation of Ritchie's that the shame translated into a literal dying of shame.

Davies handles it well, without judgement. In giving it to Jill, he says it as an observer, an outsider, and that feels right – to have one of the other gay men say it would have felt wrong, been jarring, felt like a judgement from Davies inside the community. Jill, as she is a genuine person, can make that observation and offer the truth to the community. It's also the virtue of writing later than the other AIDS narratives; with the distance to the moment's emotion, there is the opportunity to say that. Not only to say that some men did wilfully but dangerously act in defiance of advice and common sense, but, also, to acknowledge they did so out of fear, defiance, ignorance, and, tragically, shame. It's not Davies ascribing shame to sex but crucially acknowledging that it exists for gay men.

It's a Sin is a bookend or a counterpoint to *Queer as Folk* in a way, with its attitude to sex. In *Queer as Folk*, sex was a rebellion against the past, a declaration that gay men were still here, still queer, and still having sex. It was, in some ways, a more simplistic look at the issues, but still, a worthwhile statement, that life and sex continued and was a political, social statement. In *Queer as Folk*, sex was glossing over the nuances, returning to a 1970s liberation era freedom as a statement. When it came to *It's a Sin*, a more nuanced look at sex and what it meant socially, psychologically and personally in context was needed. What we see, then, is the tricky relationship to sex that AIDS created for gay men, and interestingly, in reflecting on the work, we can see those ideas mirrored in *Queer as Folk*.

Conclusion

Davies and the legacy of queer TV

Russell T Davies has had a significant impact on British TV, which is understandable given the opportunity he's had to contribute to the TV landscape over the past twenty years – from children's TV to prime-time drama. He has also massively impacted queer, children's and Welsh TV. It is fair to say that he has become one of our leading TV writers and a significant influence on the TV landscape. Over the past two decades, his work has shaped much of the TV culture and the stories told by queer writers.

Had Davies not followed his passion projects (*Doctor Who*) and made a stand in queer writing, the approach and inclusivity of British TV today might be hugely different. It was also the tragic personal twist of fate, through the death of his partner, Andrew, that kept Davies working in the UK rather than making a permanent move to the US. That has ultimately allowed him more freedom in his work. Indeed, it was a benefit for TV in the UK.

Davies's work of course exists in the broader web of queer culture (including music, fashion and art, which also give queer artists a voice in popular culture). Before TV was able to, theatre told gay stories. In theatre the way was paved by writers like Mart Crowley with *The Boys in the Band* (1968), the first 'mainstream' Broadway play about openly gay men. Or a little later, by *La Cage aux Folles* (1984), the musical with an early contender for gay 'happy endings' and positive depictions of gay relationships.

There's a whole host of queer stories in theatre, eventually fuelling the quiet and not-so-quiet revolutions of the stories on TV. Of course, in all formats, the 1980s and the impact of AIDS, drastically altered the trajectory of representation and inclusion of gay stories, shifting towards activist works about the AIDS epidemic. But out of this, seminal game-changing works like Tony Kushner's *Angels in America* (1994) shifted conversations by showing that works about gay people could also be dramatic masterpieces. As ever a step ahead of TV and film, theatre paved the way for telling new gay stories with relative freedom. This has also resulted in, particularly in recent years, more and more 'happy' gay stories on stage, particularly in musical theatre – from *The Prom* (2018) to the adaptation of Alison Bechdel's seminal coming-of-age story *Fun Home* (2014) or even *&Juliet* (2019).

What have these all got to do with Davies's work? They're linked by queerness. That's not to say that queerness is homogenous, but because queer people are a minority telling stories, we are not the dominant cultural narrative. So, we become interlinked, consciously or otherwise, in writing and reading these stories. Therefore, even if in the subject matter they seem worlds apart, the existence of work like *Angels in America* has allowed work like *Schitt's Creek* (2015–20) to exist. The existence of *The Boys in the Band* on stage eventually led to *Queer as Folk*, or the fact that Larry Kramer wrote *The Normal Heart* meant Davies could write *It's a Sin*. As a minority culture, all the work is connected, owing a debt to one another and opening doors for the next generation.

In the same way, as we have any rights as queer people, we needed people before us to kick down that door, so we could ask for more. That's why the through-line of theatre and TV is so important. The theatre often did a lot of that door-kicking for queer representation so TV and film could follow. But it's not been easy to get to this point, and Davies was, it can be argued, utterly intrinsic to this. A part of kicking down the door so others could follow.

Queer TV legacy

Queer TV can mimic queer culture by showing the kind of 'chosen family' many people look for and find in real life. *Queer as Folk* is the obvious archetype and origin story on TV. Seen before this in the 1970s in Armistead Maupin's *Tales of the City*, in the books and the TV show, it was continued with the US *Queer as Folk* and later *The L Word*. All these show the 'urban' queer family, the idea that friends and lovers become an extended family away from blood relatives. Many queer people experience life – leaving home, perhaps under a cloud of rejection, finding an adopted family in their new homes – in urban centres that are tolerant of gay people like Manchester or LA. From a group of friends, they then form a kind of family unit, and in that unit there are parental figures looking after younger members of the group. Also, there are dynamics that mirror family life, like sibling rivalry. We see a formalised, historical version of this in *Pose*, too, where the 'houses' of ballroom culture provide a formalised version of a family, with mothers and daughters of the houses. This unit acts like an adopted family in place of the actual families who may have rejected the characters for being queer. This dynamic draws on lived and documented experience via the documentary *Paris Is Burning* (1990). Informal or non-exclusively queer versions of this are also seen in shows where the wider friendship group adopts and takes care of its queer characters – we see this in everything from *Buffy* to *Brooklyn Nine-Nine*. These shows offer roadmaps; the coming-of-age narratives for queer people, including how to find your people. They are essential because they offer hope that these family groups exist. They might not be slick and cool and witty, or maybe they will be, and that's aspirational but also vital for queer viewers to imagine their future that way.

Davies's queer TV model has evolved, too. Those audiences who were teens with *Will & Grace* and *Queer as Folk* and thirty-something adults with *It's a Sin* and *Schitt's Creek* felt that they finally had a set of shows and actors who spoke to their experiences. Davies was right; it was a political act. It's more nuanced than just 'acting gay' but more about the source – who is writing, directing and helping create this representation of identity and community.

This is why this idea of 'queer TV' ending up as both an act of performance of authenticity and activism is important. Queer narratives are both a tool for activism and an act of activism in themselves –

both on and off screen. When they challenge the status quo, queer narratives themselves are inherently political, so even queer represent-ations in, say, American sitcoms of the 1990s like *Friends* or *Seinfeld*, which might not hold up to current scrutiny, were political and part of the process, by simply including references to queer lives. Similarly, we saw this with overly queer stories or series, to stick with sitcom examples, like *Ellen* whose coming out episode was monumental, or *Will & Grace* which in parts hasn't aged well but alongside *Ellen*, put queer characters centre-stage in TV comedy for the first time. Every time a soap includes a new queer character it's still (sadly) a political statement. We also include bigger things like *It's a Sin* telling stories that were hidden, or *Orange is the New Black* (2013–19) including trans actors in its cast, and *Pose* doing the same, platforming trans performers of colour, in roles that tell their history. All of these are political acts on-screen that challenge audiences and affirm identities.

Queer as Folk kick-started a generation, who watched it late at night in their bedrooms alone, fearful of being caught. But many of that gen-eration went on to watch *Schitt's Creek* with their families – real and chosen – and were able to celebrate how far TV – and they – had come as a generation and individuals. Through these two decades of queer TV, we can see what has changed, what still needs to change, and, more importantly, the impact it might have had. And with it, Davies evolved.

He's now giving us historical narratives (*Scandal* and *Sin*) that reclaim histories for queer people. Still, these also aimed beyond queer people to educate and engage straight audiences with a history they have been deprived of. They're still told from a queer point of view; they're still queer-centred in their approach. These stories are essential across both types of audiences in retelling the queer stories lost, and ensuring those who missed them (queer and not) know the stories.

But Davies hasn't moved over into simply telling 'mainstream' queer stories: as the idea of *Sin* as complex queer TV shows, even the more 'toned down' approach, still doesn't sit well within the mainstream. Davies leans into that still; he's subversive in what he writes and the unapologetic nature of his queerness, as he was in *Queer as Folk*. The content and reception of *Cucumber* and *Banana* illustrate this.

These very queer shows did not perform as well as expected or have the same cultural resonance. More accurately, they didn't have the same resonance in the straight viewership as expected. Like *Sin* being 'difficult' queer TV, they both fell into that bracket. They were received well by the people they were targeted at. They were also recognised for the calibre of writing (as Davies quoted earlier in this book, he won a BAFTA for *Cucumber* after all), so were *Cucumber* and *Banana* just brilliantly queer? Yes. Did they 'break through' in the way *Queer as Folk* did? No. But other factors are at play – firstly, a proliferation of queer stories that, in part, we have Davies to thank for by that point. Secondly, *Cucumber* specifically was aimed at an older demographic, one that perhaps isn't as headline-grabbing and interesting, or indeed marketable, as the younger demographic.

But his work in *Cucumber* and *Sin* is also unflinchingly honest about queer experiences and stories. Not filtering or pandering to refined sensibilities might mean that, conversely, with this branch of writing, Davies never 'breaks through' into the mainstream. Indeed, had the fates allowed, if he had gone to the US, would he have been forced to temper what he wrote? Maybe. But having carved out a niche in British TV, Davies unapologetically writes queer TV. That's important. While we've evolved on TV to have a plethora of queer stories, from *Heartstopper* to *Schitt's Creek*, both loved by queer and straight audiences alike, the heart of queerness has always been subversion, and we need subversive stories.

We also need sex. The elephant in the room of Davies's stories is the sexual content. That, for some, will always be a barrier to the mainstream. Even if we have seen highly explicit straight content for decades, the line between gay and straight sex will always be there for some. That Davies refuses to tone this down, that he includes sex in his storytelling, is an ongoing political, social and somewhat rebellious streak in his work. Could he tell some of the stories with slightly less sex? Sure. Should he have to? Absolutely not. And should queer audiences have to compromise on what they see on screen? No. Once again, if it's ok for *Bridgerton* because it's straight and they put a Taylor Swift instrumental over the top, then why isn't it ok for Russell T Davies to show a Top getting down to the Pet Shop Boys? Suppose *Bridgerton* makes it acceptable to lust after the duke, why is that so different from queer audiences delighting in rimming scenes? These are questions that go beyond Davies's writing. Still, by defiantly keeping those rimming scenes in his work, from *Queer as Folk* to *It's a Sin*, Davies has, defiantly and loudly, declared he would not dilute his stories for anyone. Quite right, too, as another character of his might say.

Queer TV by queer creators

Suppose TV can help queer audiences imagine a better, more accepting version of their reality. If this is true, it can and should be telling their stories. Who, then, gets to tell those stories? In recent years, this debate has raged, dividing the community, creators and audiences alike. Should queer TV be made by queer people only? Davies has leaned into this in recent years and continues to cause debate across all areas. In 2017, Andrew Garfield was the cause of debate when he starred in the iconic queer play *Angels in America* by declaring that he had been 'watching a lot of *Drag Race*' to prepare.[82] In 2022, Harry Styles caused controversy by queer-coding his performances and saying all gay movies were 'just sex'.[83] This glossing over the nuances of queer performance and queer culture supports Davies's take that it requires an 'insider' to understand the culture.

Davies, it could be argued, has been instrumental in creating that culture on TV, and therefore has the right to comment on it. In terms of sheer breadth, only Ryan Murphy (who has led several queer programmes in the US) has contributed quite as much to queer narratives on TV as Davies. Davies made his contribution when nobody else was around to, and, essentially, he set his own rules within the parameters and restrictions of the industry at the time. So now that he's at a point where he gets to set the rules, it seems fair that he can ask others to play by them.

Times change, so why not elevate our queer actors and other artists and enable them to be part of telling their stories? In essence, that's what Davies has worked for. *Queer as Folk* was seminal 'gay' TV, but the three main actors were straight men. This was an acceptable compromise twenty years ago, maybe, to get the story made, but the idea of openly gay actors taking on gay roles at that time was unthinkable. Skip ahead twenty years, and *It's a Sin* cast all openly gay actors in gay roles, something Russell T Davies saw as a political move, righting past wrongs. It might not seem necessary for straight audiences, because acting is acting. Still, for queer audiences, knowing those actors fully understood the world and the experiences they were depicting, this was crucial. Also, having those people to look up to as role models can also be necessary for audiences and the queer performers coming through the ranks.

What about when queer TV becomes history?

Of course, when a creator has been writing as long as Davies has, naturally, things will shift and, indeed, move into history. On a personal level, he perhaps won't like the idea that his early work, *Queer as Folk*, has become an historical piece. But that Davies is still writing, still creating queer work, and therefore spans contemporary queer TV history, is quite the achievement. If, as a result, some of what is written becomes 'outdated', is that such a bad thing? Or just the inevitable consequence of a longer career than others?

When we look at *Queer as Folk*, it looks dated. It's an historical representation of a community that no longer exists. That version of Canal Street doesn't exist; that version of a group of friends, how they find lovers, even how they are perceived by society, no longer exists. In the real world, that's a good thing. It is good that we should evolve, our communities need to, and we will change as a result of life, technology and everything. So that version of life is as historic as Davies's depiction of Jeremy Thorpe is now, and that's ok.

But with it, things like terminology and attitudes change. That's inevitable as we learn; even work written on the queer community ten years ago will have used what is now outdated terminology because we are learning fast and changing fast. We have the new vocabulary, new visibility, and hopefully new, understanding. Some of Davies's characters use words we wouldn't use today. Some of them behave in a way or do things that we wouldn't agree were acceptable today (though, as the chapter on it expands, they aren't held up as role models either).

Evolving as a writer as queer representation evolves

As one of the forerunners in depicting queer characters, previous writing will likely look different from those writing today dealing with the backlash. With the availability of streaming shows, more of our TV history is now available at a click, it's easy to view older shows. In a way this is great, but also leaves shows from decades before open to critique by today's standards. While critical reading is good, with an understanding that older shows don't always reflect current attitudes, it's something that needs some degree of nuance, particularly when considering minority groups like the LGBTQ+ community and how they are represented.

Why does it matter? History. Where, then, are the queer people in historical drama? And why also do they not have as much sex as their straight counterparts? More importantly, why is it indeed a 'very English scandal' when they do? The generation in the UK who grew up under Section 28 (so those in school between 1989 and 2003, but also beyond, as the attitudes and culture it created reached further) saw LGBTQ+ people erased from their basic history lessons in school. What impact did the idea that there were few queer people in fiction have?

Why does this matter? Because in watching TV, we are fed a diet of historical drama – even in history classes at school, teachers will resort to TV drama to tell stories in an exciting, more engaging way. Queer characters are often removed from that narrative; not only are their stories more rarely told, but they are erased even as part of the fabric of life in historical dramas. The idea that gay didn't exist in history, something that legislation like Section 28 tried to ensure, is also often supported by the stories we are told on TV.

Davies wrote a new TV history by creating those first queer characters. But now they're dated, history, and in part, the kind of queer characters slightly judged by new audiences. But that's ok because being part of history shows you probably were part of that conversation, certainly part of the through-line. So, what now?

Evolution in writing

Things have changed drastically in the last few years. When Davies announced Yasmin Finney – a young trans actress – for a role in *Doctor Who*, it was not an isolated incident of queer representation but more part of an ongoing, steady, quiet revolution. Finney had just been seen in *Heartstopper*, the adaptation of Alice Oseman's Young Adult comic series about teen boys in love. It's British, set in a British school, and the wholesome version of what Nathan in *Queer as Folk* could have had twenty years earlier.

What's that got to do with Davies, aside from giving him another brilliantly talented young actress to cast? It shows that things have changed not only since *Queer as Folk*, but since he wrote kids' TV. While Davies wrote one-off references to AIDS as a political moment in *Children's Ward*, there are now whole queer TV dramas – from *Heartstopper* to *Love, Victor*, and many more. They are the '*Heartstopper* generation' who grew up with Young Adult novels and TV adaptations. Things have changed, even from when an incidentally queer character in *Doctor Who* was a huge deal or Captain Jack felt scandalous.

That's brilliant, as the Tenth Doctor might say. But of course, it also means that the old guard, like Davies, have had to change their approach. It's no longer *just* a big deal to be queer on screen; audiences are demanding more from their queer representation, and rightly so. This means that moving forward, queer characters can be more nuanced because they aren't carrying the weight of being the only queer representation out there.

So that's why in *It's a Sin* Ritchie could be a bit of a Tory or Roscoe could make questionable sexual choices; they aren't speaking for all queer people. Of course, they never were, as we saw when Davies wrote *Queer as Folk*, unapologetically. Rather than being *solely* from a place of defiance (though, of course, that's still there), it now comes from a place of, 'Don't like this queer story? Watch another one?'

But now, with the *Heartstopper* generation looking for adult drama to watch with a queer angle, some of that generation will be in a position to write their own queer stories. It's a freeing moment for writers like Davies, no longer being the only queer voice on TV in a room (again, not that he ever was, but it sometimes felt like it). Rather than competition, the proliferation of queer voices offers an opportunity; to finally be able to represent the broadest stories possible.

For writers like Davies, it offers a chance to lean into personal interest and political conviction.

What now?

Davies was, in a way, part of a quietly queer revolution that would later become a small explosion. Is this because some of those who lost out on TV as a kid channelled that pain into humour? Maybe. But in doing it, they also asked what kinder humour, where minorities and particularly queer people aren't the punchlines, would look like.

An array of queer characters across gender/sexuality representation happened in American comedy programmes post-2010. Shows like *Modern Family*, *One Day at a Time*, or *Schitt's Creek* show a shift in queer TV from when Davies started. They represent the chance to feel represented in 'normal' TV rather than 'queer TV'. It wasn't the TV to keep hidden in the bedroom, but TV your mum could watch and laugh at, too – and ultimately shed a tear over, and understand their queer kids more. They reach beyond just a niche queer audience. This both normalises the existence of queer characters on screen and has the potential to open questions – if viewers can be comfortable with fictional characters in a show, who love being queer, what, then, of the people in their real lives? Humour has a disarming quality; if characters can laugh at themselves, then audiences have permission to laugh with – not at – the queer characters. It's the shift, crucially, from not just telling queer jokes but queer stories.

In TV terms, we moved from the adaptation of Waugh's *Brideshead Revisited* – all coded and hidden sexuality – to 1990s works like *Queer as Folk* and *Will & Grace*. This shifted what queer characters looked like on screen. Russell T Davies gave us some of the most important contributions to queer TV in the last twenty years. That contribution cannot be in dispute. Without *Queer as Folk* bursting out unapologetically and confrontationally, the slower drip, drip of queer representation would have taken far longer. That Channel 4 took that leap with Davies was seismic for his career and for queer TV, and paved the way for what we would see next.

Queer as Folk mattered to the people who watched it, those who watched it on TV and saw people like them. The American version, too, impacted those that tuned in.

Cucumber and *Bob & Rose* resonated with the viewers who saw people like them in those shows. *A Very English Scandal* mattered to those who saw some of history through their lens for once, not one blocked by Margaret Thatcher. *Years and Years* impacted those that saw Daniel and thought, 'that could be my family', and those who shared the fear of 'that could be me', and appreciated vocalising it. *It's a Sin* mattered to viewers who may have realised they didn't know their history or that they had closed their minds off it, or, perhaps more importantly, those who finally saw the story of what their friends, lovers and relatives went through and thought people would finally see. Or perhaps Captain Jack's story was crucial to his fans who thought, maybe, just maybe, they could be a gay hero, too. Most likely, it's a mix of all those.

For many queer people, Russell T Davies raised them in queer TV. Because it's not just TV, it's so much more. It's seeing yourself, or a version of yourself. TV provides friends you don't yet have or used to have. It's seeing who you'd like to be (though Stuart Jones probably shouldn't be a literal role model). It is for all the kids who couldn't get to Canal Street, they could dream.

In the same way, we can't escape in a real TARDIS; we can dream. Not everyone has that community in real life or at all times in their lives. TV can be that community. That's what Russell T Davies's queer TV was for, for so many: the community. Even for those who hid the VHS of *Queer as Folk* from their parents, but eventually found friends who did the same; it was imagining what that community could be, knowing that other queer people and queer viewers existed, knowing they weren't alone. TV has power, and Russell T Davies used that power to connect people, even if they didn't know it. He might not love the analogy, but in a community that lost so many elders, he became an elder by proxy through the stories he told and continues to tell. He is so important for that.

Twenty years ago, still, queer audiences accepted their lack of representation – confirmed by the 'gay drama' of Chapter One: 'Canal Street to the TARDIS' or 'token gays' of sitcoms. However, things have evolved, and LGBTQ+ writers are starting to demand representation in their work. But twenty years on, has scripted drama managed to move beyond tokenistic storylines? Is the generation which grew up starting to see itself represented finally getting what it wanted? Or are there still clear divides between drama for 'gay people' and 'regular drama'? In the two decades that have passed since young people watched *Queer as Folk* alone in their bedrooms, we can see a real evolution in queer TV. Through these two decades of queer TV, we can see what has changed, what still needs to change, and, more significantly, the impact it might have had. And ask: what next from Russell T Davies?

A Personal Reflection

'Paul McGann, *allons-y*'

'Paul McGann doesn't count'
Adventures in nerdy TV

That's the first Russell T Davies quote I remember. Stuart and Vince are making a joke about the Eighth Doctor at the end of season one of *Queer as Folk*. For years I said it, not really knowing a great deal about *Doctor Who*. You see, I was the 'lost generation': born in the 1980s, growing up without a Doctor of my own, and educated under Section 28. I was a part of that generation which grew up without queerness acknowledged in my life.

So as a teenager, when I finally stumbled across *Queer as Folk*, it was another world being opened to me, as if I'd stepped out of the TARDIS somewhere. Vince and Stuart were the start of an insight into a world where maybe I could exist. I didn't think much more of them at the time, not until a madman with a blue box crashed back onto TV when I was 20.

I was in the *Who* 'lost generation'. I grew up with a passing knowledge of Tom Baker and his scarf and Daleks. But when the TARDIS crashed into Cardiff for the first time, I was swept away, like Rose Tyler. It's almost impossible to explain exactly how magical those fandom days were. It was a mysterious in-between time of online fandom, before social media became dominant. I felt part of something, it was the nerdy thing, and being part of it, I loved being, actually, kinda sorta cool. I saw my hometown on TV screens, heard rumours from friends that 'they' were filming nearby. It was an exciting time to be a nerd.

More than that, though, in that weird age of early twenties, a transitional period, I got to escape in the TARDIS. The Doctor gave me a safe space, a chosen family, a feeling of being accepted. I didn't have the words for it then, but the Doctor's asexual attitude to romance and sex in a sex-charged world, was a welcome escape for my asexual brain. The Doctor and the TARDIS were a place where sex and romance didn't matter, only cleverness and adventures did. Subconsciously I started dressing like Ten: fashion, like Time Lords, should know no gender.

When *Torchwood* arrived, 'home' was on TV again, pansexual Captain Jack made it ok to love whoever you wanted, and the Welsh could, in fact, save the world. What's more, it was possible to be a queer superhero, too. I hadn't seen queer people on British TV quite like that before. I hadn't really seen two men share a romantic kiss, let alone in a sci-fi show. I hadn't seen two guys get together on TV and being a couple like everyone else. For that, Captain Jack and Ianto Jones will forever be special.

I got to see my hometown become 'cool' too: I've talked to fellow nerds across the years, and they feel a connection to where I'm from, and that's a nice feeling. While I lived in London, I sometimes would see a bus with a *Torchwood* advert on it go past the coffee shop I worked in, and I would feel a mix of pride and homesickness, or more like *hiraeth*. That felt important, too. Because if you're not a Welsh person who feels connection to, say, rugby, or particulars of Welsh culture in other ways, if you were brought up in English speaking Cardiff in the 1990s and you're queer but not sporty, maybe there was nothing for you. But what if your favourite TV show, the nerdiest of TV shows and the best of them, suddenly had a very large connection to where you're from?

I've never been a person who has felt deeply connected to Wales. I'm probably not supposed to say that in a book published by a Welsh press. I put this largely down to having zero interest in rugby, something which had long since seemed my countryfolk's main connection to the lands – at least during the Six Nations (for legal purposes and the risk of not being run out, this is a joke). But Russell T Davies gave this queer, non-sporty, non-rugby-loving Welsh nerd a reason to be excited about their Welshness. Of course, there are, and have been many reasons for excitement. *Doctor Who*, as a nerdy Welsh adult, gave me a pretty good one. It's really fun to have a TV show your friends (yes, your internet, nerd friends) from around the world love, too, that's connected to where you're from. And for you to be able to go, 'Hey that's made where I live.' How often do you get to talk about the biggest sci-fi show of the moment and casually go, 'Oh yeah them, saw them filming on my lunch break on Tuesday'. It might be nerdy; it might be silly to some, but, those years? They were pretty good years to be a Cardiff-based Welsh nerd.

They also gave me an attachment to particular times and places that also mean something sometimes. It's not always that deep, granted. I drive through the Butetown tunnels at least once a week and have a laugh thinking about the *Who* fans who had to pay for overnight parking while they spied on filming from the carpark adjacent to them. I think of driving to yet another crappy job, seeing Sarah Jane's house, or coming back from a late-night evening shift seeing the Weeping Angels (not great for driving). Or, I think of the time I was walking my dog on a snowy day and when I saw the TARDIS outside the Wales Millennium Centre, and having a crew member stop and say hello to her. The dog isn't around anymore, but every time I watch that episode, I think of her.

There's emotion, too. I will forever remember where I was when I heard that Elisabeth Sladen had died. I will always cry when I write about her (yes, even now). She wasn't part of my childhood, but Russell T Davies made her part of my Whoniverse and she's special to me.

What does the Doctor mean to me? Many things.

The Doctor feels like a particular moment in my twenties. A moment when, like many, I was more than a bit lost in the world. The idea of running away with a mad person in a blue box was of course appealing. As a long-time nerd, too, the Doctor made nerds cool again. The Doctor made being a bit clever cool again. And, ok, yes, it helped that for a big chunk of that time I was doing a PhD and could demand a TARDIS if I was a Doctor at the end of it. The Doctor was a friend, the Doctor is actually the companion of many a lost soul in the universe.

For anyone who ever felt a bit hopeless, a bit lost, the Doctor is something important, the Doctor is hope. The Doctor teaches us that we can all be extraordinary, even in our ordinariness. That's something you take with you. We all have our Doctor, and mine was Ten, who always spoke to me with Russell's voice as much as David's. That period was a defining one in my life. Russell T Davies gave me adventures in time and space, and said I'd be welcomed whoever I was.

'The maybe'

That's the quote I use most often when talking about writing. It comes, of course, from Russell T Davies. I learned more about writing from that man, from watching his work, from reading his thoughts on writing, than I did from any writing class I've taken. In Davies's chaotic writing style on screen, and the way he describes it in his brain, I saw myself in writing. What's more, I saw for the first time someone *real* about writing; there isn't a formula or a mystical thing, it's about hours bashing out ideas, and sometimes chaotic tumbling nonsense condensed into something workable. Davies's insights gave me hope for my own chaotic brain.

Finally, after writing a PhD on AIDS and how we've written about it, the man I'd waited to write about it finally did. While I sat watching it, moved, I also watched the unfolding social media and traditional media response with a tinge of sadness, even anger, because everyone was discovering this like it was news. I am less angry at my fellow Section 28 generation, who had the truth hidden from them. I am angry at the systems that kept the truth from the younger generations.

But my frustration aside, there was a sense of 'Listen to Uncle Russell' in this, a lesson that has served me well over the years. Listen to Russell T Davies; let him tell you the story you need to hear. This personal reflection isn't a balanced analysis of his pros and cons as a TV writer; instead, this is a testament to what he did – he told a story and moved people – and why that was critical. Because Russell, in telling this story, in casting Olly Alexander and Keeley Hawes respectively, got the attention of different demographics and got them to sit their butts on the sofa and watch a story about AIDS. And isn't that amazing?

Russell T Davies's work has been a backdrop to my life. I was too young to be shaped by *Queer as Folk*, but its existence let me peek behind a curtain, to return later, to see a world I sort of missed, one that led me to who I am now. Later, *Doctor Who* would be formative for me, not as a child as for many, but as a young adult, because Davies let the TARDIS be a safe space, one where anyone could be themselves. That version of the TARDIS will always feel like home, thanks to him.

I've laughed with Russell T Davies, and I've cried because of him a whole lot more. Often at the same time. In a TV landscape that tries to relegate people like me, queer people, to the side, Davies has always let us be front and centre: often confrontational, often subversive, always honest. Always real. When he told the story that had been the back-drop to my professional life for so many years, it felt like full circle. He opened the door to queerness to this teenager, then told the stories I'd been writing about, too.

Some writers are just able to tap into something in your brain. There's a wavelength, a certain frequency Davies taps into with me. Yes, the part that makes me laugh and cry, the part that makes me feel seen. But also, the part that says, you get me, you get people like me. And the part that also wants to be just a fraction of the writer he is.

Epilogue

Back to the TARDIS

On Friday 24 September 2021, a moment of 'wibbly wobbly timey wimey'-ness was happening. The rift in Cardiff opened, and the parallel universe was back.

The *Radio Times* reported Russell T Davies was coming back to *Doctor Who*.[84]

In an article that made it seem like we'd all time-travelled to 2005, it was reported that Davies was to take on the sixtieth anniversary episode and 'series beyond', taking over from Chris Chibnall, who along with the then Doctor, played by Jodie Whittaker, was due to depart at the end of the current run of episodes.

It's fair to say that *Doctor Who* fans the world over echoed the Tenth Doctor with cries of 'What? What? What?' at the news. After bringing the show to arguably its highest point, Davies had been finished with adventures in the TARDIS, his job there done.

But, of course, the lifelong Whovian had never truly stepped away, not entirely; from a cameo appearance in Peter Davison's spoof special 'The Five(ish) Doctors Reboot' in 2013 to also writing *Who* again when his novel *Damaged Goods* was adapted by Big Finish into an audio drama. He also illustrated a *Doctor Who* poetry book (*Now We Are Six Hundred: A Collection of Time Lord Verse*) and a novelisation of 'Rose' for Target Books.

Davies leaned into his *Who* roots in 2020 and, for the first time, entirely took to social media to engage with fans, utilising the time isolated by Covid as we all were at that point, to reconnect with *Who* fans on social media. First, this was via sharing sketches based on *Who*. He tweeted behind-the-scenes information and general reflections for a series of rewatches of his episodes. He also continued writing *Who* by releasing an old short story originally destined for *Doctor Who Magazine*. He wrote a script for an animated feature in which David Tennant and Anna Hope reprised their roles as voice actors ('The Secret of Novice Hame'). Finally, during the watch party for *The Runaway Bride*, Davies shared extracts of a script he wrote in 1986, which was eventually made into an audio play by Big Finish and released in 2022.

So, did Russell T Davies ever leave the TARDIS? Yes and no. And after all, time is wibbly wobbly timey wimey…either way, he's back in the TARDIS, and this was probably the most excited many Whovians had been in years.

Until Davies started making announcements, of course.

Teasing fans on social media with TARDIS, diamond, and heart emojis (for the Doctor, the diamond anniversary, and the Doctor's two hearts), Davies made an announcement it's fair to say most fans didn't see coming: David Tennant was coming back to the TARDIS. Not just Tennant, but Catherine Tate as well. As part of the sixtieth anniversary, the Tenth Doctor and Donna Noble were to be reunited.

It's always dangerous to make statements about how *Doctor Who* fans feel because they will always be a loud dissenting bunch. It's safe to say that the Tennant/Tate return was met on social media with great enthusiasm. Things continued to be exciting with sightings of them filming shortly after, as well as rumoured sightings of Bernard Cribbins (who played Donna's grandad Wilf and who sadly passed away not long after filming his scenes). The sixtieth got another exciting announcement with the casting of Neil Patrick Harris in the special (Harris, of course, had recently starred in *It's a Sin*, too). With the return of Rachel Talalay as director for the sixtieth, fans were excited about the potential for the story as much as the nostalgia.

Not content with this level of excitement, the BBC unexpectedly announced the new Doctor. With zero build-ups or even a hint that an announcement was impending, they took to social media to announce Ncuti Gatwa as the Fifteenth Doctor. Gatwa, best known for his role in

Netflix's *Sex Education* (2019–), will be the first actor of colour to play the role. Gatwa, who was born in Rwanda and raised in Scotland, has expressed his pride in the character he plays on *Sex Education* (a gay man), saying: 'It matters, I hope, that other little black boys round the world can be like – "Oh, Eric is like this, and it's cool".'[85]

And while he chooses to keep his personal life private, it's safe to say he is on board with Davies's inclusive, positive ethos in terms of inclusivity. That Gatwa gets to extend that and be an icon for all the Black boys and girls, all the non-white kids, who wanted to fly the TARDIS, is truly an exciting moment.

So, what happens next? All of time and space are a possibility at the time of writing. There is a feeling like 'coming home' in having Davies back in charge of *Who*. Even if he had not decided to stay for a subsequent series, there's something right about having him take the helm for the sixtieth anniversary. Steven Moffat taking charge for the fiftieth felt ok, in that he, too, was a huge 'fanboy', like Davies. His series of *Who* was different but no less imbued with that childhood spent chasing imaginary Daleks in the playground. It feels right to hand that baton back to Davies for the sixtieth. But, also, who would have thought, when Davies first rebooted it, that we'd have seen another eighteen years of *Doctor Who* in the interim? That's whole childhoods with *their* Doctor, for so many. For those from the 'missing generation' of *Who* fans who never had it growing up, that's astounding. It's for that that having Davies at the helm for the sixtieth feels right.

What will he have done? Oh, to have a TARDIS to know, a planned reunion of Doctors and companions past seems to be on the cards, with the revelation that David Tennant and Catherine Tate are back. In summer 2022, at a fan convention, Tennant teased that the fans don't know half of what's going on…was he hinting maybe at more Doctors and companions converging on a studio somewhere outside Cardiff? Only time will tell…

Notes

1. Mark Aldridge and Andy Murray, *T is for Television: the small screen adventures of Russell T Davies* (Cheltenham: Reynolds and Hearn, 2008), p. 32.

2. Aldridge and Murray, *T is for Television*, p. 33.

3. Aldridge and Murray, *T is for Television*, p. 32.

4. Russell T Davies, 'Transmission was madness. Honestly', *Guardian*, 15 September 2003.

5. Davies, *Guardian*, 15 September 2003.

6. Davies, *Guardian*, 15 September 2003.

7. Aldridge and Murray, *T is for Television*, p. 61.

8. Russell T Davies, quoted in Andrew Billen, 'As queer as Dr Who? No, just Daleks in chains', *The Times*, 23 November 2004.

9. Russell T Davies, 'The whole nation will be gawping at his fruit'n'veg', *The Sunday Times*, 28 December 2014.

10. Davies, *The Sunday Times*, 28 December 2014.

11. Davies, *The Sunday Times*, 28 December 2014.

12. Aldridge and Murray, *T is for Television*, p. 98.

13. Sally R. Munt, 'Shame/Pride Dichotomies in *Queer as Folk*', *Textual Practice*, 14/3 (2000), 534.

14. David Alderson, 'Queer Cosmopolitanism: Place, Politics, Citizenship and *Queer as Folk*', *New Formations*, 55(2005).

15. Munt, *Textual Practice*, 531–46.

16. Davies quoted in Andrew Billen, *The Times*, 23 November 2004.

17. Hannah Jones, 'Hold the Front Page…for Doctor Who', *IC Wales*, 4 June 2005.

18. Cardiff Shoot, *Doctor Who* website, 29 June 2011.

19. Davies, *The Sunday Times*, 28 December 2014.

20. Phil Wickham, *Understanding TV Texts* (London: BFI Publishing, 2007), p. 120.

21. Glyn Davis and Gary Needham, *Queer TV* (Abingdon: Routledge, 2009), pp. 153–6.

22. 'Fit But You Know It', *Doctor Who Magazine*, 398, 20 August 2008.

23. Neil Wilkes, 'Chris Chibnall talks "Torchwood", "L&O: London"', *Digital Spy*, 1 April 2008.

24. Glyn Davis and Gary Needham, *Queer TV*, pp. 153–6.

25. Cityseeker tourism, 'Ianto's Shrine', *<https://cityseeker.com/cardiff/854641-ianto-s-shrine>*.

26. Kristina Busse, *Framing Fan Fiction: Literary and Social Practices in Fan Fiction Communities* (Iowa City: University of Iowa Press, 2017), p. 47.

27. Davies to Cook, 6 March 2007, in Benjamin Cook and Russell T Davies, *The Writer's Tale: The Final Chapter* (London: BBC Books, 2008).

28. Ken Plummer, 'Gay Cultures/Straight Borders', in D. Morley and K. Robins (eds), *British Cultural Studies* (Oxford: Oxford University Press, 2001), p. 393.

29. Ken Plummer, *British Cultural Studies*, p. 392.

30. Ellen E. Jones, 'Cucumber, Channel 4 – review: Russell T Davies is on top form in this universal slice of gay life', *Independent*, 22 January 2015.

31. Sam Wollaston, 'Cucumber, Banana and Tofu review – "gloriously, triumphantly, explicitly gay and the television event of the week"', *Guardian*, 22 January 2015.

32. Nick Levine, 'Russell T Davies talks LGBTQ visibility, Queer As Folk's legacy, and the commercialisation of Pride', *Gay Times*, 2019.

33. Davies and Cook, *The Writer's Tale*, pp. 34–5.

34. Audio commentary, 'Tooth and Claw', *Doctor Who*, DVD edition, 2006.

35. Brian Silliman, 'Doctor Who has always been political, and it has the right to be', *SyFy*, 2 February 2020.

36. Silliman, *SyFy*, 2 February 2020.

37. Levine, *Gay Times*, 2019.

38. Morgan Jeffery, 'Russell T Davies: "Love, Simon is extraordinary but we're nowhere near equality for gay people"', *Digital Spy*, 14 May 2018.

39. Yohana Desta, 'Hugh Grant Gets Comfortable with Controversy in *A Very English Scandal*', *Vanity Fair*, 29 June 2018.

40. '"A Very English Scandal": Russell T Davies Interview', *We are Cult Rocks*, 16 May 2018.

41. Russell T Davies quoted in Liz Shannon Miller, 'How to Make Very British TV Like a Very English Scandal, According to Russell T Davies', *IndieWire*, 1 July 2018.

42. Davies, *IndieWire*, 1 July 2018.

43. Adam Sherwin, 'Hugh Grant was my first choice to play Doctor Who says Russell T Davies', *I News*, 8 May 2018.

44. Sherwin, *I News*, 8 May 2018.

45. Davies, *IndieWire*, 1 July 2018.

46. Davies, *IndieWire*, 1 July 2018.

47. Norman Scott, 'Norman Scott criticises "weakling" portrayal in BBC's A Very English Scandal', *Irish Times*, 6 May 2018.

48. Davies, *IndieWire*, 1 July 2018.

49. Davies, *IndieWire*, 1 July 2018.

50. David Shariatmadari, 'The quiet revolution; why Britain has more gay MPs than anywhere else', *Guardian*, 15 May 2015.

51. Jeffery, *Digital Spy*, 14 May 2018.

52. Jeffery, *Digital Spy*, 14 May 2018.

53. Sean O'Grady, 'Years and Years review: Emma Thompson is brilliant in dystopian drama', *Independent*, 14 May 2019.

54. Ben Travers, 'Years and Years Review: HBO's Cautionary Drama Only Really Works as a Black Comedy', *IndieWire*, 24 June 2019.

55. Daniel D'Addario, 'TV Review: Years and Years', *Variety*, 22 June 2019.

56. Jigsaw Research, 'News Consumption in the UK: 2022', 21 July 2022.

57. Sam Damshenas, 'Russell Tovey defends Jack Whitehall's decision

to play a gay character', *Gay Times*, 2019.

58. Helen Lewis, 'Russell T Davies: Living as a gay man is a political act', *New Statesman*, 14 May 2018. <https://www.newstatesman.com/long-reads/2018/05/russell-t-da-vies-living-gay-man-political-act>

59. <*www.instagram.com/p/BxvXBZtn2Hh/*>, 21 May 2019.

60. Peter Goodwin, 'Channel Four and More', in *Television Under the Tories: Broadcasting Policy 1979–1997* (London: British Film Institute, 1998), p. 34.

61. AfterElton, 12 October 2013.

62. Russell T Davies, 'What I've Learned', *The Times*, 25 May 2019.

63. Davies, *The Times*, 25 May 2019.

64. Davies, *Guardian*, 15 September 2003.

65. Decca Aitkenhead, 'Russell T Davies on It's a Sin; "AIDS was like everything people said about you came true in the shape of a virus"', *The Times*, 17 January 2021.

66. Russell T Davies in L. Goldberg '"Queer as Folk" Folks: Four Creators on 23 Years of Three Groundbreaking Shows', *The Hollywood Reporter*, 9 June 2022.

67. Davies in Aitkenhead, *The Times*, 17 January 2021.

68. Davies, *The Hollywood Reporter*, 9 June 2022.

69. Davies, *The Hollywood Reporter*, 9 June 2022.

70. Davies, *The Hollywood Reporter*, 9 June 2022.

71. Ben Dowell, 'Russell T Davies: I want to show what life was like for gay men during the 1980s AIDS crisis', *Radio Times*, 20 June 2016.

72. James Milton, 'Russell T Davies "literally refused" to write this "unbelievably crass" It's a Sin scene', *PinkNews*, 3 March 2021.

73. Davies in Milton, *PinkNews*, 3 March 2021.

74. Lucy Mangan, 'It's a Sin review – Russell T Davies Aids drama is a poignant masterpiece', *Guardian*, 22 January 2021.

75. Mangan, *Guardian*, 22 January 2021.

76. Davies in Aitkenhead, *The Times*, 17 January 2021.

77. David Roman, *Acts of Intervention* (Bloomington: University of Indiana Press, 1998), p. 59.

78. Davies in Aitkenhead, *The Times*, 17 January 2021.

79. Scarlett Russell, 'It's a Sin star Lydia West on the hit Channel 4 drama: "It's a celebration of life"', *The Times*, 31 January 2021.
80. <*www.channel4.com/press/news/channel-4s-its-sin-hits-189m-all-4-views-and-helps-drive-increase-hiv-testing*>, 1 March 2021.
81. Larry Kramer, '1983: 1,112 and Counting', *The Native*, 27 March 1983.
82. Andrew Garfield, National Theatre Platform, 2017.
83. Harry Styles quoted in Brittany Spanos, 'How Harry Styles Became the World's Most Wanted Man', *Rolling Stone*, 22 August 2022.
84. Huw Fullerton, 'Russell T Davies to return as Doctor Who showrunner', *Radio Times*, 24 September 2021.
85. Judi Dry, '"Sex Education" Star Ncuti Gatwa on Why His Character Is So Important for Black Gay Visibility', *IndieWire*, 5 February 2020.

References

Abbott, Paul, 'What Do You Want To Watch Tomorrow?', Royal Television Society, annual lecture (2005).

Aitkenhead, Decca, 'Russell T Davies on *It's a Sin*: "Aids was like everything people said about you became true in the shape of a virus"', *The Times*, 17 January 2021.

Alderson, David, 'Queer Cosmopolitanism: Place, Politics, Citizenship and Queer as Folk', *New Formations*, 55 (2005), 73–88.

Aldridge, Mark and Murray, Andy, *T is for Television: the small screen adventures of Russell T Davies* (Cheltenham: Reynolds and Hearn, 2008).

Billen, Andrew, 'As queer as Dr Who? No, just Daleks in chains', *The Times*, 23 November 2004.

Channel 4's remit [online]. <*www.channel4.com/corporate/about-4/who-we-are/about-channel-4*> accessed 1 April 2015.

Cook, Benjamin and Davies, Russell T, *The Writer's Tale: The Final Chapter* (London: BBC Books, 2008).

D'Addario, Daniel, 'TV Review: Years and Years', *Variety*, 22 June 2019.

Damshenas, Sam, 'Russell Tovey defends Jack Whitehall's decision to play a gay character', *Gay Times* [online]. <*www.gaytimes.co.uk/culture/russell-tovey-defends-jack-whitehalls-decision-to-play-a-gay-character*>.

Davies, Russell T, 'Transmission was madness. Honestly', *Guardian*, 15 September 2003.

Davies, Russell T, 'The whole nation will be gawping at his fruit'n'veg', *The Sunday Times*, 28 December 2014.

Davies, Russell T, '"A Very English Scandal": Russell T Davies Interview', *We are Cult Rocks*, 16 May 2018 [online]. <*https://wearecult.rocks/a-very-english-scandal-russell-t-davies-interview*>.

Davies, Russell T, 'What I've Learned', *The Times*, 25 May 2019.

Davies, Russell T, in L. Goldberg '"Queer as Folk" Folks: Four Creators on 23 Years of Three Groundbreaking Shows', *The Hollywood Reporter*, 9 June 2022.

Denham, Jess, 'Cucumber and Banana: What to expect from Russell T Davies' new gay dramas', *Independent*, 22 February 2015.

Desta, Yohana, 'Hugh Grant Gets Comfortable with Controversy in *A Very English Scandal*', *Vanity Fair*, 29 June 2018.

Dowell, Ben, 'Russell T Davies: I want to show what life was like for gay men during the 1980s AIDS crisis', *Radio Times*, 20 June 2016.

Dry, Judi, '"Sex Education" Star Ncuti Gatwa on Why His Character Is So Important for Black Gay Visibility', *IndieWire*, 5 February 2020.

Flett, Kathryn, 'Television: It's that man again', *Observer,* 16 February 2003.

Fountain, Alan, 'Opening Channels: Channel Four and After', in Huw Beynon and Sheila Rowbotham (eds), *Looking at Class: Film, Television and the Working Class in Britain* (London: Rivers Oram Press, 2001).

Fullerton, Huw, 'Russell T Davies to return as Doctor Who showrunner', *Radio Times*, 24 September 2021.

Goodwin, Peter, 'Channel Four and More', in Peter Goodwin, *Television Under the Tories: Broadcasting Policy 1979–1997* (London: British Film Institute, 1998).

References

Jaffe, Harold, CDC for *Newsweek* D. McGinn, 'MSNBC: AIDS at 20: Anatomy of a Plague: An Oral History', *Newsweek* Web Exclusive, from AVERT AIDS Timeline, 1982.

Jeffery, Morgan, 'Russell T Davies: "Love, Simon is extraordinary but we're nowhere near equality for gay people"', *Digital Spy*, 14 May 2018.

Jones, Ellen E., 'Cucumber, Channel 4 – review: Russell T Davies is on top form in this universal slice of gay life', *Independent*, 22 January 2015.

Lawson, Mark, 'Cucumber-Banana-Tofu trilogy – first-look review', *Guardian*, 16 January 2015.

Levine, Nick, 'Russell T Davies talks LGBTQ visibility, Queer As Folk's legacy, and the commercialisation of Pride', *Gay Times* [online]. *<www.gaytimes.co.uk/culture/russell-t-davies-interview/>*.

Lewis, Helen, 'Russell T Davies: Living as a gay man is a political act', *New Statesman*, 14 May 2018.

<https://www.newstatesman.com/long-reads/2018/05/russell-t-davies-living-gay-man-political-act>

Mangan, Lucy, 'It's a Sin review – Russell T Davies Aids drama is a poignant masterpiece', *Guardian*, 22 January 2021.

Miller, Liz Shannon, 'How to Make Very British TV like "A Very English Scandal" a great sensation according to Russell T Davies', *IndieWire*, 1 July 2018.

Milton, James, 'Russell T Davies "literally refused" to write this "unbelievably crass" It's a Sin scene', *PinkNews*, 3 March 2021.

Munt, Sally R., 'Shame/Pride Dichotomies in Queer as Folk', *Textual Practice*, 14/3 (2000), 531–46.

O'Grady, Sean, 'Years and Years review: Emma Thompson is brilliant in dystopian drama', *Independent*, 14 May 2019.

O'Hara, Mary, 'How comedy makes up better people', BBC, 30 August 2016 [online]. <*www.bbc.com/future/article/20160829-how-laughter-makes-us-better-people*>.

Peirse, Alison, 'A Broken Tradition? British Telefantasy and Children's Television in the 1980s and 1990s', *Visual Culture in Britain*, 11/1 (2010), 109–24.

Plummer, Ken, 'Gay Cultures/Straight Borders', in D. Morley and K. Robins (eds), *British Cultural Studies* (Oxford: Oxford University Press, 2001).

Roman, David, *Acts of Intervention* (Bloomington: Indiana University Press, 1995).

Russell, Scarlett, 'It's a Sin star Lydia West on the hit Channel 4 drama: "It's a celebration of life"', *The Times*, 31 January 2021.

Sherwin, Adam, 'Hugh Grant was my first choice to play Doctor Who says Russell T Davies', *I News*, 8 May 2018.

Spanos, Brittany, 'How Harry Styles Became the World's Most Wanted Man', *Rolling Stone*, 22 August 2022.

Travers, Ben, '"Years and Years" Review: HBO's Cautionary Drama Only Really Works as a Black Comedy', *IndieWire*, 24 June 2019.

Wilkes, Neil, 'Chris Chibnall talks "Torchwood", "L&O: London"', *Digital Spy*, 1 April 2008.

Wollaston, Sam, 'Cucumber, Banana and Tofu review – "gloriously, triumphantly, explicitly gay and the television event of the week"', *Guardian*, 22 January 2015.

Writing Credits

On the Waterfront (1989)
Dark Season (1991)
Allsorts (1992)
ChuckleVision
'Spooks and Gardens' (1992)
'Rich for a Day' (1992)
Century Falls (1993)
Coronation Street (1993)
Coronation Street: Viva Las Vegas! (1997)
The House of Windsor (1994)
Revelations (1994–5)
Touching Evil (1997)
The Grand (1997–8)
Queer as Folk (1999–2000)
Bob & Rose (2001)
Linda Green (2001)
The Private Life of a Masterpiece (2001)
The Second Coming (2003)
Mine All Mine (2004)
Casanova (2005)
Children in Need Special (2005)
Wizards vs Aliens (2013)
Old Jack's Boat (2013–14)
Tofu (2015)
Cucumber (2015)
Banana (2015)
A Midsummer Night's Dream (2016)

Gay Aliens and Queer Folk

A Very English Scandal (2018)
Years and Years (2019)
It's a Sin (2021)
Nolly (2022)

Doctor Who and *Torchwood* (up until 2022)

Doctor Who (as writer)

Series One (2005)
'Rose'
'The End of the World'
'Aliens of London'
'World War Three'
'The Long Game'
'Boom Town'
'Bad Wolf'
'The Parting of the Ways'

Series Two (2006)
'The Christmas Invasion'
'New Earth'
'Tooth and Claw'
'Love and Monsters'
'Army of Ghosts'
'Doomsday'

Series Three (2007)
'The Runaway Bride'
'Smith and Jones'
'Gridlock'
'Utopia'
'The Sound of Drums'
'The Last of the Time Lords'

Writing Credits

Series Four (2008)
'The Voyage of the Damned'
'Partners in Crime'
'Midnight'
'Turn Left'
'The Stolen Earth'
'Journey's End'

The 'Specials' (2008–10)
'The Next Doctor' (2008)
'The Planet of the Dead' (with Gareth Roberts, 2009)
'The Waters of Mars' (with Phil Collinson, 2009)
'The End of Time Part One' (2009)
'The End of Time Part Two' (2010)

Torchwood (as writer)

Series One (2006)
'Everything Changes'

Series Three (2009)
'Children of Earth: Day One'
'Children of Earth: Day Three' (with James Moran)
'Children of Earth: Day Five'

Series Four 'Miracle Day' (2011)
'The New World'
'The Blood Line' (with Jane Espenson)

The Sarah Jane Adventures (as writer)

Series One (2007)
'Invasion of the Bane' (with Gareth Roberts)

Series Four (2010)
'Death of the Doctor'

Online Special (2020)
'Farewell, Sarah Jane'

Other *Doctor Who* spinoffs (as a writer)

Doctor Who Music of the Spheres (2008)
Doctor Who at the Proms (2008)